Sir Walter Scott

THE LAY

D1825187

OF

THE LAST MINSTREL

CANTOS I.–VI.

WITH INTRODUCTION AND NOTES

BAILEY, E.C.

PREFACE

The Notes in this edition, being intended particularly for young students, consist largely of simple explanations of words and expressions likely to be unfamiliar. Allusions, historical and antiquarian, are freely explained, Scott's own notes being in many cases reprinted verbatim. Some hints are given towards the literary appreciation of the poem. The Introduction will, it is hoped, in the hands of the teacher, enable the student to gain some comprehension of Scott's literary position, besides providing all necessary information as to the composition and the form of *The Lay*. Lord Jeffrey's account of the plot is included in order that the student may the more easily follow the course of the story.

INTRODUCTION.

1. BIOGRAPHICAL SKETCH.

WALTER SCOTT was born in Edinburgh on August 15, 1771. His father was one of a class of lawyers known there as Writers to the Signet, but his ancestors had followed more active and boisterous careers in the Borderland. As a boy, in spite of a constitutional lameness, Scott distinguished himself by his activity and feats of daring. At school he won no great honours, but he made himself popular among his schoolmates by his readiness for frolic, and by the stories which he told them from his reading or weaved for them out of his own imagination. On leaving school he was apprenticed to his father, and entered the law classes of Edinburgh University, in due course becoming an advocate, and then a sheriff, and a clerk of session. But as a lawyer he did not attain the success which his abilities might have won if they had been concentrated on his profession. From boyhood ballads and romances fascinated him, and he spent much of his time in reading such literature as Percy's *Reliques of Ancient Poetry*, storing all that he read in a memory of extraordinary capacity. He also studied German, and his first serious poetical efforts were made in translations of German ballads.

In 1797 he married Charlotte Margaret Charpentier or Carpenter, the daughter of a French Huguenot refugee. Two years later his translations from German appeared. For some years he had been collecting the ballads which were familiar as household words among the people of the Border country. This collection, in which were included some imitatory pieces of his own, and some valuable introductions and notes to the old poems, was published in 1802

under the title of *The Minstrelsy of the Scottish Border*, and
was a great success. *The Lay of the Last Minstrel*, begun
in the same year, did not appear until 1805. Three years
later again, *Marmion* was published, which is the greatest
of Scott's poems, and gave him, in the opinion of most
men, a title to be called Britain's greatest living poet.
The superiority of *Marmion* to *The Lay* was in great part
due to its subject, a well-planned and interesting story.
In 1810 came *The Lady of the Lake*, which was followed
at intervals by *Rokeby* and the other poems.

A greater poet was now beginning to oust Scott from his
throne. Scott himself recognized a superior in Lord Byron,
and accepted a lower place gracefully, telling his publisher
that if he failed in one thing he must stick to another. By
that time *Waverley* had been published, in 1814, anonymous-
ly, and had met with wonderful success. It had been begun
nine years before, and Scott told a friend that, happening to
come across the mislaid manuscript of the early chapters, he
"took the fancy of finishing it", and accomplished the feat in
three weeks. *Waverley* was the first of that long series of
novels and romances which still keep Scott secure as monarch
of English fiction.

In 1820 Scott was made a baronet. Five years later a
calamity fell on him which would have utterly crushed a man
of less splendid courage. Many years before, he had entered
into partnership with two printing and publishing houses.
Owing to the business incapacity of some of the partners, and
a lack of the necessary firmness on Scott's part, these firms
had long been on the verge of bankruptcy, and only the con-
tinued success of the novels had so far averted ruin. Mean-
while Scott had been anticipating his income, spending
largely on his buildings at Abbotsford, and on his family,
and saving little. When the crash came, he was involved to
the extent of considerably more than £100,000. Though
now fifty-five years old, he set to work with energy and
determination to "write off" his debts. By January 1828 he
had earned nearly £40,000. But illness came upon him, and
there were signs of brain disease. Though he manfully

struggled on, in 1831 his health completely broke down, and
he left Scotland in the hope of gaining benefit from foreign
travel. Returning worse, he begged to be taken to Abbots-
ford, and died there on September 21, 1832, four days after
his arrival, aged 61. Fifteen years after his death his works
had realized enough to pay his debts in full.

Scott would not now, perhaps, be regarded as one of the
greatest poets. He lacked the keen vision into the souls of
men that Shakespeare had; he did not see in Nature what
Wordsworth saw and taught others to see; he could not
make wonderful verse-music like Tennyson; he had not even
the formal perfection of which Dryden was the first and Pope
the greatest master. He was a strong, simple, healthy-
minded gentleman, with deep feelings but a hatred of showing
them, with a love for things old and strange, a delight in the
pomp and circumstance of chivalry, in weird legends and the
picturesqueness of romance, and a power of expressing and
communicating his enthusiasm in vigorous and stirring verse.
Of poetry of a tenderer sort he has, however, left one delicate
gem.

> The Violet in her greenwood bower,
>   Where birchen boughs with hazels mingle,
> May boast itself the fairest flower
>   In glen, or copse, or forest dingle.
>
> Though fair her gems of azure hue
>   Beneath the dewdrop's weight reclining,
> I've seen an eye of lovelier blue,
>   More sweet, through watery lustre shining.
>
> The summer sun that dew shall dry,
>   Ere yet the day be past its morrow;
> Nor longer in my false love's eye,
>   Remain'd the tear of parting sorrow.

His best poems are his songs, but it is by his novels that he
will be longest remembered—and by the unflinching courage
with which he met adversity, and the heroic efforts that he
made to leave an unstained name.

2. THE COMPOSITION OF *THE LAY.*

In the years 1800–1802 Scott was engaged in the publication of his *Minstrelsy of the Scottish Border*, which was, as has been said, a collection of old Border ballads and romances, with copious historical and antiquarian notes, and some original ballads in imitation of the old. It was suggested to Scott by the beautiful Countess of Dalkeith, wife of the Duke of Buccleuch's heir, that he should write a poem, for inclusion in the *Minstrelsy*, on the legend of Gilpin Horner, a traditionary goblin whose antics the lady had heard of with delight from one of her husband's tenants. "To hear was to obey", Scott tells us in his Introduction to the edition of 1830; his admiration for the young countess was so enthusiastic that, as he told Miss Seward, if she had asked him to write a ballad on a broomstick he must have attempted it. He therefore wrote a few stanzas, intending to work up a short romance for the third volume of his *Minstrelsy*. These opening stanzas he showed to two friends of whose literary judgment he had a high opinion. Their remarks were so guarded that Scott imagined they could not conscientiously praise his verses, and would have censured them but for regard for his feelings. With some natural chagrin he threw the manuscript on the fire when his friends were gone, and resolved to abandon the project.

Meeting one of the two friends a few days later, he learnt to his surprise that their silence was due not to disapproval but to their reluctance to give an immediate judgment upon a poem with so odd a subject and in so novel a style. But their curiosity had been awakened to see what Scott would make of it, and they strongly advised him to proceed. He did not at once follow this advice, but some time after, being confined to his house through a kick from his horse, he finished the first canto and planned the whole poem. It grew under his hands until it was too long for its intended setting in the *Border Minstrelsy*. Friends whom he had taken into confidence all alike expressed admiration of what he had written, and he proceeded to finish the poem at the rate of about a canto a week.

Early in 1805, Scott's thirty-fourth year, *The Lay of the Last Minstrel*, with notes, was published, in London and Edinburgh, in a handsome quarto volume, at the price of twenty-five shillings. It was inscribed "To the Right Honourable Charles, Earl of Dalkeith", and bore the motto—

> *Dum relego, scripsisse pudet, quia plurima cerno,*
> *Me quoque, qui feci, judice, digna lini.*[1]

Its success was immediate, unquestioned, and lasting. Within twenty-five years, at the date of Scott's Introduction to the edition of 1830, it had had the unprecedented sale of some 44,000 copies. It was very profitable to the publishers, and the sum of money which Scott gained by it was in all £769, 6s.

3. THE FORM OF THE POEM.

The poem, as Scott originally conceived it, was to have been a refinement on the ancient ballad, dealing with the tradition of Gilpin Horner. But its final form was due to the suggestion of one of the friends before mentioned. His suggestion, after reading the first stanzas of the romance proper, was "that some sort of prologue might be necessary to place the mind of the hearers in the situation to understand and enjoy the poem". Scott says: "I entirely agreed with my friendly critic in the necessity of having some sort of pitch-pipe, which might make readers aware of the object, or rather the tone of the publication.... I therefore introduced the old minstrel as an appropriate prolocutor by whom the lay might be sung or spoken, and the introduction of whom betwixt the cantos might remind the reader at intervals of the time, place, and circumstances of the recitation. This species of *cadre*, or frame, afterwards afforded the poem its name".

---

[1] Ovid, *Epist. ex Ponto*, i. 5. 16: "As I read my lines again, I am ashamed that ever I wrote them; for many things I see which, even in the judgment of me who made them, are worthy only to be blotted out".

Scott had been attracted by the irregular rhythms of *Thalaba* and other poems of Southey, which had won general admiration in Scotland. But he acknowledged a more definite obligation to Coleridge's *Christabel*, the famous fragment of a romance, which, though not published until 1816, had been written mainly in 1797, and was in part recited to Scott by a mutual friend. *Christabel* is written in stanzas of unequal length, and in a metre which, Coleridge says in his Preface, "is not properly speaking irregular, though it may seem so from its being founded on a new principle, namely, that of counting in each line the accents, not the syllables. Though the latter may vary from seven to twelve, yet in each line the accents will be found to be only four. Nevertheless this occasional variation in the number of syllables is not introduced wantonly, or for the mere ends of convenience, but in correspondence with some transition in the nature of the imagery or passion".[1] Scott partially adopted the same principle. The irregular stanza, he said, "and the liberty which it allowed the author to adapt the sound to the sense, seemed to be exactly suited to such an extravaganza as I meditated on the subject of Gilpin Horner".

The metre of *The Lay* is the romantic riming measure of English poetry, often called iambic tetrameter, though that name is more proper to poetry scanned by quantity. The normal verse is of four feet, each consisting of an unaccented or unstressed, followed by an accented or stressed syllable.

This octo-syllabic metre is one that soon becomes monotonous and mechanical if the lines succeed one another with perfect uniformity of rhythm. It was Scott's great merit, according to Lord Byron, that he had "completely triumphed over the fatal facility of the octo-syllabic verse". This he did by a judicious variation of the rhythm, in accordance with Coleridge's four-beat principle, and of the disposition of the rimes. Compare the following lines :—

---

[1] It is curious that this principle, on which Scott founded a poem so universally admired, should in Coleridge's case have evoked the vehement displeasure of the *Edinburgh Review*, which condemned it as "the most notable piece of impertinence of which the press has lately been guilty".

(1) The way' | was long', | the wind' | was cold'

(2) The min' | strel wãs | infirm" | and old'

(3) And the La' | dye had gone' | to her se' | cret bower'

(4) Knight' | and page' | and house' | hold squire'

(5) Such' is | the cus' | tom of Brank' | some Hall'

(6) Pen' | ance, fa' | ther, will' | I none'

(7) And the silk' | en knots', | which in hur' | ry she would make'

All these lines contain four stresses, but a variable number
of syllables. Line (1) is regular. In (2) the loss of emphasis
on *was* gives the second syllable of *infirm* additional em-
phasis. In (3) the first three feet consist of two unstressed
and one stressed syllable (technically known as *anapaestic*).
(Note that *bower* and such words are treated as mono-
syllables.) Line (4) begins with a defective foot, consisting
of one long monosyllable. In (5) the first foot has the stress
inverted to the first syllable, while the third foot is like the
first in (3); or the first foot may be regarded as defective,
as in line (4), the second and third feet then being both
anapaests. Line (6) is suited to the rude character of the
Borderer; in line (7) the seven syllables of the last two feet
are very expressive of hurry.

With regard to the disposition of the rimes it will be
observed that the introduction, and the interludes between
the cantos, are in rimed couplets; in the *Lay* proper couplets
are variously combined with trimeters and quatrains. The
songs in the sixth canto have of course their own individual
forms.

4. CRITICAL.

In accounting for the brilliant success of Scott's *Lay*, we
must remember the circumstances and the spirit of the time
in which he lived, and the circumstances of his own poetical
training. The poetry of the 18th century had been dis-
tinguished by high excellence of artistic form, but had
exhibited two great defects: it ignored Nature, and it treated
man as having intellect, but no feeling; it could please his
mind but not touch his heart. In the subject-matter of

poetry were included religion, morals, politics, the manners of fine ladies, the squabbles of fine writers; treated in odes, essays, satires, and epistles in verse, but better, and properly, in the matchless prose of the Augustan writers. The subjects which we are accustomed to find in poetry, the beauty of Nature, the deepest soul-experiences of man, did not appeal to the writers of Pope's school. The insensibility to Nature which characterized the age drew from Keats the following denunciation:—

> Ah, dismal-soul'd!
> The winds of heaven blew, the ocean roll'd
> Its gathering waves,—ye felt it not; the blue
> Bared its eternal bosom, and the dew
> Of summer night collected still to make
> The morning precious. Beauty was awake—
> Why were ye not awake? But ye were dead
> To things ye knew not of—were closely wed
> To musty laws lined out with wretched rule
> And compass vile; so that ye taught a school
> Of dolts to smoothe, inlay, and chip, and fit,
> Till—like the certain wands of Jacob's wit—
> Their verses tallied.[1]

But even in this dead time there were signs of an awakening, the promise of another May in English song. Thomson wrote *The Seasons*, and Collins his *Odes*; Gray put into perfect words thoughts and feelings that never leave mankind; Cowper wrote "God made the country" and showed his readers the charm of country scenery; Crabbe drew pathetic stories from the "simple annals of the poor"; Blake sang happy songs of innocence. Above all, Burns, born twelve years before Scott, enshrined in verse for ever the passions common to men. These all led the way to that final breaking with old traditions which Wordsworth and Coleridge achieved by the publication of their *Lyrical Ballads* in 1798.

The new tendency took also another direction. The "marvellous boy", Thomas Chatterton, set flowing that stream

---

[1] *Sleep and Poetry.*

of romance which has not ceased to run through all succeeding poetry. It was from Chatterton that Coleridge got his new four-beat principle, from Coleridge that Scott stole it, from Scott that Byron lifted it; it was Chatterton from whom Shelley and Keats drew so much inspiration, and Tennyson owes not a little to Keats. Chatterton died in 1770; in 1765 was published Bishop Percy's *Reliques*, which set the minds of Scott and innumerable other children agog with enthusiasm. These were the influences under which Scott's genius developed; these influences were at the same time preparing for him readers who should appreciate his work. Hence, when *The Lay* came, with its pictures of romance, its legendary lore, its life and movement, its hints of the beauty of Nature, its sympathy with human feeling, it appealed, by this combination of manifold qualities, to a very large number of readers.

It would be wrong to say that Scott belonged wholly to the new school. His mind was too far in the past for that to be so. The scenes of his poems, and even of his novels, are all laid in bygone times, either remote as in *Ivanhoe*, or in the middle distance as *The Lay*, or within the memory of his grandfather, as *Old Mortality*. In dealing with these antique subjects, it was almost inevitable that he should exhibit some of the features of the discarded poetic style. So it is that his language is neither so expressive nor does it mean so much as that of some other poets of his own time. His epithets are often conventional and his diction artificial. He was in truth a link between the old and the new poetry, combining in his own many of the excellences and some of the defects of both. And always he was a romancer first and a poet afterwards.

The Lay owed much of its success to its simplicity. There is no subtle mental analysis; the characters are easily understood. The figure of the Minstrel,—old, poor, saddened by memories of the brighter past, beset by conflicting impulses as he came in sight of Branksome,—seized the attention of the reader, who felt at once a sympathy with the pathetic figure, and an interest in the tale he wished to tell. His picture was so naturally and so vividly drawn. The lines in which is depicted his embarrassment when he tries to recall the old half-forgotten strain delighted Pitt, who said : " This is a sort of thing which I might have expected in painting, but could never have fancied capable of being given in poetry ". This simplicity and naturalness is maintained throughout the poem, joined with a vividness of imagination, a descriptive power, a briskness of narrative, and a genuine love of nature, which enable the reader to see the scenes as Scott saw them, and with the same enjoyment. We have a wonderful picture of Melrose Abbey ; we see the rough Borderer, and dash along with him on his midnight ride ; we hear the bugle-note and the clash of arms ; we are carried right into the midst of scenes of mediæval romance. But we also feel the freshness and brightness of the still morning as we watch fair Margaret stealing through the wood to meet her lover, and we see the young lord, face to face with the baying blood-hound, his cheeks wet with tears but his courage undismayed, raising his little bat on high as one day he will raise a more for-midable weapon. Nothing is more admirable than the way in which these varying and contrasted scenes are set before us by means of varying rhythm and diction.

The defects of *The Lay*, as a work of art, are manifest. The style is in many places rough and unpolished. Scott wrote at a great pace, and though his language always flows easily on, the words are not always well chosen from an artistic point of view. Scott had little natural ear for music, and was not fastidious as to the harmony of his verse. The un-couth names here and there introduced would be a great blemish on the work if it were not that Scott himself made no great pretensions. " I am sensible ", he said, " that if there be anything good about my poetry ... it is a hurried frankness of composition which pleases soldiers, sailors, and young people of bold and active disposition." This " hurried frankness " is no doubt responsible for other defects in versification. Unlike Coleridge, Scott perhaps considered " the mere ends of convenience ". Hence the occurrence of faulty rimes, of the same words over and over

gain at the end of lines, of instances of inconsistency in the
sequence of tenses. Scott said himself, in explaining the
rapidity with which the poem was completed, "There was
ttle occasion for pause or hesitation, when a troublesome
rhyme might be accommodated by an alteration of the
stanza, or where an incorrect measure might be remedied by
variation of the rhyme".

The great defect of the poem, according to Jeffrey, was the
introduction of the goblin page. "The page", he says, "is
perpetual burden to the poet and to the reader; it is an
undignified and improbable fiction, which excites neither
error, admiration, nor astonishment, but needlessly debases
he strain of the whole work." Mr. R. H. Hutton says, " I
venture to say that no reader of the poem ever has distinctly
understood what the goblin page did or did not do, what it
was that was 'lost' throughout the poem and 'found' at the
conclusion, what was the object of his personating the young
heir of the house of Scott, and whether or not that object
was answered:—what use, if any, the magic book of Michael
Scott was to the Lady of Branksome, or whether it was only
harm to her; and I doubt, moreover, whether anyone ever
cared an iota what answer, or whether any answer, might be
given to any of these questions".

On the other hand, Professor Minto, besides pointing out
that the goblin was no afterthought, but the occasion of the
poem, and that it is due to Scott to take the superstitious
element at least as seriously as he did, adds: "his super-
natural machinery is really very closely jointed into the
movement of human affairs in his story. The goblin's pranks
in the kitchen are episodical, but the incidents on which the
story turns are all brought about by his help. His prying
into the mighty book of Michael Scott; his secret return of
the wounded and stunned Deloraine to the castle; his luring
away of the heir of Buccleuch to fall into English hands;
his substitution of Cranstoun for Deloraine in the combat,
are all necessary links in the main chain of events. The
discourse between the River Spirit and the Mountain Spirit;
the Lady's knowledge of this through her witchcraft; her

determination to baffle Fate with the help of Michael Scott
mighty book; the irony with which this instrument is turne
against her; her vengeance on the goblin, whose impish
tricks have marred her plans, are all essential parts of th
tale as told, and must all be taken seriously if we are to rea
it in the spirit in which it was conceived. It was meant t
be ' a tale of wonder' as well as a tale of rugged character
and picturesque adventures." But that Scott himself wa
conscious of the confusion and inconsistency into which th
enlargement of his original plan led him may be seen fror
his own plain statement in a letter to Miss Seward. H
wrote: "At length the story appeared so uncouth that I wa
fain to put it into the mouth of an old minstrel, lest th
nature of it should be misunderstood, and I should b
suspected of setting up a new school of poetry instead of
feeble attempt to imitate the old. In the process of th
romance, the page, intended to be a principal person in th
work, contrived (from the baseness of his natural propensities
I suppose) to slink downstairs into the kitchen, and now h
must e'en abide there." And unquestionably the figure tha
stands clearest to our eye, and holds the firmest place in ou
memory and our affection, is the Minstrel, and not the goblin
page.

4. THE STORY OF THE LAY.[1]

Sir Walter Scott of Buccleuch, the Lord of Branksome
was slain in a skirmish with the Carrs, about the middl
of the sixteenth century. He left a daughter of matchles
beauty, an infant son, and a high-minded widow, who, thoug
a very virtuous and devout person, was privately addicted t
the study of magic, in which she had been initiated by he
father. Lord Cranstoun, their neighbour, was at feud wit
the whole clan of Scott, but had fallen desperately in lov
with the daughter, who returned his passion with equa
sincerity and ardour, though withheld, by her duty to he
mother, from uniting her destiny with his.

---

[1] From Lord Jeffrey's article in the *Edinburgh Review*.

Canto I.—The poem opens with a description of the war-ike establishment of Branksome Hall, and the first incident hat occurs is a dialogue between the Spirits of the adjoining nountain and river, who, after consulting the stars, declare hat no good fortune can ever bless the mansion "till pride be quelled, and love be free". The lady, whose forbidden studies had taught her to understand the language of such speakers, overhears their conversation, and vows, if possible, to retain her purpose in spite of it. She calls a gallant knight of her train therefore, and directs him to ride immediately to the Abbey of Melrose, and there to ask from the Monk of St. Mary's Aisle, the mighty book that was hid n the tomb of the Wizard, Michael Scott. The remainder of the First Canto is occupied with the night journey of the warrior.

Canto II.—When he delivers his message the monk appears filled with consternation and terror, but leads him at last through many galleries and chapels to the spot where the Wizard was interred; and, after some account of his life and character, the warrior heaves up the tombstone, and is dazzled by the streaming splendour of an ever-burning lamp, which illuminates the sepulchre of the enchanter. With trembling hand he takes the book from the side of the deceased, and hurries home with it in his bosom. In the meantime, Lord Cranstoun and the lovely Margaret have met at dawn in the woods adjacent to the castle, and are repeating their vows of true love, when they are startled by the approach of a horseman. The lady retreats, and the lover rides away.

Canto III.—Advancing, he finds it to be the messenger from Branksome, with whom, as an hereditary enemy, he thinks it necessary to enter immediately into combat. The poor knight, fatigued with his nocturnal adventures, is dismounted at the first shock, and falls desperately wounded to the ground; while Lord Cranstoun, relenting to the kinsman of his beloved, directs his page to attend him to the castle, and gallops home before any alarm can be given. Lord Cranstoun's page is something unearthly. It is a little misshapen dwarf whom he found one day when he

was hunting in a solitary glen, and took home with him
It never speaks except now and then to cry "lost! lost
lost!" and is, on the whole, a hateful, malicious little urchin
with no one good quality but his unaccountable attachmen
and fidelity to his master. This personage, on approaching
the wounded Borderer, discovers the mighty book in hi:
bosom, which he finds some difficulty in opening, and ha:
hardly had time to read a single spell in it when he is strucl
down by an invisible hand, and the clasps of the magi(
volume shut suddenly more closely than ever. This on(
spell, however, enables him to practise every kind of illusion
He lays the wounded knight on his horse and leads him int(
the castle, while the warders see nothing but a wain of hay
He throws him down unperceived at the door of the lady':
chamber, and turns to make good his retreat. In passin§
through the court, however, he sees the young heir of Buc
cleuch at play, and, assuming the form of one of his com
panions, tempts him to go out with him to the woods, where
as soon as they pass a rivulet, he assumes his own shape an(
bounds away. The bewildered child is met by two Englisl
archers, who make prize of him, and carry him off, while th(
goblin page returns to the castle, where he personates th(
young baron to the great annoyance of the whole inhabitants
The lady finds the wounded knight, and eagerly employ
charms for his recovery, that she may learn the story of th(
disaster. The lovely Margaret in the meantime is sitting i1
her turret gazing on the western star, and musing on th(
scenes of the morning, when she discovers the blazin§
beacons that announce the approach of an English enemy
The alarm is immediately given, and bustling preparation
made throughout the mansion for defence.

Canto IV.—The English force, under the command of th
Lords Howard and Dacre, speedily appears before the castl(
leading with them the young Buccleuch, and propose tha
the lady should either give up Sir William of Deloraine (wh(
had been her messenger to Melrose), as having incurred th
guilt of March treason, or receive an English garrison withi1
her walls. She answers, with much spirit, that her kinsma1

will clear himself of the imputation of treason by single combat, and that no foe shall ever get admittance into her fortress. The English lords being secretly apprised of the approach of powerful succours to the besieged, agree to the proposal of the combat, and stipulate that the boy shall be restored to liberty or detained in bondage according to the issue of the battle. The lists are appointed for the ensuing day, and a truce being proclaimed in the meantime, the opposing bands mingle in hospitality and friendship.

Canto V.—Deloraine being wounded was expected to appear by a champion, and some contention arises for the honour of that substitution. This, however, is speedily terminated by a person in the armour of the warrior himself, who encounters the English champion, slays him, and leads the captive young chieftain to the embraces of his mother. At this moment Deloraine himself appears, half clothed and unarmed, to claim the combat which has terminated in his absence; and all flock around the stranger who had personated him so successfully. He unclasps his helmet, and behold! Lord Cranstoun of Teviotdale! The lady, overcome with gratitude, and the remembrance of the Spirit's prophecy, consents to forgo the feud, and to give the fair hand of Margaret to the enamoured baron.

Canto VI.—The rites of betrothment are then celebrated with great magnificence, and a splendid entertainment given to all the English and Scottish chieftains whom the alarm had assembled at Branksome. Lord Cranstoun's page plays several unlucky tricks during the festival, and breeds some dissension among the warriors. To soothe their ireful mood the minstrels are introduced, who recite three ballad pieces of considerable merit. Just as their songs are ended a supernatural darkness spreads itself through the hall; a tremendous flash of lightning and peal of thunder ensue, which break just on the spot where the goblin page had been seated, who is heard to say "found! found! found!" and is no more to be seen when the darkness clears away. The whole party is chilled with terror at this extraordinary incident, and Deloraine protests that he distinctly saw the figure of the ancient wizard, Michael Scott, in the middle of the lightning. The lady renounces for ever the unhallowed study of magic; and all the chieftains, struck with awe and consternation, vow to make a pilgrimage to Melrose to implore rest and forgiveness for the spirit of the departed sorcerer. With the description of this ceremony the Minstrel closes his lay.

THE
LAY OF THE LAST MINSTREL.

INTRODUCTION.

THE way was long, the wind was cold,
The Minstrel was infirm and old;
His wither'd cheek, and tresses gray,
Seem'd to have known a better day;
The harp, his sole remaining joy,   5
Was carried by an orphan boy.
The last of all the Bards was he,
Who sung of Border chivalry;
For, well-a-day! their date was fled,
His tuneful brethren all were dead;   10
And he, neglected and oppress'd,
Wish'd to be with them, and at rest.
No more, on prancing palfrey borne,
He caroll'd light as lark at morn;
No longer courted and caress'd,   15
High placed in hall, a welcome guest,
He pour'd, to lord and lady gay,
The unpremeditated lay:
Old times were changed, old manners gone;
A stranger fill'd the Stuarts' throne;   20
The bigots of the iron time
Had call'd his harmless art a crime.
A wandering Harper, scorn'd and poor,
He begg'd his bread from door to door;
And tuned, to please a peasant's ear,   25
The harp a king had loved to hear.

He pass'd where Newark's stately tower
Looks out from Yarrow's birchen bower:
The Minstrel gazed with wishful eye—
No humbler resting-place was nigh.   30
With hesitating step, at last,
The embattled portal arch he pass'd,
Whose ponderous grate and massy bar
Had oft roll'd back the tide of war,

But never closed the iron door   35
Against the desolate and poor.
The Duchess mark'd his weary pace,
His timid mien, and reverend face,
And bade her page the menials tell,
That they should tend the old man well: 40
For she had known adversity,
Though born in such a high degree;
In pride of power, in beauty's bloom,
Had wept o'er Monmouth's bloody tomb.

When kindness had his wants supplied,   45
And the old man was gratified,
Began to rise his minstrel pride:
And he began to talk anon,
Of good Earl Francis, dead and gone,
And of Earl Walter, rest him, God!   50
A braver ne'er to battle rode;
And how full many a tale he knew,
Of the old warriors of Buccleuch:
And, would the noble Duchess deign
To listen to an old man's strain,   55
Though stiff his hand, his voice though weak,
He thought even yet, the sooth to speak,
That, if she loved the harp to hear,
He could make music to her ear.

The humble boon was soon obtain'd;   60
The Aged Minstrel audience gain'd.
But, when he reach'd the room of state,
Where she, with all her ladies, sate,
Perchance he wish'd his boon denied:
For, when to tune his harp he tried,   65
His trembling hand had lost the ease,
Which marks security to please;
And scenes, long past, of joy and pain,
Came wildering o'er his aged brain—
He tried to tune his harp in vain!   70
The pitying Duchess praised its chime,
And gave him heart, and gave him time,
Till every string's according glee
Was blended into harmony.
And then, he said, he would full fain   75
He could recall an ancient strain,
He never thought to sing again.

It was not framed for village churls,
But for high dames and mighty earls;
He had play'd it to King Charles the Good,   80
When he kept court in Holyrood;
And much he wish'd, yet fear'd, to try
The long-forgotten melody.
Amid the strings his fingers stray'd,
And an uncertain warbling made,   85
And oft he shook his hoary head.
But when he caught the measure wild,
The old man raised his face, and smiled;
And lighten'd up his faded eye,
With all a poet's ecstasy!   90
In varying cadence, soft or strong,
He swept the sounding chords along:
The present scene, the future lot,
His toils, his wants, were all forgot:
Cold diffidence, and age's frost,   95
In the full tide of song were lost;
Each blank, in faithless memory void,
The poet's glowing thought supplied;
And, while his harp responsive rung,
'Twas thus the LATEST MINSTREL sung.   100

CANTO FIRST.

I.

THE feast was over in Branksome tower,
And the Ladye had gone to her secret bower;
Her bower that was guarded by word and by spell,
Deadly to hear, and deadly to tell—
Jesu Maria, shield us well!   5
No living wight, save the Ladye alone,
Had dared to cross the threshold stone.

II.

The tables were drawn, it was idlesse all;
    Knight, and page, and household squire,
Loiter'd through the lofty hall,   10
    Or crowded round the ample fire:

The stag-hounds, weary with the chase,
  Lay stretch'd upon the rushy floor,
And urged, in dreams, the forest race,
  From Teviot-stone to Eskdale-moor.   15

III.

Nine-and-twenty knights of fame
  Hung their shields in Branksome-Hall;
Nine-and-twenty squires of name
  Brought them their steeds to bower from stall;
    Nine-and-twenty yeomen tall   20
    Waited, duteous, on them all:
    They were all knights of mettle true,
    Kinsmen to the bold Buccleuch.

IV.

Ten of them were sheath'd in steel,
With belted sword, and spur on heel: 25
They quitted not their harness bright,
Neither by day, nor yet by night:
    They lay down to rest,
    With corslet laced,
Pillow'd on buckler cold and hard;   30
    They carved at the meal
    With gloves of steel,
And they drank the red wine through the helmet barr'd.

V.

Ten squires, ten yeomen, mail-clad men,
Waited the beck of the warders ten;   35
Thirty steeds, both fleet and wight,
Stood saddled in stable day and night,
Barbed with frontlet of steel, I trow,
And with Jedwood-axe at saddle-bow;
A hundred more fed free in stall:—   40
Such was the custom of Branksome-Hall.

VI.

Why do these steeds stand ready dight?
Why watch these warriors, arm'd, by night?—
They watch, to hear the blood-hound baying:
They watch, to hear the war-horn braying;   45

To see St. George's red cross streaming,
To see the midnight beacon gleaming:
They watch, against Southern force and guile,
    Lest Scroop, or Howard, or Percy's powers,
    Threaten Branksome's lordly towers,   50
From Warkworth, or Naworth, or merry Carlisle.

VII.

Such is the custom of Branksome-Hall.—
    Many a valiant knight is here;
But He, the Chieftain of them all,
His sword hangs rusting on the wall,   55
    Beside his broken spear.
    Bards long shall tell
    How Lord Walter fell!
When startled burghers fled, afar,
The furies of the Border war;   60
When the streets of high Dunedin
Saw lances gleam, and falchions redden,
And heard the slogan's deadly yell—
Then the Chief of Branksome fell.

VIII.

Can piety the discord heal,   65
    Or stanch the death-feud's enmity?
Can Christian lore, can patriot zeal,
    Can love of blessed charity?
No! vainly to each holy shrine,
    In mutual pilgrimage, they drew;   70
Implored, in vain, the grace divine
    For chiefs, their own red falchions slew:
While Cessford owns the rule of Carr,
    While Ettrick boasts the line of Scott,
The slaughter'd chiefs, the mortal jar,   75
The havoc of the feudal war,
    Shall never, never be forgot!

IX.

In sorrow o'er Lord Walter's bier
    The warlike foresters had bent;
And many a flower, and many a tear,   80
    Old Teviot's maids and matrons lent:

But o'er her warrior's bloody bier
The Ladye dropp'd nor flower nor tear!
Vengeance, deep-brooding o'er the slain,
    Had lock'd the source of softer woe;   85
And burning pride, and high disdain,
    Forbade the rising tear to flow;
Until, amid his sorrowing clan,
    Her son lisp'd from the nurse's knee—
" And if I live to be a man,   90
    My father's death revenged shall be!"
Then fast the mother's tears did seek
To dew the infant's kindling cheek.

X.

All loose her negligent attire,
    All loose her golden hair,   95
Hung Margaret o'er her slaughter'd sire,
    And wept in wild despair,
But not alone the bitter tear
    Had filial grief supplied;
For hopeless love, and anxious fear,   100
    Had lent their mingled tide:
Nor in her mother's alter'd eye
Dared she to look for sympathy.
Her lover, 'gainst her father's clan,
    With Carr in arms had stood,   105
When Mathouse-burn to Melrose ran,
    All purple with their blood;
And well she knew, her mother dread,
Before Lord Cranstoun she should wed,
Would see her on her dying bed.   110

XI.

Of noble race the Ladye came,
Her father was a clerk of fame,
    Of Bethune's line of Picardie:
He learn'd the art that none may name,
    In Padua, far beyond the sea.   115
Men said, he changed his mortal frame
    By feat of magic mystery;
For when, in studious mood, he paced
    St. Andrew's cloister'd hall,
His form no darkening shadow traced   120
    Upon the sunny wall!

XII.

And of his skill, as bards avow,
  He taught that Ladye fair,
Till to her bidding she could bow
  The viewless forms of air.   125
And now she sits in secret bower,
In old Lord David's western tower,
And listens to a heavy sound,
That moans the mossy turrets round.
Is it the roar of Teviot's tide,   130
That chafes against the scaur's red side?
Is it the wind, that swings the oaks?
Is it the echo from the rocks?
What may it be, the heavy sound,
That moans old Branksome's turrets round?   135

XIII.

At the sullen, moaning sound,
  The ban-dogs bay and howl;
And, from the turrets round,
  Loud whoops the startled owl.
In the hall, both squire and knight   140
  Swore that a storm was near,
And looked forth to view the night;
  But the night was still and clear!

XIV.

From the sound of Teviot's tide,
Chafing with the mountain's side,   145
From the groan of the wind-swung oak,
From the sullen echo of the rock,
From the voice of the coming storm,
  The Ladye knew it well!
It was the Spirit of the Flood that spoke,   150
  And he call'd on the Spirit of the Fell.

XV.

RIVER SPIRIT.

"Sleep'st thou, brother?"—

MOUNTAIN SPIRIT.

        —"Brother, nay—
On my hills the moonbeams play.

From Craik-cross to Skelfhill-pen,
By every rill, in every glen,   155
  Merry elves their morris pacing,
    To aërial minstrelsy,
  Emerald rings on brown heath tracing,
    Trip it deft and merrily.
Up, and mark their nimble feet!   160
Up, and list their music sweet!"—

XVI.

RIVER SPIRIT.

"Tears of an imprison'd maiden
  Mix with my polluted stream;
Margaret of Branksome, sorrow-laden,
  Mourns beneath the moon's pale beam.   165
Tell me, thou, who view'st the stars,
When shall cease these feudal jars?
What shall be the maiden's fate?
Who shall be the maiden's mate?"—

XVII.

MOUNTAIN SPIRIT.

"Arthur's slow wain his course doth roll,   170
In utter darkness round the pole;
The Northern Bear lowers black and grim;
Orion's studded belt is dim;
Twinkling faint, and distant far,
Shimmers through mist each planet star;   175
  Ill may I read their high decree!
But no kind influence deign they shower
On Teviot's tide, and Branksome's tower,
  Till pride be quell'd, and love be free."—

XVIII.

The unearthly voices ceast,   180
  And the heavy sound was still;
It died on the river's breast,
  It died on the side of the hill.
But round Lord David's tower
  The sound still floated near;   185
For it rung in the Ladye's bower,
  And it rung in the Ladye's ear.

She raised her stately head,
　　And her heart throbb'd high with pride:—
" Your mountains shall bend, 190
And your streams ascend,
　　Ere Margaret be our foeman's bride!"

XIX.

The Ladye sought the lofty hall,
　　Where many a bold retainer lay,
And, with jocund din, among them all, 195
　　Her son pursued his infant play.
A fancied moss-trooper, the boy
　　The truncheon of a spear bestrode,
And round the hall, right merrily,
　　In mimic foray rode. 200
Even bearded knights, in arms grown old,
　　Share in his frolic gambols bore,
Albeit their hearts of rugged mould,
　　Were stubborn as the steel they wore.
For the gray warriors prophesied, 205
　　How the brave boy, in future war,
Should tame the Unicorn's pride,
　　Exalt the Crescent and the Star.

XX.

The Ladye forgot her purpose high,
　　One moment, and no more; 210
One moment gazed with a mother's eye,
　　As she paused at the arched door:
Then from amid the armed train,
She call'd to her William of Deloraine.

XXI.

A stark moss-trooping Scott was he, 215
As e'er couch'd Border lance by knee;
Through Solway sands, through Tarras moss,
Blindfold, he knew the paths to cross;
By wily turns, by desperate bounds,
Had baffled Percy's best blood-hounds; 220
In Eske, or Liddel, fords were none,
But he would ride them, one by one;
Alike to him was time or tide,
December's snow, or July's pride;

Alike to him was tide or time,   225
Moonless midnight, or matin prime :
Steady of heart and stout of hand,
As ever drove prey from Cumberland ;
Five times outlawed had he been,
By England's King, and Scotland's Queen.   230

XXII

" Sir William of Deloraine, good at need,
Mount thee on the wightest steed ;
Spare not to spur, nor stint to ride,
Until thou come to fair Tweedside ;
And in Melrose's holy pile   235
Seek thou the Monk of St. Mary's aisle.
 Greet the Father well from me ;
  Say that the fated hour is come,
 And to-night he shall watch with thee,
  To win the treasure of the tomb :   240
For this will be St. Michael's night,
And, though stars be dim, the moon is bright ;
And the Cross, of bloody red,
Will point to the grave of the mighty dead.

XXIII.

" What he gives thee, see thou keep ;   245
Stay not thou for food or sleep :
Be it scroll, or be it book,
Into it, Knight, thou must not look ;
If thou readest, thou art lorn !
Better had'st thou ne'er been born."—   250

XXIV.

" O swiftly can speed my dapple-gray steed,
 Which drinks of the Teviot clear ;
Ere break of day," the Warrior 'gan say,
 " Again will I be here :
And safer by none may thy errand be done,   255
 Than, noble dame, by me ;
Letter nor line know I never a one,
 Were 't my neck-verse at Hairibee."

XXV.

Soon in his saddle sate he fast,
And soon the steep descent he past, 260
Soon cross'd the sounding barbican,
And soon the Teviot side he won.
Eastward the wooded path he rode,
Green hazels o'er his basnet nod;
He pass'd the Peel of Goldiland, 265
And cross'd old Borthwick's roaring strand;
Dimly he view'd the Moat-hill's mound,
Where Druid shades still flitted round;
In Hawick twinkled many a light;
Behind him soon they set in night; 270
And soon he spurr'd his courser keen
Beneath the tower of Hazeldean.

XXVI.

The clattering hoofs the watchmen mark;—
" Stand, ho! thou courier of the dark."—
" For Branksome, ho!" the knight rejoin'd, 275
And left the friendly tower behind.
    He turn'd him now from Teviotside,
    And, guided by the tinkling rill,
    Northward the dark ascent did ride,
    And gain'd the moor at Horsliehill; 280
Broad on the left before him lay,
For many a mile, the Roman way.

XXVII.

A moment now he slack'd his speed,
A moment breathed his panting steed;
Drew saddle-girth and corslet-band, 285
And loosen'd in the sheath his brand.
On Minto-crags the moonbeams glint,
Where Barnhill hew'd his bed of flint;
Who flung his outlaw'd limbs to rest,
Where falcons hang their giddy nest, 290
Mid cliffs, from whence his eagle eye
For many a league his prey could spy;
Cliffs, doubling, on their echoes borne,
The terrors of the robber's horn;

Cliffs, which, for many a later year,   295
The warbling Doric reed shall hear,
When some sad swain shall teach the grove,
Ambition is no cure for love!

XXVIII.

Unchallenged, thence pass'd Deloraine,
To ancient Riddel's fair domain,   300
    Where Aill, from mountains freed,
Down from the lakes did raving come;
Each wave was crested with tawny foam,
    Like the mane of a chestnut steed.
In vain! no torrent, deep or broad,   305
Might bar the bold moss-trooper's road.

XXIX.

At the first plunge the horse sunk low,
And the water broke o'er the saddle-bow;
Above the foaming tide, I ween,
Scarce half the charger's neck was seen;   310
For he was barded from counter to tail,
And the rider was arm'd complete in mail;
Never heavier man and horse
Stemm'd a midnight torrent's force.
The warrior's very plume, I say,   315
Was daggled by the dashing spray;
Yet, through good heart, and Our Ladye's grace,
At length he gain'd the landing-place.

XXX.

Now Bowden Moor the march-man won,
    And sternly shook his plumed head,   320
As glanced his eye o'er Halidon;
    For on his soul the slaughter red
Of that unhallow'd morn arose
When first the Scott and Carr were foes;
When royal James beheld the fray,   325
Prize to the victor of the day;
When Home and Douglas, in the van,
Bore down Buccleuch's retiring clan,
Till gallant Cessford's heart-blood dear
Reek'd on dark Elliot's Border spear.   330

XXXI.

In bitter mood he spurred fast,
And soon the hated heath was past;
And far beneath, in lustre wan,
Old Melros' rose, and fair Tweed ran :
Like some tall rock with lichens gray,   335
Seem'd dimly huge, the dark Abbaye.
When Hawick he pass'd, had curfew rung,
Now midnight lauds were in Melrose sung.
The sound, upon the fitful gale,
In solemn wise did rise and fail,   340
Like that wild harp, whose magic tone
Is waken'd by the winds alone.
But when Melrose he reach'd, 'twas silence all;
He meetly stabled his steed in stall,
And sought the convent's lonely wall.   345

HERE paused the harp; and with its swell
The Master's fire and courage fell:
Dejectedly, and low, he bow'd,
And, gazing timid on the crowd,
He seem'd to seek, in every eye,   350
If they approved his minstrelsy;
And, diffident of present praise,
Somewhat he spoke of former days,
And how old age, and wand'ring long,
Had done his hand and harp some wrong.   355
The Duchess, and her daughters fair,
And every gentle lady there,
Each after each, in due degree,
Gave praises to his melody;
His hand was true, his voice was clear,   360
And much they long'd the rest to hear.
Encouraged thus, the Aged Man,
After meet rest, again began.

NOTES.

INTRODUCTION.

Lay, song, narrative poem with or without music. (O. F. *lai*, from a Celtic root.)

2. Minstrel. See note on *Bards*, line 7, which in Scott mean much the same. From O. F. *menestral*, a servant or retainer. In the late middle ages and thenceforward, the word was applied to 'musicians'.

3. tresses, curls of hair. (From a Greek word meaning 'in three parts', because braiding the hair in three plaits was common; through F. *tresse*.) Notice how the Minstrel's *cheek* and *hair* are spoken of as having known a better day, when the Minstrel himself is meant. This is the figure of speech known as *metonymy*, *i.e.* change of name.

7. Bards. Celtic name for poets: given especially to the poets of Wales and Ireland.

In early English times, many a nobleman had his own bard or *scóp*, who was a kind of upper servant, employed to celebrate in song his master's prowess. Such long remained the custom in Scotland: cf. *Waverley*, ch. xxii. "...those family bards whom chieftains of more distinguished name and power retain as the poets and historians of their tribes"; and Scott's note to *Lady of the Lake*, ii. 7. With the Normans the minstrel was in high repute: Taillefer, minstrel and warrior, rode into the battle of Hastings chanting the *Song of Roland*: cf. the story of Richard I. and Blondel. Minstrels were often in the king's retinue. We hear also of unattached wandering harpers, singing of battles and heroic deeds, and depending on the bounty of those for whom they sang. Cf. the story of Alfred singing in the Danish camp.

8. Border chivalry. The barons and knights on the English and Scotch border spent much of their time in raiding on one another's domains. Their rough robber-warfare was sometimes illumined by chivalrous deeds. *Chivalry* means both 'knighthood', and 'the body of knights', collectively. (O. F. *chevalerie*, knighthood, horsemanship; *cheval*, a horse.)

9. well-a-day, alas! (corruption of *well-a-way*, from O. E. *wá lá wá*).

13–18. Notice that in these lines several words that are near one another begin with the same letter: *p*rancing *p*alfrey, *l*ight as *l*ark, *c*ourted and *c*aress'd, &c. This is called *alliteration*, and it was very common in old poems and ballads. It is intentional, and has a good effect on the melody of the verse.

13. palfrey, a saddle-horse, as distinct from a war-horse. (O. F. *palefrei.*) The word is generally applied to a lady's horse: cf. *Marmion*, vi. 7, "The Ancient Earl, with stately grace, Would Clara on her palfrey place".

14. caroll'd, sang. *Carol* meant originally a kind of dance.

14. light may be taken as = *lightly*, thus an adverb qualifying *caroll'd*, or it may be taken as an adjective in apposition with *he*, meaning then 'as light-hearted'.

16. high placed in hall. In the period of the Lay, the nobleman dined with his family and guests in the same hall with his servants and retainers (see *A Legend of Montrose*, ch. iv.). His own table was raised above the servants' table, and between the two was placed a huge salt-cellar, which separated the gentry from the lower classes. (Hence the expression "to sit above or below the salt".) The place at table depended on the guest's social rank. In England the noble's chaplain was often placed first of the servants below the salt. The family minstrel similarly was ranked among the retainers. A travelling minstrel would possibly be treated as a guest.

17. pour'd. This expresses the ease and freedom with which the Minstrel sang his song. It went on without pause like a rushing river.

18. unpremeditated, composed at the time; not the result of previous thought. (Lat. *prae*, before; *meditari*, to think about.)

It was not uncommon in the middle ages for bards to sing "unpremeditated lays"; it is still common in Italy, where the peasantry are skilful in the art, the Italian language being very fertile in rimes. Such singers are called *improvvisatori*.

20. a stranger. William III., Stadtholder of Holland, became king of England in 1689; this fixes the date of the supposed Last Minstrel: see line 80.

21, 22. The disfavour which the Puritans in the time of the Commonwealth showed to amusements and arts, music among them, is well known. Bishop Percy (*Reliques*, 5th edition, p. ciii) quotes an ordinance of 1656 declaring strolling "fidlers and minstrels" to be "rogues, vagabonds, and sturdy beggars". During the Commonwealth, organs, whose tones were likened to the whining of pigs, were removed from the churches. But the more cultured class of the nation still practised music, instrumental and vocal, in their own homes. Weekly musical parties were kept up at Oxford, where, as Anthony Wood tells us, "the Presbyterians used to love and encourage instrumental musick, but did not care for vocall, because that was used in church by the prelaticall partie". Cromwell was fond of music, and had the organ that was removed from Magdalen College re-erected at Hampton Court, where he paid his organist £100 a year. Milton, the Puritan poet, was also passionately fond of music, and a performer on the organ.

21. bigots, those who obstinately believe in certain things, and think that all who do not believe as they do must be wrong. The derivation of the word is disputed.

21. iron time. Iron is typical of hardness. Cf. the classical "age of iron"; the term 'iron-hearted'; see "iron door", line 35 below.

26. Notice the omission of the relative: cf. line 77, &c.

26. a king; see line 80.

27. Newark, in Selkirkshire, on the Yarrow. Newark Castle was built by James II. of Scotland. It came into the possession of the Buccleuch family, who retained it as an occasional seat for more than a century. The Duchess of Monmouth (see line 37) was brought up there. The neighbouring Bowhill was the favourite residence of Lady Dalkeith, who suggested the subject of the *Lay* to Scott: see Editorial Introduction.

28. Yarrow, a river in Selkirkshire. It is rich in poetical associations. See William Hamilton's *The Braes of Yarrow*, and Wordsworth's three Yarrow poems, the rhythm and metre of which he derived from *Leader Haughs and Yarrow*, the work of Nicol Burne, a 17th-century poet. James Hogg lived his shepherd life near Yarrow's banks.

28. birchen bower, garden-like nook formed by the branches of the birches. The suffix *-en* forms an adjective of material. *Bower* has several meanings: (1) a dwelling-place (O.E. *búr*); cf. canto vi. line 559, "Arose the Minstrel's lowly bower; A simple hut"; (2) an inner private room, especially a lady's room; cf. canto i. line 2, "And the Ladye had gone to her secret bower"; (3) as here.

29, 30. Notice how much is expressed in these lines. The Minstrel was weary and desired to rest: when he saw Newark towers he longed to enter there, but feared it might seem presumptuous in so poor and lowly a man. He would have asked leave to rest in a poorer place, but there was none, so he at last made up his mind to go to the castle, though even then he went "with hesitating step".

32. embattled portal arch, arched gateway, defended against attack by the **ponderous grate,** or portcullis, a grating that could be lowered and raised at will. *Embattled* properly means 'set in battle array'; then it means furnished with battlements; and lastly, fortified in general.

32. Notice the inversion of the natural order of the words. This is common in poetry, and particularly in Scott's.

34. roll'd back ... war. This is what is called a *metaphor*, the figure of speech in which one thing is put for another because of some real or fancied likeness between them. Here, attacking armies are likened to the waves of the sea, and just as a sea-wall would roll back waves advancing against it, so the "ponderous grate" is here represented as rolling back the soldiers.

35. Another instance of inversion : "the iron door never closed ".

35. **iron.** The door was made of iron, but it is implied here that the heart of the Duchess was not ‘iron’ in the same sense as the word is used in line 21.

37. **The Duchess.** Anne, Countess of Buccleuch (1651-1732), widow of James, Duke of Monmouth, who was beheaded for treason by order of James II., his uncle, in July, 1685, after the defeat of his rebellion at the Battle of Sedgemoor.

38. **mien,** look, appearance.

39. **menials,** household servants. (*Menial* is strictly an adjective: O. F. *meignal*, belonging to a *meisnee*, household.) The word has now a contemptuous meaning, and is given to those who do the lowest kind of work.

45. **kindness.** Another figure of speech, *metonymy*. The feeling which prompted the Duchess is put for the Duchess herself.

48. **anon, soon.** The original meaning was *at once*. (O. E. *on án*, in one.)

49, 50. **Earl Francis** was the father, **Earl Walter** the grandfather of the Duchess. Both were earls of Buccleuch.

50. **rest him, God!**, may God give him rest. *Rest* is here used transitively. Cf. the old Christmas Carol, "God rest ye, merry gentlemen".

51. **a braver,** *i.e.* a braver soldier.

52. **full,** very. *Full* is often used to strengthen and emphasize an adjective or adverb.

54. **would,** *i.e. if* she would.

55. **strain,** song, tune. (Through F. from Lat. *stringere*, to stretch.)

57. **sooth,** truth. (O. E. *sóth*.)

59. **to her ear,** *i.e.* that would please her.

60. **boon,** favour asked for. Originally a prayer, petition.

63. **with all her ladies.** It was common for the lady of the house to pass her time among her bower-maidens, engaged in music, or spinning, or fine needle-work.

63. **sate.** The *e* lengthens the preceding vowel *a*.

64. **wished his boon denied,** short for ‘wished (*that*) his boon (*had been*) denied’.

67. **security to please,** confidence in his power to please. Scott often uses *secure* in its classical sense of freedom from care or anxiety. (Lat. *se*, apart from; *cura*, care.)

69. **wildering,** in a bewildering, puzzling way.

71. chime, harmonious sound.   (O. E. *chimbe*, cymbal; Lat. *cymbalum.*)

73. according glee, joyful note sounding in harmony.   Or *according* might possibly be taken as 'agreeing with' or 'responding to' the minstrel's rising gaiety of heart.—*Glee* is an old word meaning 'music' (O. E. *gleó*, joy, music).   *Gleeman* is an old name for minstrel.   *Glee-maiden* occurs in *Lady of the Lake*, vi. 129.

75. he would full fain, he heartily wished.   See note on *full*, line 52 above.   *Fain* is O. E. *fægen*, glad.   "I would fain" = I should be glad to.

77. He never thought to sing, *i.e. which* he never expected to sing: omission of relative.

78. churls. The churls (O. E. *ceorl*) formed originally the lowest rank of freemen.   Then the word came to be applied generally to all men not of gentle birth; then to rustics and peasantry.   It now means a surly boorish man.

80, 81. Charles I. visited Scotland for the first time in June, 1633, with a large and brilliant train, among whom was Laud, then Bishop of London.   He lived in the royal palace of Holyrood, at the eastern border of Edinburgh, in the Abbey Church of which the ceremony of coronation was performed.

85. warbling, quavering sound.   Usually applied to the singing of birds.   (O. F. *werbler*, to whirl.)

86. hoary, white.   (O. E. *hár.*)

87. measure = rhythm, 'swing' of the music.   Or possibly here the music itself.

89. lighten'd. The subject is *eye.*

90. ecstasy, the state of being 'beside oneself' with emotion. (From a Greek word meaning to put out of place.)   The word is often applied to the effect of music.

91. cadence is properly the fall or modulation of tone in speaking or singing; it often means rhythmical movement: cf. *Old Mortality*, v., "the occasional boom of the kettledrum, to mark the cadence".   Here there seems to be a suggestion of rhythm as well as of tone.

92. swept expresses rapid free movement.   Cf. *Lycidas*, 17, "Begin, and somewhat loudly sweep the string".

92. chords, *i.e.* the music produced by striking the strings of his instrument.   (Lat. *chorda*, a string.)

93. future lot, future life; what would be *allotted* to him by Providence.   (O. E. *hlot*, a share, portion.)

94. forgot. The past part. is properly *forgotten*.   There was, and indeed is, a tendency to clip the inflectional endings.

95. age's frost. As frost hardens the ground and renders it for the time useless, so time is represented as having a chilling, hardening, deadening influence on a man's spirits and powers.

97. void, empty. *Void* is not a good rime to *supplied.*

99, 100. rung, sung. The correct past tenses are *rang* and *sang.*

100. Latest, *i.e.* last, which is a contraction of *latst.*

CANTO FIRST.

1. Branksome Tower. In the reign of James I. (of Scotland), the head of the Buccleuch clan came into possession of Branksome, and made it the principal seat of his family. "The castle was enlarged and strengthened by Sir David Scott, the grandson of Sir William, its first possessor." In 1570–71 it was destroyed by the English; the work of repair was begun in the same year by a Sir Walter Scott, and finished by his widow in 1574. Branksome, or *Branxholm*, is in the valley of the Teviot, 3 miles above Hawick.

2. Ladye. See note to line 113 below. She was the widow of the Sir Walter referred to in stanza vii.—A look of antiquity is given to the word by the final *e.* The O. E. original was *hláfdige,* 'loaf-kneader'.

2. bower. See Introduction, line 28, note.

3. by word and by spell. The *glosse* to Spenser's *Shepheards Calender, March,* gives: "Spelle is a kinde of verse or charme, that in elder tymes they used to say over everything that they would have preserved, as the Nightspel for theeves". *Spell* is therefore a form of words, supposed to possess magical protective power. Scott also uses the word for *substances* superstitiously supposed to be remedies against various ailments.

5. Taken from Coleridge's *Christabel,* line 54.

5. Jesu Maria. Originally a petition to or invocation of Jesus and His Mother, this became a mere exclamation.

6. wight, person. Also spelt *whit,* meaning 'thing' or 'bit', from O. E. *wiht,* the *h* having been misplaced.

7. had dared, *i.e.* would have dared.

8. drawn = removed or pushed back.

8. idlesse. A modern poetical word formed to look like *humblesse* and *noblesse,* which are genuine Old French words used by Chaucer.

8. all, perhaps 'altogether', or merely an intensive particle; cf. Coleridge, *Ancient Mariner,* 111, "All in a hot and copper sky".

9. **page ... squire.** A well-born boy was placed at the age of twelve among the household of a knight, where as a *page* he fulfilled lowly offices. In two years he became a *squire*, and engaged in higher duties in attendance on the knight, whose arms he carried. Then at the age of twenty-one he might himself become a *knight*, thus attaining the last of the degrees of chivalry.—The derivation of *page* is uncertain. *Squire* is from Fr. *escuyer*, Low Lat. *scutarius*, a shield-bearer.

13. **rushy floor.** The floors were then covered with rushes.

14. **urged ... the ... race**, ran rapidly. *Urge* means to press on: Lat. *urgere*.

15. **Teviot**, river of Roxburghshire, flowing N.E. to the Tweed. **Eskdale-moor**, mountainous district in the N.W. of the Esk valley.

16. "The ancient Barons of Buccleuch, both from feudal splendour and from their frontier situation, retained in their household at Branksome a number of gentlemen of their own name, who held lands from their chief for the military service of watching and warding the castle."

18. **of name** = well-born.

19. **to bower from stall;** *i.e.* from the stables to the door of the private apartments, where the knights mounted after bidding the ladies farewell.

20. **yeomen.** The title *yeoman* was given to a servant next above a groom, and below a sergeant. It was also given to a bailiff's attendant. In a secondary sense the word was applied "to people of middling rank not in service; and in more modern times it came to signify a small landholder" (Morris). The *yeomen* formed part of the army.—Much conjecture has been exercised in deriving the word. Tyrwhitt and Morris refer it (most probably) to *yeongeman*, a young man. "The A. S. *geongra* = a vassal, and *geongorscipe* = service. It is the latter etymology that explains the modern form *yeoman*." (Morris.)

22. **mettle.** The same word as *metal* (Lat. *metallum*). It here means high courage, a metaphorical meaning derived from the literal meaning. In its metaphorical senses the spelling *mettle* is now exclusively employed.

24-33. These lines indicate, with some exaggeration, the state of watchfulness and readiness in which the knights constantly were. Sudden attacks were common on the Borders.

24. **sheath'd in steel**, completely covered with steel armour, as a sword is completely covered by its sheath.

26. **harness** = armour. So used in the Bible. Cf. *1 Kings*, xxii. 34, "A certain man drew a bow at a venture, and smote the king of Israel between the joints of the harness".

29. **corslet,** armour covering for breast and back. (O. F. *cors*, the body.)

30. **buckler,** small round shield with a boss or knob in the centre. (O. F. *boucler*, from L. Lat. *bucula*, the boss of a shield, Lat. *buculla*, dim. of *bucca*, the cheek.)

32. **gloves of steel,** the gauntlets which they wore to protect their hands in battle. They were probably made of a kind of steel netting.

33. **helmet barr'd.** The front part or visor of the helmet had bars through which the knights might see and breathe, but which would protect the face from injury.

34. **mail-clad,** dressed in mail armour. There were two kinds of armour, mail and plate. The latter consisted of plates of metal, the former consisted of a fine steel network. (Lat. *macula*, small hole, through F. *maille*.)

35. **waited the beck,** were ready instantly to obey orders. Cf. the common phrase, "at beck and call". Shortened form of *beckon*, O. E. *béacn*, a sign.

36. **wight,** nimble, swift. Quite a different word from *wight* in line 6, being derived from Icelandic *vigr*, in fighting condition.

38. **barbed with frontlet,** protected with a head-covering. *Barbed* is a corruption of *barded* (O. F. *barde*, horse armour); see line 311. *Frontlet*, a covering for the forehead = *frontal-et*, dim. of *frontal*, O. F. *frontale*, from Lat. *frons*.

39. **Jedwood-axe,** an axe mounted on a long staff. "The Jedwood-axe was ... used by horsemen, as appears from the arms of Jedburgh. ... It is also called a Jedwood or Jeddart staff." (Scott.)

42. **dight,** saddled and furnished with armour. *Dighted* is the true past participle. The proper meaning of *dight* is 'to set in order'. (O. E. *dihtan*, from Lat. *dictare*, to prescribe.)

42, 43. The questions are introduced in order to draw special attention to the facts.

44. "The kings and heroes of Scotland, as well as the border-riders, were sometimes obliged to study how to evade the pursuit of blood-hounds. Barbour informs us that Robert Bruce was repeatedly tracked by sleuth-dogs." (Scott.)

46. **St. George's red cross,** the English banner. *St. George* is the English patron saint: English knights frequently bore the red cross woven on their outer garment. The Union Jack contains the combined crosses of St. George for England and St. Andrew for Scotland.

47. beacon, from O. E. *béacn*: see note on line 35. *Beacon*, or signal, fires were lighted upon hill-tops to give warning of an approaching enemy. Cf. Macaulay's *Armada.*

48-51. "Branksome Castle was continually exposed to the attacks of the English, both from its situation and the restless military disposition of its inhabitants, who were seldom on good terms with their neighbours." (Scott.) **Scroop, Howard, Percy** were lords on the English side at different times Wardens of the Marches.

49. powers, forces, troops, as often in Shakespeare.

51. Warkworth, a castle on the Coquet, in Northumberland; the seat of the Percies. **Naworth,** near Carlisle. **Carlisle,** being so near the Border, was continually subject to attack, and was a centre for the Border warfare. It had a bustling trade, and was the scene of some romantic adventures. Hence its permanent epithet **merry.**

54, 55. he, the Chieftain ... his sword. Notice the emphatic change in the construction, *his sword* becoming subject instead of *he.*

57, 58. "Sir Walter Scott of Buccleuch succeeded to his grandfather, Sir David, in 1492. He was a brave and powerful baron, and warden of the west marches of Scotland. His death was the consequence of a feud betwixt the Scotts and the Carrs." (Scott.)

The feud arose thus:—In 1526 James V., then a minor, was governed by the Douglases, and wished to escape their control. He therefore wrote secretly to Buccleuch, asking him to meet him at Melrose on his home-coming, and take him out of the Douglases' hands. Buccleuch obeyed, but his company was completely routed by the Douglases with the aid of the Carrs and others, though in the pursuit the chief of the Carrs was slain by Elliot, one of Buccleuch's servants. Twenty-six years later, in 1552, this Sir Walter Scott was slain by the Carrs in the streets of Edinburgh.

59. burghers, citizens, men of a burgh or borough. (O. E. *burg,* a town.)

59. fled, *i.e.* fled from.

61. Dunedin = Edinburgh, Edwin's town. *Dun* = a hill fort. *Dunedin* therefore = Edwin's fort, named after a Northumbrian prince to whom it belonged in 628.

62. falchions, straight blades curved at the point. (O. F. *fauchon,* Lat. *falx,* sickle.)

63. slogan, the war-cry of a clan. (Gaelic *sluagh,* army; *gairm,* outcry.)

66. death-feud, a feud between two clans, in which, if a member of one clan were killed, it would become the duty of every kinsman to avenge him, either on the actual murderer or on any of his kin.

67. lore, learning. (O. E. *lár*, from the stem of *læran*, to teach.)

69, 72. With a view to end the feud between the Scotts and the Carrs, an agreement was made in 1529 between the heads of the clans, binding themselves to go on pilgrimage to the four principal shrines of Scotland, "for the benefit of the souls of those of the opposite name who had fallen in the quarrel. ... But either it never took effect, or else the feud was renewed shortly afterwards." (Scott.)

72. Note the omission of the relative.

73. Cessford, village in Roxburghshire, 5 miles from the English border. Its castle was the seat of the Carr (or *Ker*) family. The *place* is here put for the *inhabitants*. It is the people who *own the rule of (i.e.* acknowledge feudal submission to) the Carrs.

74. Ettrick, district in Selkirkshire, where the Buccleuchs had one of their earliest estates.

74. boasts the line, glories in the fact that the Scott family had been settled there for generations.

75. mortal jar, deadly quarrel. *Mortal* is here used in the same sense as in 'mortal wound'. *Jar* is properly a musical term, 'discord'.

76. feudal war. *Feudal* here has two senses combined: (1) the ordinary sense, as in 'feudal system': *feudal war* meaning a war in which the dependants of the noble family were involved because they held their lands on condition of doing service in war: this *feud* is from O. H. G. *fihu*, property, through O. F. *fieu* and L. Lat. *feudum*: (2) belonging to a *feud*, a strife between families. This *feud* is from O. E. *fæhth*, enmity, and owes its spelling, though really an older word, to confusion with the former word.—In this case probably the second meaning is the stronger. Cf. iii. 36, "feudal hate".

81. lent, gave. (O. E. *lenan,* to lend or give.)

83. nor ... nor=neither ... nor; frequent in poetry.

84. deep-brooding, belongs *grammatically* to **vengeance,** but *actually* to the person who cherished thoughts of revenge. *Vengeance* is personified.

85. softer woe, *i.e.* tears; abstract for concrete.

86. high=haughty.

87–93. Tennyson has a similar incident in his song *Home they brought her warrior dead*, in *The Princess*—

> "Home they brought her warrior dead,
>   She nor swoon'd, nor uttered cry;
> All her maidens, watching, said,
>   'She must weep, or she will die'.

.   .   .   .

Rose a nurse of ninety years,
Set his child upon her knee;
Like summer tempest came her tears—
'Sweet my child, I live for thee.'"

90. **and if.** *And* is an old word meaning 'if', often spelt *an* to distinguish it from the copulative conjunction.

94. **All.** See i. 8, note.

96. **sire,** often used by the poets for *father.* It is another form of *sir,* and comes from Lat. *senior,* elder, through French.

98. **alone** goes with filial grief.

98. **filial grief,** the grief of a daughter for her father. (Lat. *filia,* a daughter.)

102. **alter'd eye,** *i.e.* eye that no longer looked on her with the same affection as before. Cf. line 211.

104. **clan,** the descendants of a common ancestor, united under a chief.

106. **Mathouse-burn.** *Burn,* a brook (O.E. *burna*). *Burn* is the form common in the north; the form *bourn* occurs in the south of England, as in *Bournemouth.*

106. **Melrose,** in the N. of Roxburghshire, near the Tweed. The battle of Melrose, here probably alluded to, was in 1526.

108. **her mother dread,** her terrible mother.

109, 110. "The Cranstouns are an ancient border family, whose chief seat was at Crailing, in Teviotdale. They were at this time at feud with the clan of Scott." (Scott.)

112. **clerk of fame** = famous scholar. *Clerk* (Lat. *clerus*) originally meant a clergyman. Since, in the middle ages, learning was almost entirely confined to the clergy, the word came to mean *scholar*; and, generally, man of learning.

113. Lady Buccleuch was Dame Janet Beaton, of the same family as the famous Cardinal Beaton. The Scotch branch of the family were settled in Fifeshire, but were of French origin, appearing as the Bethunes in Picardy, deriving their name from a small town in Artois.

114. **the art that none may name,** magic, necromancy, the "black art". Those who professed the art pretended to have spirits at their beck and call, with whom they might take counsel, and by whose aid they could foretell events, &c.

115. **in Padua.** "Padua was long supposed, by the Scottish peasants, to be the principal school of necromancy." (Scott.) The University of Padua, founded in 1221, was famous in the middle ages.

117. feat, extraordinary deed. (Fr. *fait*; Lat. *factum*.)

119. St. Andrew's cloister'd hall, the hall of the monastery at St. Andrews. *Cloister* means a covered walk (Lat. *claustrum*, from *claudere*, to shut).

120, 121. It was a popular belief "that when a class of students have made a certain progress in their mystic studies, they are obliged to run through a subterraneous hall, when the devil literally catches the hindmost in the race, unless he crosses the hall so speedily that the arch-enemy can only apprehend his shadow. In the latter case the person of the sage never after throws any shade." (Scott.)

122. of his skill, *i.e.* something of his skill—*partitive* use of the preposition.

124. bow, *cause* to bow, *i.e.* to obey. Cf. *rest*, Introduction, line 50.

125. viewless forms of air, invisible spirits supposed to hover in the air, whence they did good or ill to men.

127. Lord David. "Branksome Castle was enlarged and strengthened by Sir David Scott, the grandson of Sir William, its first possessor." (Scott.)

128. heavy, deep-toned. There is probably also a hint of fore-boding ill. Cf. 195, "that heavy sound breaks in once more".

129. Notice the inverted order; and the alliteration in this line and the next. R o und is a preposition.

131. chafes, dashes in commotion like boiling water. (F. *chauffer*, to warm.) See line 145.

131. scaur, precipitous rocky bank, bare hill-side. The same as English *scar*, as in *Scarborough*, &c. (Icel. *sker*.)

137-139. The howling of dogs and the screeching of owls were held to portend death or some disaster.

137. ban-dogs, mastiffs. Originally *band-dogs*, because they were chained up. In iii. 185 and 206 the same dog is called 'ban-dog' and 'blood-hound', but the former was properly a watch-dog, while the latter was employed in the chase.

138. round is here an adverb.

150, 151. Simple people personify the powers of nature: they regard the commonest natural events as the deeds of invisible divinities, who inhabit streams and groves, &c. In Scotland, as late as Scott's day, the belief in spirits, fairies, and elves was rife. Poets have made large use of the superstition.

151. Fell=hill, as in *Crossfell*. (Icel. *fjall*.)

154. pen, a hill-summit, as in *Pen-i-gant*, &c.   (A Celtic word.)
Craik-cross and **Skelfhill-pen** are hills on opposite sides of the
Teviot.

156. elves, supernatural beings, of dwarfish shape, possessing
magical powers.   They differ from *fairies* in that they exercise their
powers more mischievously and harmfully than the latter.   See note
on line 158 below.   (O. E. *ælf.*)

156. morris.   The morris-dance was a dance performed by
persons in fantastic costume, having bells attached to their hoods
and other parts of their dress.   "Another name was *morisco*, *i.e.*
Moorish dance.   It is said to have been introduced into England
in the reign of Edward III. when John of Gaunt returned from
Spain."

157. aerial minstrelsy, music in the air.

158. "The Elves are extremely fond of dancing in the meadows,
where they form those circles of a livelier green which from them
are called Elf-dance" (Keightley).   Cf. Scott's Introduction to
the *Tale of Tamlane* (*Border Minstrelsy*, ii. 162): "The Fairies
of Scotland ... inhabit the interior of green hills ... on which they
lead their dances by moonlight; impressing on the surface the marks
of circles, which sometimes appear yellow and blasted, sometimes
of a deep green hue".

159. trip it.   Cf. *L'Allegro*, 33, "Come, and trip it as ye go".
The *it* is equivalent to a cognate accusative, *i.e.* a substantive implied
in the governing verb.

159. deft, *i.e.* deftly, adjective for adverb; cf. *timid*, line 349.
Deft means skilful, clever.

161. list = listen to.   O. E. *hlystan* was an active verb.

163. polluted, *i.e.* by the blood shed in "feudal hate".

170. Arthur's slow wain, commonly called *Charles's Wain* or the
Plough; the seven brightest stars in the constellation Ursa Major.
Arthur's is a popular corruption of *Arcturus*, the Latin name.   In
early times the British Arthur was associated in popular hero-worship
with the Frankish Charlemagne: hence the term *Charles's wain.*
Wain is from O. E. *wægn*, wagon.

171. utter, extreme, complete.   Appears as *outer* in the Biblical
"outer darkness."   Comparative of O. E. *út*, out.

172, 173. Northern Bear, Orion; names of constellations.

172. lowers, frowns.   (D. *loeren*.)   The constellations are per-
sonified.

173. studded belt.   The constellation *Orion* is figured as a man
with a sword at his side, the belt of which is formed by three stars.

175. planet, used adjectivally = wandering.   (Gk. *planētēs*, wan-
derer.)

176. **Ill may I read**, I can ill interpret (because they faintly twinkle and shimmer through mist).

176. **may.** O. E. *mægon* meant 'to be strong, able,' and was used where we now use 'can'. There are numerous instances of the word so used in Scott.

176. **read**, interpret by looking at.

176. **their high decree.** In the middle ages the belief in astrology was almost universal. The stars were believed not only to appear as *signs* of future events, but even to influence them. Many references occur in the poets.

177. **influence**, an astrological term, denoting the *inflowing* power of the heavenly bodies on the lives of men.

177. **shower.** When the O. E. infinitive ending -*an* or -*en* was lost and was beginning to be replaced by *to*, auxiliary verbs were used with another verb without being followed by *to*. But the distinction between auxiliary and non-auxiliary verbs not being at first clear, there was inconsistency in the usage. Scott here adopts the license of omitting *to*.

191. A typical impossibility.

194. **retainer**, an armed servant, wearing the livery of a nobleman, but of higher rank and owning less obedience than the domestic servants.

195. **jocund**, merry, light-hearted. (Lat. *jucundus*, connected with *juvenis*, a youth.)

197. **fancied**; he was "playing at soldiers".

197. **moss-trooper.** "This was the usual appellation of the marauders upon the Borders; a profession diligently pursued by the inhabitants on both sides." (Scott.) The name arises from the fact that the border-lands were marshy (*moss*=marsh); cf. line 271, "Through Solway sands, through Tarras moss".

198. **truncheon**, the wooden shaft. (O. F. *tronçon*, a piece cut off, diminutive of *tronc*.)

200. **foray**, raid, expedition in quest of plunder. *Foray* is a northern form of *forage*, O. F. *fourage*, from Low Latin *fodrum*, food. The word is applied generally to marauding expeditions.

202. **frolic**, gay, merry. Now usually a noun, but the adjectival use is the earlier.

203. **Albeit**, although.

203. **mould**, make, material. A metaphor from metal-casting.

207, 208. **Unicorn's pride, Crescent and the Star**: a reference to the coats of arms of the Carrs and Buccleuchs respectively.

Unicorn must be pronounced with a strongly trilled *r* to make the two syllables required by the metre. Cf. iv. 258, where *Rangleburn* must be similarly pronounced.

209. high, important, serious, far removed from child's play. Notice how often *high* is used in this poem, and compare the different expressions in which it occurs.

213. train, company of retainers. (Fr. *traîner*, Lat. *trahere*, to draw along.)

214. William of Deloraine. William Scott, commonly called " Cut-at-the-Black ", a kinsman of the Buccleuchs. He had a grant of the lands of Deloraine in Ettrick Forest, which belonged to the Buccleuchs, in return for services rendered. Sir Walter Scott has invested him with the attributes of the typical borderer of the time.

215. stark, stiff, strong. Cf. *Lady of the Lake*, canto v. stanza xx., " King James shall mark, If age has tamed these sinews stark ".— Now used only in the sense of ' completely ', as in ' stark naked ', &c.

216. couch'd, grasped and held firmly in a horizontal position in readiness for the charge.

217. Tarras moss, marshy district about the Tarras, a rivulet of Dumfriesshire, running into the Esk.

218. to cross = for crossing, to be crossed.

221. Eske (or *Esk*), river of Dumfriesshire, flowing into the Solway Firth. **Liddel,** tributary of the Esk.

221, 222. fords were none, but he would ride them = there was no ford that he would not ride through.

224. July's pride, the glory of a July day. Accent *July* on the first syllable, as it is still accented in Scotland.

226. matin prime, early morning. (L. *matutinus*, pertaining to morning; *primus*, first.)

229. outlawed, declared to be without the protection of the law. A price was set on an outlaw's head; he had no rights; if captured, he might be punished without trial.

230. England's King, and Scotland's Queen. At this time (1552) Edward VI. was King of England, and Mary Stuart, daughter of James V., Queen of Scotland. But Mary was in France. The queen-mother, Mary of Lorraine, daughter of the Duke of Guise, was all-powerful.

231. good at need, a man to rely on in an emergency. A perpetual epithet, like *pius Aeneas*. Cf. canto ii. **178.**

232. mount thee. *Thee* is dative (see ii. 69, note). In O. E., verbs of motion were generally reflexive.

233. stint to ride. *To ride* is equivalent to a verbal noun. *Stint*, cease (O. E. *styntan*, to make short). *Stint* is usually followed by a noun.

235, 236. Melrose's holy pile ... St. Mary's aisle. The abbey of the monastery at Melrose was founded by King David I. in 1136, and dedicated to St. Mary. It is situated about two furlongs south of the Tweed. The original building was destroyed by fire in 1322; its successor was a magnificent Gothic structure, remarkable for its exquisite stone carvings, which have in measure defied the wear of time and weather. See Scott's fine description in canto ii.

238-250. Explained in canto ii. stanza xv. Michael Scott's magic book was buried with him, the monk who buried him swearing not to remove it except in the urgent need of the chief of the Scott clan, *i.e.* Buccleuch.

240. win, get. *Win* also means to 'reach', 'get to', as in line 262.

241. St. Michael's night, September 29th (Michaelmas). St. Michael the Archangel was the leader of the hosts of heaven against Satan; see *Paradise Lost*, books xi. and xii. especially. He is represented as holding a flaming sword; this is probably the **cross of bloody red** in line 243.

245. see thou keep, see *that* thou keep, be sure to keep.

247. scroll, roll of parchment.

249. lorn, lost. Past participle of O. E. *leosan*, to lose.

250. Better, *i.e.* it would have been better.

251. Notice how expressive this line is of a horse's galloping.

253. 'gan. The O. E. verb is *ginnan*, so that strictly the apostrophe is unnecessary. *Gan* is auxiliary and means *did*. When it means *began* it is always followed by *to*.

258. neck-verse, the verse set to be read by a malefactor claiming benefit of clergy. The clergy could not be punished by the civil courts, but only by ecclesiastical courts; this exemption was called "benefit of clergy". Any one claiming to escape execution for this reason had to prove his clerkly scholarship by reading a verse of the Latin Bible, usually Psalm li. 1, *Miserere mei, Domine*. If he could do this, he saved his neck.

258. Hairibee, an eminence outside Carlisle, on which criminals were executed. See *The Heart of Midlothian*, ch. xl.

259-345. Notice how rapidly and vividly Scott describes the march-man's ride and the various scenes through which he passed.

261. barbican, "generally a small round tower for the station of an advanced guard placed just before the outward gate of the castle-yard" (Nares' *Glossary*). It was properly a watch-tower. But Scott appears to use the word indifferently for a tower and an extensive outwork—more often the latter. Cf. *Ivanhoe*, ch. xxi.: "The access, as usual in castles of the period, lay through an arched barbican, or outwork, which was terminated and defended by a small turret at each corner"; *id.* ch. xxvii.: "Passing the moat on a single plank, they reached a small barbican, or exterior defence, which communicated with the open field by a well-defended sally-port".—Cf. canto iv. 53, "echoing barbican".

262. won, reached. See note on line 240.

264. basnet, shortened form of *basinet*, a light steel helmet, fitting close to the skull. (O. F. *bacinet*, dim. of *bacin*, basin.)

265. peel, small square tower. There were formerly many of these towers on the Borders.

265. Goldiland, on right bank of Teviot, 1½ miles above Hawick: so called because it belonged to a family named Goldie.

266. Borthwick, rapid stream flowing into the Teviot between Branxholm and Hawick.

266. strand, shore. Hence *Strand*, the name of the street in London, because it runs along parallel with and near to the shore of the Thames.

267. Moat-hill's mound. "This is a round artificial mound near Hawick, which, from its name [O. E. *gemôt*, meeting], was probably anciently used as a place for assembling a national council of the adjacent tribes." (Scott.)

268. Druid shades, the ghosts of dead Druids. *Shades*, the souls of men separated from their bodies, were supposed to haunt the spots frequented by the men in life.

269. Hawick, town 50 miles S.E. of Edinburgh, in Roxburgh-shire, at confluence of Teviot with Slitrig.

271. courser keen, swift, eager horse; from O. F. *corsier*; Lat. *cursus*, a running.

272. Hazeldean. "The estate of Hazeldean belonged formerly to a family of Scotts." (Scott.) Hazeldean, or *Hassendean*, is on the left bank of Teviot.

274. courier of the dark. Deloraine, riding in haste just as the evening shades are gathering, is hailed as though he were a messenger sent to tell of the advance of night. *Courier*, a swift messenger. (F. *courrier*, from Lat. *currere*, to run. See note on line 271.)

278. tinkling, an imitative word, expressing the *tink tink* of falling water. A *tinker* is a man who makes a *tinking* sound as he mends his pots.

280. Horsliehill, N.W. of Hazeldean, between that and Minto-crags.

282. Roman way. "An ancient Roman road, crossing through part of Roxburghshire."

284. breathed, gave time for taking breath.

286. brand, sword, so called probably from its flashing in light (O. E. *brand*; *beornan*, to burn).

287. Minto-crags, rocks about 2 miles north of Hassendean

287. glint, glance, flash.

288. Barnhill, a robber.

290. giddy, suggesting giddiness to an onlooker, by its extreme height.

291. eagle eye. The eagle is said to have very keen sight, and to be able to look with open eye at the bright sun; hence the use of the word *eagle* adjectivally in the sense 'keen-sighted'.

295–298. These lines refer to Sir Gilbert Elliot of Minto (1722–1777), an able statesman and orator, who also wrote verses. The poem particularly referred to is a song entitled *Amynta*, two lines of which are as follows: "Ambition, I said, would soon cure me of love"..."Ah! what had my youth with ambition to do?"

296. warbling Doric reed. Pastoral poetry (*i.e.* poetry describing pastoral scenes or written in the person of an imaginary shepherd) is often described as *Doric*, because the first poets who used the style wrote in the Doric dialect of Greek. The shepherd's pipe was formed out of a reed: cf. canto iii. 11.

297. swain, properly, a young countryman.

299. Unchallenged, not called upon from Minto-crags to give an account of himself.

300. "The family of Riddel have been very long in possession of the barony called Riddell, or Ryedale." (Scott.)

301. Aill, stream rising on high ground in Selkirkshire, flowing into the Teviot.

306. might. See note on *may*, line 176.

309. ween, think, imagine (O. E. *wenan*).

311. barded. See note on *barbed*, line 38.

311. counter, breast. Strictly, the part of the breast between the shoulders and under the neck. (Lat. *contra*, opposite.)

315. very plume, actually, his plume. *Very* is used to give emphasis, to show more vividly the heavy splashing of horse and rider in the stream.

316. daggled, wetted. (Sw. *dagga*, dew.)

317. Our Ladye, the Virgin Mary.

317. grace, favour. (Lat. *gratia*.)

319. Bowden Moor, in Roxburghshire, crossed by the Hawick and Melrose road.

319. march-man, man of the *marches* or borders.

321. "Halidon was an ancient seat of the Carrs." On Halidon Hill the battle of Melrose was fought, 1333.

322. slaughter red. *Slaughter* is strictly an abstract noun, and therefore incapable of being qualified by an adjective of colour. It is an instance of personification. The adjective signifies the *effect*, *i.e.* the shedding of blood.

323-330. See note on lines 57, 58.

327. van, foremost part of the army. An abbreviation of *vanguard*, from Fr. *avant-garde*.

330. Reek'd, steamed.

334. Melros': the *e* is omitted to avoid the repetition of the long vowel sound in *rose*. This form is nearer the original Gaelic *maol-ross*, a bald projection, or Celtic *mel-rhos*, a meadow-projection.

335. lichens, mosses. gray qualifies *rock*, not *lichens*.

336. Abbaye. The French word from which *abbey* is derived. It looks antique, and it rimes with *gray*; hence its choice here.

337. curfew, evening bell. *Curfew* is from O. F. *covre-feu*, cover fire. The Normans introduced into England the practice of ringing a bell as a signal for lights and fires to be put out—a beneficial practice, for the houses were made of wood. The time of ringing was usually eight o'clock, but the custom varied, nine and even ten o'clock being common for a long time in Scotland.

338. lauds. The first service in monastic houses after midnight was called *matins*, and consisted of two parts, *nocturns* (Lat. *nocturnus*, of the night) and *lauds* (Lat. *laus*, praise): lauds was followed by *prime* one hour after sunrise.

340. wise, manner (O. E. *wise*). We still have it in this sense in compounds: *e.g. likewise, otherwise*; in the phrase *in no wise*, &c.

341. that wild harp, &c.: the Æolian harp, an instrument made by stretching eight or ten strings of wire or catgut of the same length across an oblong box. The box is placed slantwise in a spot exposed to the wind, which passing over the chords produces weird sounds. So called from *Æolus*, the god of winds.

344. meetly, fitly, properly. (O. E. *gemet*.) Cf. *Luke* xv. 32, "It was meet that we should make merry." See line 363.—Notice the alliteration in this line.

349. timid, adjective for adverb, *timidly*.

CANTO SECOND.

I.

IF thou would'st view fair Melrose aright,
Go visit it by the pale moonlight;
For the gay beams of lightsome day
Gild, but to flout, the ruins gray.
When the broken arches are black in night,　　5
And each shafted oriel glimmers white;
When the cold light's uncertain shower
Streams on the ruin'd central tower;
When buttress and buttress, alternately,
Seem framed of ebon and ivory;　　10
When silver edges the imagery,
And the scrolls that teach thee to live and die;
When distant Tweed is heard to rave,
And the owlet to hoot o'er the dead man's grave,
Then go—but go alone the while---　　15
Then view St. David's ruin'd pile;
And, home returning, soothly swear,
Was never scene so sad and fair!

II.

Short halt did Deloraine make there;
Little reck'd he of the scene so fair:　　20
With dagger's hilt, on the wicket strong,
He struck full loud, and struck full long.
The porter hurried to the gate—
"Who knocks so loud, and knocks so late?"
"From Branksome I!" the Warrior cried;　　25
And straight the wicket open'd wide;
For Branksome's Chiefs had in battle stood,
　　To fence the rights of fair Melrose;
And lands and livings, many a rood,
　　Had gifted the shrine for their souls' repose.　　30

III.

Bold Deloraine his errand said;
The porter bent his humble head;
With torch in hand, and feet unshod,
And noiseless step, the path he trod;
(814)　　　　　　　　　　　　　　　B

The arched cloisters, far and wide,   35
Rang to the Warrior's clanking stride;
Till, stooping low his lofty crest,
He enter'd the cell of the ancient priest,
And lifted his barred aventayle,
To hail the Monk of St. Mary's aisle.   40

IV.

"The Ladye of Branksome greets thee by me;
    Says, that the fated hour is come,
And that to-night I shall watch with thee,
    To win the treasure of the tomb."—
From sackcloth couch the Monk arose,   45
    With toil his stiffen'd limbs he rear'd;
A hundred years had flung their snows
    On his thin locks and floating beard.

V.

And strangely on the Knight look'd he,
    And his blue eyes gleam'd wild and wide;   50
"And, dar'st thou, Warrior! seek to see
    What heaven and hell alike would hide?
My breast, in belt of iron pent,
    With shirt of hair and scourge of thorn;
For threescore years, in penance spent,   55
    My knees those flinty stones have worn;
Yet all too little to atone
For knowing what should ne'er be known.
    Would'st thou thy every future year
        In ceaseless prayer and penance drie,   60
    Yet wait thy latter end with fear—
        Then, daring Warrior, follow me!"—

VI.

"Penance, Father, will I none;
Prayer know I hardly one;
For mass or prayer can I rarely tarry,   65
Save to patter an Ave Mary,
When I ride on a Border foray:
Other prayer can I none;
So speed me my errand, and let me be gone."—

VII.

Again on the Knight look'd the Churchman old,   70
  And again he sighed heavily ;
For he had himself been a warrior bold,
  And fought in Spain and Italy.
And he thought on the days that were long since by,
When his limbs were strong, and his courage was high:—
Now, slow and faint, he led the way,   76
Where, cloister'd round, the garden lay ;
The pillar'd arches were over their head,
And beneath their feet were the bones of the dead.

VIII.

Spreading herbs, and flowerets bright,   80
Glisten'd with the dew of night ;
Nor herb, nor floweret, glisten'd there,
But was carved in the cloister-arches as fair.
  The Monk gazed long on the lovely moon,
    Then into the night he looked forth ;   85
  And red and bright the streamers light
    Were dancing in the glowing north.
  So had he seen, in fair Castile,
    The youth in glittering squadrons start ;
  Sudden the flying jennet wheel,   90
    And hurl the unexpected dart.
He knew, by the streamers that shot so brignt,
That spirits were riding the northern light.

IX.

By a steel-clench'd postern door,
  They enter'd now the chancel tall ;   95
The darken'd roof rose high aloof
  On pillars lofty and light and small :
The key-stone, that lock'd each ribbed aisle,
Was a fleur-de-lys, or a quatre-feuille ;
The corbells were carved grotesque and grim ;   100
And the pillars, with cluster'd shafts so trim,
With base and with capital flourish'd around,
Seem'd bundles of lances which garlands had bound.

X.

Full many a scutcheon and banner riven
Shook to the cold night-wind of heaven   105
  Around the screened altar's pale ;

And there the dying lamps did burn,
Before thy low and lonely urn,
   O gallant Chief of Otterburne!
And thine, dark Knight of Liddesdale!   110
O fading honours of the dead!
O high ambition, lowly laid!

XI.

The moon on the east oriel shone
Through slender shafts of shapely stone,
   By foliaged tracery combined;   115
Thou would'st have thought some fairy's hand
'Twixt poplars straight the ozier wand,
   In many a freakish knot, had twined;
Then framed a spell, when the work was done,
And changed the willow-wreaths to stone.   120
The silver light, so pale and faint,
Shew'd many a prophet, and many a saint,
   Whose image on the glass was dyed;
Full in the midst, his Cross of Red
Triumphant Michael brandished,   125
   And trampled the Apostate's pride.
The moon-beam kiss'd the holy pane,
And threw on the pavement a bloody stain.

XII.

They sate them down on a marble stone,
   A Scottish monarch slept below;   130
Thus spoke the Monk, in solemn tone:—
   "I was not always a man of woe;
For Paynim countries I have trod,
And fought beneath the Cross of God:
Now, strange to my eyes thine arms appear,   135
And their iron clang sounds strange to my ear.

XIII.

"In these far climes it was my lot
To meet the wondrous Michael Scott;
   A wizard of such dreaded fame,
That when, in Salamanca's cave,   140
Him listed his magic wand to wave,
   The bells would ring in Notre Dame!

Some of his skill he taught to me;
And, Warrior, I could say to thee
The words that cleft Eildon 'hills in three,   145
    And bridled the Tweed with a curb of stone:
But to speak them were a deadly sin;
And for having but thought them my heart within,
    A treble penance must be done.

XIV.

"When Michael lay on his dying bed,   150
His conscience was awakened:
He bethought him of his sinful deed,
And he gave me a sign to come with speed:
I was in Spain when the morning rose,
But I stood by his bed ere evening close.   155
The words may not again be said,
That he spoke to me, on death-bed laid;
They would rend this Abbaye's massy nave,
And pile it in heaps above his grave.

XV.

"I swore to bury his Mighty Book,   160
That never mortal might therein look;
And never to tell where it was hid,
Save at his Chief of Branksome's need:
And when that need was past and o'er,
Again the volume to restore.   165
I buried him on St. Michael's night,
When the bell toll'd one, and the moon was bright,
And I dug his chamber among the dead,
When the floor of the chancel was stained red,
That his patron's cross might over him wave,   170
And scare the fiends from the Wizard's grave.

XVI.

"It was a night of woe and dread,
When Michael in the tomb I laid!
Strange sounds along the chancel pass'd,
The banners waved without a blast"—   175
—Still spoke the Monk, when the bell toll'd one!—
I tell you, that a braver man
Than William of Deloraine, good at need,
Against a foe ne'er spurr'd a steed;

Yet somewhat was he chill'd with dread,   180
And his hair did bristle upon his head.

XVII.

"Lo, Warrior! now, the Cross of Red
Points to the grave of the mighty dead;
Within it burns a wondrous light,
To chase the spirits that love the night: 185
That lamp shall burn unquenchably,
Until the eternal doom shall be."—
Slow moved the Monk to the broad flag-stone,
Which the bloody Cross was traced upon:
He pointed to a secret nook;   190
An iron bar the Warrior took;
And the Monk made a sign with his wither'd hand,
The grave's huge portal to expand.

XVIII.

With beating heart to the task he went;
His sinewy frame o'er the grave-stone bent;   195
With bar of iron heaved amain,
Till the toil-drops fell from his brows, like rain.
It was by dint of passing strength,
That he moved the massy stone at length.
I would you had been there to see   200
How the light broke forth so gloriously,
Stream'd upward to the chancel roof,
And through the galleries far aloof!
No earthly flame blazed e'er so bright:
It shone like heaven's own blessed light,   205
    And, issuing from the tomb,
Show'd the Monk's cowl, and visage pale,
Danced on the dark-brow'd Warrior's mail,
    And kiss'd his waving plume.

XIX.

Before their eyes the Wizard lay,   210
As if he had not been dead a day.
His hoary beard in silver roll'd,
He seem'd some seventy winters old;
    A palmer's amice wrapp'd him round,
    With a wrought Spanish baldric bound,   215
    Like a pilgrim from beyond the sea:

His left hand held his Book of Might;
A silver cross was in his right;
The lamp was placed beside his knee:
High and majestic was his look,   220
At which the fellest fiends had shook,
And all unruffled was his face:
They trusted his soul had gotten grace.

XX.

Often had William of Deloraine
Rode through the battle's bloody plain,   225
And trampled down the warriors slain,
   And neither known remorse nor awe;
Yet now remorse and awe he own'd;
His breath came thick, his head swam round,
   When this strange scene of death he saw.   230
Bewilder'd and unnerved he stood,
And the priest pray'd fervently and loud:
With eyes averted prayed he;
He might not endure the sight to see,
Of the man he had loved so brotherly.   235

XXI.

And when the priest his death-prayer had pray'd,
Thus unto Deloraine he said:—
" Now speed thee what thou hast to do,
Or, Warrior, we may dearly rue;
For those, thou may'st not look upon,   240
Are gathering fast round the yawning stone!"—
Then Deloraine, in terror, took
From the cold hand the Mighty Book,
With iron clasp'd, and with iron bound:
He thought, as he took it, the dead man frown'd;   245
But the glare of the sepulchral light,
Perchance, had dazzled the Warrior's sight.

XXII.

When the huge stone sunk o'er the tomb,
The night return'd in double gloom;
For the moon had gone down, and the stars were few;
And, as the Knight and Priest withdrew,   251
With wavering steps and dizzy brain,
They hardly might the postern gain.

'Tis said, as through the aisles they pass'd,
They heard strange noises on the blast;   255
And through the cloister-galleries small,
Which at mid-height thread the chancel wall,
Loud sobs, and laughter louder, ran,
And voices unlike the voice of man;
As if the fiends kept holiday,   260
Because these spells were brought to day.
I cannot tell how the truth may be;
I say the tale as 'twas said to me.

XXIII.

" Now, hie thee hence," the Father said,
" And when we are on death-bed laid,   265
O may our dear Ladye, and sweet St. John,
Forgive our souls for the deed we have done!"—
    The Monk return'd him to his cell,
        And many a prayer and penance sped;
    When the convent met at the noontide bell—   270
        The Monk of St. Mary's aisle was dead!
Before the cross was the body laid,
With hands clasp'd fast, as if still he pray'd.

XXIV.

The Knight breathed free in the morning wind,
And strove his hardihood to find: 275
He was glad when he pass'd the tombstones gray,
Which girdle round the fair Abbaye;
For the mystic Book, to his bosom prest,
Felt like a load upon his breast;
And his joints, with nerves of iron twined,   280
Shook, like the aspen leaves in wind.
Full fain was he when the dawn of day
Began to brighten Cheviot gray;
He joy'd to see the cheerful light,
And he said Ave Mary, as well as he might.   285

XXV.

The sun had brighten'd Cheviot gray,
    The sun had brighten'd the Carter's side;
And soon beneath the rising day
    Smiled Branksome Towers and Teviot's tide.

The wild birds told their warbling tale, 290
 And waken'd every flower that blows;
And peeped forth the violet pale,
 And spread her breast the mountain rose.
And lovelier than the rose so red,
 Yet paler than the violet pale, 295
She early left her sleepless bed,
 The fairest maid of Teviotdale.

XXVI.

Why does fair Margaret so early awake,
 And don her kirtle so hastilie;
And the silken knots, which in hurry she would make, 300
 Why tremble her slender fingers to tie;
Why does she stop, and look often around,
 As she glides down the secret stair;
And why does she pat the shaggy blood-hound,
 As he rouses him up from his lair; 305
And, though she passes the postern alone,
Why is not the watchman's bugle blown?

XXVII.

The ladye steps in doubt and dread,
Lest her watchful mother hear her tread;
The ladye caresses the rough blood-hound, 310
Lest his voice should waken the castle round;
The watchman's bugle is not blown,
For he was her foster-father's son;
And she glides through the greenwood at dawn of light,
To meet Baron Henry, her own true knight. 315

XXVIII.

The knight and ladye fair are met,
And under the hawthorn's boughs are set.
A fairer pair were never seen
To meet beneath the hawthorn green.
He was stately, and young, and tall; 320
Dreaded in battle, and loved in hall:
And she, when love, scarce told, scarce hid,
Lent to her cheek a livelier red;
When the half sigh her swelling breast
Against the silken riband prest; 325

When her blue eyes their secret told,
Though shaded by her locks of gold—
Where would you find the peerless fair,
With Margaret of Branksome might compare!

XXIX.

And now, fair dames, methinks I see   330
You listen to my minstrelsy;
Your waving locks ye backward throw,
And sidelong bend your necks of snow;—
Ye ween to hear a melting tale,
Of two true lovers in a dale;   335
  And how the Knight, with tender fire,
    To paint his faithful passion strove;
  Swore, he might at her feet expire,
    But never, never cease to love;
And how she blush'd, and how she sigh'd,   340
And, half consenting, half denied,
And said that she would die a maid ;—
Yet, might the bloody feud be stay'd,
Henry of Cranstoun, and only he,
Margaret of Branksome's choice should be.   345

XXX.

Alas! fair dames, your hopes are vain!
My harp has lost the enchanting strain;
  Its lightness would my age reprove:
My hairs are gray, my limbs are old,
My heart is dead, my veins are cold: 350
  I may not, must not, sing of love.

XXXI.

Beneath an oak, moss'd o'er by eld,
The Baron's Dwarf his courser held,
  And held his crested helm and spear:
That Dwarf was scarce an earthly man,   355
If the tales were true that of him ran
  Through all the Border, far and near.
'Twas said, when the Baron a-hunting rode
Through Reedsdale's glens, but rarely trod,
  He heard a voice cry, "Lost! lost! lost!"   360
And, like tennis-ball by racquet toss'd,

A leap of thirty feet and three
Made from the gorse this elfin shape,
Distorted like some dwarfish ape,
　　And lighted at Lord Cranstoun's knee.   365
Lord Cranstoun was some whit dismay'd;
'Tis said that five good miles he rade,
　　To rid him of his company;
But where he rode one mile, the Dwarf ran four,
And the Dwarf was first at the castle door.   370

XXXII.

Use lessens marvel, it is said:
This elvish Dwarf with the Baron stay'd;
Little he ate, and less he spoke,
Nor mingled with the menial flock:
And oft apart his arms he toss'd,   375
And often mutter'd, " Lost! lost! lost!"
　　He was waspish, arch, and litherlie,
　　But well Lord Cranstoun served he:
And he of his service was full fain;
For once he had been ta'en or slain,   380
　　An it had not been for his ministry.
All between Home and Hermitage,
Talk'd of Lord Cranstoun's Goblin-Page.

XXXIII.

For the Baron went on pilgrimage,
And took with him this elvish Page,   385
　　To Mary's Chapel of the Lowes:
For there, beside our Ladye's lake,
An offering he had sworn to make,
　　And he would pay his vows.
But the Ladye of Branksome gather'd a band   390
Of the best that would ride at her command:
　　The trysting-place was Newark Lee.
Wat of Harden came thither amain,
And thither came John of Thirlestane,
And thither came William of Deloraine;   395
　　They were three hundred spears and three.
Through Douglas-burn, up Yarrow stream,
Their horses prance, their lances gleam.
They came to St. Mary's lake ere day;
But the chapel was void, and the Baron away.   400

They burn'd the chapel for very rage,
And cursed Lord Cranstoun's Goblin-Page.

XXXIV.

And now, in Branksome's good green wood,
As under the aged oak he stood,
The Baron's courser pricks his ears,   405
As if a distant noise he hears.
The Dwarf waves his long lean arm on high,
And signs to the lovers to part and fly;
No time was then to vow or sigh.
Fair Margaret, through the hazel grove,   410
Flew like the startled cushat-dove:
The Dwarf the stirrup held and rein;
Vaulted the Knight on his steed amain,
And, pondering deep that morning's scene,
Rode eastward through the hawthorns green.   415

WHILE thus he pour'd the lengthen'd tale,
The Minstrel's voice began to fail:
Full slyly smiled the observant page,
And gave the wither'd hand of age
A goblet, crown'd with mighty wine,   420
The blood of Velez' scorched vine.
He raised the silver cup on high,
And, while the big drop fill'd his eye,
Pray'd God to bless the Duchess long,
And all who cheer'd a son of song.   425
The attending maidens smiled to see
How long, how deep, how zealously,
The precious juice the Minstrel quaff'd;
And he, embolden'd by the draught,
Look'd gaily back to them, and laugh'd.   430
The cordial nectar of the bowl
Swell'd his old veins, and cheer'd his soul;
A lighter, livelier prelude ran,
Ere thus his tale again began.

NOTES.

CANTO SECOND.

3. lightsome, full of light; light-giving. Rare in this sense; the usual sense is 'gay', 'cheerful'. O. E. *leóht*, light, represented two distinct older words, thus giving rise to the two distinct modern meanings. *-some* is O. E. *-sum*, a suffix forming adjectives of quality.

4. gild, but to flout; *i.e.* the same light which gilds also shows up all the defects caused by time, and so seems to mock at the ruins.

6. shafted. The lights of the window are divided by *shafts* or mullions.

6. oriel, a projecting window, in shape usually half a six-sided figure, resting on a bracket or corbell. (O. F. *oriol*, M. L. *oriolum*, a recess.)

7. uncertain; (1) perhaps = fitful, intermittent; or (2) causing things to be indistinctly seen.

9. alternately: one side of each buttress shines white in the moonlight, the other is dark in shadow,—as though the buttress were composed of two different materials.

10. ebon, properly an adj. = black, here = ebony.

11. imagery, the images taken collectively; *statuary* and *minstrelsy* are similarly used in a collective sense.

12. "The buttresses ranged along the sides of the ruins of Melrose Abbey are, according to the Gothic style, richly carved and fretted, containing niches for the statues of saints, and labelled with scrolls, bearing appropriate texts of Scripture." (Scott.) *Scroll* (O. F. *escrouelle*) meant originally a roll of parchment, as in i. 247. Scrolls in stone are not uncommon on tombstones.

12. teach thee to live, *i.e. how* to live.

13. heard to rave. The *to* is very often omitted. We can say equally well 'I heard him sing', and 'I heard him singing'.

14. owlet, young owl; *-let* is the diminutive ending, as in 'brooklet', 'rivulet', 'bracelet', &c.

15. the while = then: O. E. *hwíl* meant 'a time'.

16. St. David's ruin'd pile: cf. i. 235, 236, note. "David I. of Scotland purchased the reputation of sanctity by founding and liberally endowing, not only the monastery of Melrose, but those of Kelso, Jedburgh, and many others; which led to the well-known observation of his successor [not *immediate* successor, who was Malcolm IV., but James I.: David died 1153, James reigned 1424–1437], that he was *a sore saint for the crown.*" (Scott.)

17. soothly swear was never, declare truly that there never was.

18. Scott excelled in such vivid descriptions as these, which could never have found a place in the old ballads.

20. reck'd he of, he cared for. The word *reck* was also used impersonally. (O. E. *recan*, to care.)

21. wicket, a small gate or door in a large one, capable of being opened independently. Cf. *Old Mortality*, ch. xix., "The large gate of the courtyard he barricadoed yet more strongly, leaving only a wicket open for the convenience of passage"—In cricket, the 'wicket' "was at first a small gate, being made 2 feet wide by 1 foot high (A.D. 1700)". (Skeat.)

22. full, an adverb used to intensify the meaning of the adjective or adverb it qualifies.

25. From Branksome I: the verb (*e.g. come*) is omitted. It is a common idiom.

26. straight, straightway, immediately.

28. fence, protect; guard. The word is shortened from *defence* by *apheresis, i.e.* the taking away of a letter or syllable from the beginning of a word. Another instance is *scutcheon*, line 104 below: see note there.

29, 30. "The Buccleuch family were great benefactors to the Abbey of Melrose."

29. livings, endowments for the support of clergymen.

30. gifted, presented as gifts. There are two objects: (1) *lands and livings* (direct), (2) *shrine* (indirect). In prose we might say '*endowed* the shrine (*i.e.* abbey) *with* lands and livings'. The word is thus used in Scotland to-day.—The subject is *Branksome's Chiefs*.

30. for their souls' repose. It was common for kings and nobles to make rich bequests of money and lands to religious establishments, with the object of having masses sung after their death for the repose of their souls. Richard II., for instance, made three grants of money to the famous convent of Black Friars at King's Langley, in Hertfordshire, in whose church he was buried.

31. his errand said, delivered his message, told the purpose of his coming. (O. E. *ærende*. The present form of the word perhaps due to mistaken derivation from Lat. *errare*, to wander.)

36. to, in response to.

37. stooping, bending; transitive.

37. crest. The crest was properly an ornamental addition to the helmet, and was part of the coat of arms of the family to which the wearer belonged. It was quite distinct from the plume, but it came subsequently to be used as synonymous with plume. Cf. line 354 below. (O. F. *creste*, Lat. *crista*, comb or tuft on a bird's head.)

39. aventayle, the movable front of the helmet. Also written *ventayle*. (O. F. *esventail*, air-hole; Lat. *ex*, out; *ventus*, wind. Cf. mod. *éventail*, fan.)

40. hail, greet. (Icelandic *heill*, sound, strong.)

42. the fated hour; see lines 160–164.

44. the treasure, *i.e.* the magic book.

53–56. The construction is confused. There is no predicate to *breast*. Lines 53, 54 may probably be regarded as originally an adjectival clause to a subject which was to come in line 56, but which Scott lost sight of, substituting *my knees*.

53. pent, enclosed. (O. E. *penn*, a fold.)

54. It was very common in the middle ages for men to endeavour to atone for former misdeeds, and render themselves more able to resist new temptations, by mortifying their bodies with cruel tortures such as these.

55. penance, suffering undergone by a person who is penitent. (The word is connected with Lat. *poena*, pain.)

57. atone, effect reconcilement; make amends. *Atone* = at one; to atone is therefore 'to set at one', 'to bring into accord', and intransitively 'to become reconciled'. Cf. *Acts* vii. 26, "the next day he showed himself unto them as they strove, and would have set them at one again".

60. drie, spend painfully (*thy every future year*). *Drie*, or *dree*, is commonly intransitive, in the sense of 'endure', 'hold out'. But the word is used transitively, particularly in the expression 'drie one's weird' (endure one's lot); cf. *Guy Mannering*, ch. lv., "I kenn'd he behoved to dree his weird till that day cam". (O. E. *dreogan*, Gothic *driugan*, to serve as a soldier.)

61. wait = await, wait *for*.

61. latter end, that is, death; *latter* is redundant. The expression occurs often in the Bible (cf. *Numbers* xxiv. 20) and in Shakespeare.

59–61. The monk means: 'If you insist on finding this magic book, and taking it from the grave, you will be committing a sin which you will have to atone for by ceaseless prayer and penance all the rest of your life. But even then you will await death with fear.'

63. will I none, I desire none, I will do none. *Will* was originally much more than an auxiliary verb. (O. E. *willian*, to desire.) Cf. note on *can*, line 68 below.

64-67. "The Borderers were very ignorant about religious matters. But however deficient in real religion, they regularly told their beads, and never with more zeal than when going on a plundering expedition." (Scott.)

65. mass, the Roman Catholic communion service. (O. E. *mæsse,* L. *missa.*) The name is said to be derived from the words *Ite, missa est* (Go, [the congregation] is dismissed), with which the congregation was dismissed at the close of the service, or with which those who were not yet fully members of the church were dismissed before the communion service proper.

66. patter, mumble rapidly, say indistinctly. Cf. *Marmion,* vi. stanza xxvii., "Fitz-Eustace, you with Lady Clare, May bid your beads, and patter prayer". Perhaps derived from *Paternoster,* the Latin name for the Lord's Prayer. There may be a connection with *patter,* to strike frequently, as hail—a frequentative form of *pat.*

66. Ave Mary, a devotional recitation and prayer used by Roman Catholics, composed of Gabriel's salutation to the Virgin Mary, combined with Elizabeth's: see *Luke* i. 28 and 42. The first words in the Latin are *Ave Maria, gratia plena* (Hail Mary, full of grace).

68. can, know; the original meaning of O. E. *cunnan.* Or we may understand *can I* (say) *none.*

69. speed me my errand, hasten for me the fulfilment of my errand. O. E. *spédan,* means 'to prosper' (transitive): *speed* is so used in *Julius Cæsar,* i. 2. 88, "let the gods so speed me", where Mr. Aldis Wright says in his note: "The notion of 'haste' which now belongs to the word is apparently a derived sense". *Me* is a dative implying that the person is interested in the action expressed by the verb: it is used also to give a familiar and often playful tone to the sentence.

69. be gone, used emphatically for *go.*

70. Churchman, *i.e.* the monk. *Churchman,* now used for all who belong to the church whether clergy or laymen, once meant *clergyman.*

73. in Spain and Italy. In the middle ages in Spain there was long and bitter strife between the Christians and the Moors. In Italy there were violent struggles for supremacy between rival noble families, and between the imperial and the municipal factions.

74. thought on, meditated, reflected upon.

74. since by, *i.e.* gone by, past.

77. cloister'd round, surrounded by a cloister, *i.e.* a covered stone-paved walk open to the garden. (Lat. *claustrum,* from *claudere,* to shut.)

78. pillar'd, supported on pillars.

80. **flowerets**, poetically used for *flowers*. *-et*, like *-let*, is a diminutive ending.

82, 83. **Nor herb, nor floweret ... But was**, there was no herb or floweret that was not. *But* often means 'that not'.

83. **as fair.** The carved representation was as beautiful as the actual flower. The grammar is worth noticing: *fair* cannot be regarded as an adverb modifying *carved*. The ornaments which *resulted from* the action of carving were fair: hence *fair* is an adjective used *predicatively*.

86. **streamers**, streams of lights shooting in the sky. See note on *northern light*, line 93 below.

88-91. Scott in his note quotes from Froissart some details of Castilian warfare, and adds: "This mode of fighting with darts was imitated in the military game called *Jengo de las canas*, which the Spaniards borrowed from their Moorish invaders".

88. **fair Castile**, in the centre and north of Spain. The soil is generally barren: *fair* perhaps refers to the romantic historical and legendary associations of the old kingdom.

89. **youth**, collectively, 'the bands of young warriors'.

90. **sudden**: adj. for adverb.

90. **jennet**, a small Spanish horse. (O. F. *genette*, from Sp. *ginete*, a nag; a word of Moorish origin.)

90. **wheel.** The subject is *youth*, not *jennet*.

93. **northern light**, the Aurora Borealis, the beautiful display of lights seen in northern latitudes, and believed to be due to electrical causes. The lights frequently assume the form of bands or ribbons: hence *streamers* in line 86 above.

94. **steel-clench'd**, strengthened with bands of steel fastened across.

94. **postern**, literally a back door (O. F. *posterne*, Lat. *posterus*, behind); then any small door.

96. **aloof**, properly 'far away', seems here used as meaning 'aloft'. *Aloof* is a compound of *a*, shortened form of *on*, preposition signifying onward movement, and Dutch *loef*, the windward side of a vessel. It was originally a seafaring term, equivalent to modern *luff*, to turn the ship's head towards the wind, and so away from a shore on which she might drift; from that use arose the meaning 'away', 'at a distance'.

98. **key-stone**, the stone last put in, at the apex of an arched roof: so called because in a sense it locks the whole structure.

98. **ribbed aisle.** The pieces of stone or timber supporting an arched roof are called *ribs*. *Aisle* is from Fr. *aile*, Lat. *ala*, a wing.

99. **fleur-de-lys ... quatre-feuille**; names of architectural orna-
ments. The *fleur-de-lys* (Modern Fr. *fleur-de-lis*) is a lily-shaped
ornament consisting of three leaves, separated from three short stems
by a cross-bar. The *quatre-feuille* (or *quatre-foil*, Lat. *quattuor*,
folium) contains four leaves joined with one another in the form of
a rounded cross.

100. **corbells**, "the projections from which the arches spring,
usually cut in a fantastic face, or mask". (Scott.)   They are basket-
shaped.   (O. F. *corbel*, M. Lat. *corbellus*, a little basket.)

100. **grotesque**, whimsical, odd, extraordinary.   (Ital. *grotesca*,
curious painted work, such as was employed on the walls of *grottoes*.)

101. **cluster'd shafts**, columns consisting of slender pillars
which appear to be bound together.

102. **capital**, top of a column.   (Lat. *caput*, head.)

102. **flourish'd around**, decorated all round with floral orna-
ments.   (Lat. *florescere*, to blossom.)

104.   The coats of arms, armour, and banners of dead noblemen
were often hung above their tombs in churches.   The armour of
the Black Prince is still to be seen in Canterbury cathedral.   See
note on line 109.

104. **scutcheon**, shield on which the coat of arms is painted.
(Shortened from *escutcheon*, O. Norman Fr. *escuchon*, Lat. *scutum*,
a shield.   The *e* was placed before the double consonant *sc* to soften
its harshness.)

104. **riven**, torn in battle.   Soldiers think very highly of their
tattered flags.

105. **to**, under the influence of, in response to.   Cf. Collins, *The
Passions*, 88, "To some unwearied minstrel dancing", and the
phrase "made to order".

105. **heaven**, here used for 'sky'; so we speak of the 'heavens'.

106. **screened**, divided from the rest of the church by a screen.

106. **pale**, the railing which separated the altar from the chancel.
(Lat. *palus*, a stake.)

107.   The lights were never allowed to go out, though the flame
was always low: the lamp always burning being a symbol of the
ever-living soul.

108. **urn**, tomb.   In ancient times, *e.g.* among the Romans, who
burned their dead, the ashes of the dead were enclosed in urns; hence
the derived sense *tomb*.

109.   "The famous and desperate battle of Otterburne was fought
15th August, 1388, betwixt Henry Percy, called Hotspur, and

James, Earl of Douglas. ... Percy was made prisoner, and the Scots won the day, dearly purchased by the death of their gallant general, the Earl of Douglas, who was slain in the action. He was buried at Melrose, beneath the high altar. 'His obsequye was done reverently, and on his bodye layde a tombe of stone, and his baner hangyng over hym.'" (Scott.)

110. "William Douglas, called the Knight of Liddesdale, flourished during the reign of David II., and was so distinguished by his valour, that he was called the Flower of Chivalry. Nevertheless, he tarnished his renown by the cruel murder of Sir Alexander Ramsay of Dalhousie, originally his friend and brother in arms." He was appointed "successor to his victim as Sheriff of Teviotdale. But he was soon after slain, while hunting in Ettrick Forest, by his own godson and chieftain. ... His body...was carried ... to Melrose, where he was interred with great pomp." (Scott.)

113-120. "It is impossible to conceive a more beautiful specimen of the lightness and elegance of Gothic architecture, when in its purity, than the eastern window of Melrose Abbey. Sir James Hall of Dunglas, Bart., has, with great ingenuity and plausibility, traced the Gothic order through its various forms and seemingly eccentric ornaments to an architectural imitation of wicker-work, of which, as we learn from some of the legends, the earliest Christian churches were constructed. In such an edifice, the original of the clustered pillars is traced to a set of round posts, begirt with slender rods of willow, whose loose summits were brought to meet from all quarters, and bound together artificially, so as to produce the framework of the roof: and the tracery of our Gothic windows is displayed in the meeting and interlacing of rods and hoops, affording an inexhaustible variety of beautiful forms of open work. This ingenious system is alluded to in the romance." (Scott.)

113. **east oriel**, the projecting three-sided window at the east end of the abbey.

115. **by foliaged tracery combined**, connected by ornamental stone-work delicately carved. See note on lines 113-120.

117. **ozier wand.** See note on lines 113-120. The *osier* is a species of willow, often used in basket-work.

118. **freakish**, fanciful—as though the fairy had done the work in joke.

119. **framed a spell**, composed a charm or a form of words which had magical power.

124-126. Satan is styled "the Apostate" by Milton in *Paradise Lost*, in book vi. of which the combat between Michael and Satan is described. An *apostate* is one who has forsaken his faith.

124. Cross of Red, his gleaming sword, cross-shaped. It was coloured red in the stained window.

129, 130. "A large marble stone, in the chancel of Melrose, is pointed out as the monument of Alexander II., one of the greatest of our early kings." (Scott.) He reigned 1216–1249.

132. man of woe, penitent.

133, 134. See lines 72, 73, and 88–91. A ten-years' war (1481–1491) in the reign of Ferdinand and Isabella was closed by the capture of Granada, the last stronghold of Mahometanism in Spain. As this was more than sixty years before the incidents of Scott's poem, the description "ancient priest" in line 38 is very appropriate.

133. Paynim, heathen. (O. F. *paienime*, Lat. *pagani*, dwellers in a *pagus*, village.) The word (as Trench shows in his *Select Glossary*, 22nd edition, p. 136) came to have its meaning 'unchristian' because "the Church fixed itself first in the seats and centres of intelligence, ... while ... heathen superstitions and idolatries lingered on in the obscure hamlets and villages".

134. beneath the Cross of God, *i.e.* in the Christian army : a reference to the religious wars. The last Crusade proper ended in 1291.

137. far climes, far countries. (*Clime* is a poetical word, from Lat. *clima*, a zone of the earth: whence also comes *climate*.)

138. the wondrous Michael Scott. "Sir Michael Scott of Balwearie flourished during the 13th century, and was one of the ambassadors sent to bring the maid of Norway to Scotland upon the death of Alexander III. By a poetical anachronism, he is here placed in a later era. He was a man of much learning, and wrote ... several treatises upon natural philosophy, from which he appears to have been addicted to the abstruse studies of judicial astrology, alchymy, physiognomy, and chiromancy. Hence he passed among his contemporaries for a skilful magician. Dempster informs us (*Ecclesiastical History*, 1627) that he remembers to have heard in his youth, that the magic books of Michael Scott were still in existence, but could not be opened without danger, on account of the malignant fiends who were thereby invoked ... Dante also mentions him as a renowned wizard (*Inferno*, canto xx.)." (Scott.)

139. wizard, magician. The word also meant simply 'wise man', but in this sense is uncommon. (O. F. *wischard*, Icelandic *viskr*, wise, and intensive suffix *-ard*, which usually has a depreciatory effect, as in *drunkard*, *dotard*, &c.) *Wizard* is not grammatically connected with *witch*, which was originally of common gender.

140. Salamanca's cave. "Spain, from the reliques, doubt-less, of Arabian learning and superstition, was accounted a favourite residence of magicians. ... There were public schools, where magic, or rather the sciences supposed to involve its mysteries, were regularly taught, at Toledo, Seville, and Salamanca. In the latter city they were held in a deep cavern, the mouth of which was walled up by Queen Isabella, wife of King Ferdinand. ... In a romantic history of Roderic, the last Gothic king of Spain, he is said to have entered one of those enchanted caverns. It was situated beneath an ancient tower near Toledo; and, when the iron gates which secured the entrance were unfolded, there rushed forth so dreadful a whirlwind that hitherto no one had dared to penetrate into its recesses. But Roderic ... resolved to enter ... and with great difficulty penetrated into a square hall. ... In the midst stood a colossal statue of brass, representing a Saracen wielding a Moorish mace, with which it discharged furious blows on all sides, and seemed thus to excite the tempest which raged around. Being conjured by Roderic, it ceased from striking until he read, inscribed on the right hand, '*Wretched monarch! for thy evil hast thou come hither*'; on the left hand, '*Thou shalt be dispossessed by a strange people.*' ... When the king had decyphered these ominous inscriptions, the statue returned to its exercise, the tempest commenced anew, and Roderic retired, to mourn over the predicted evils which approached his throne. He caused the gates of the cavern to be locked and barricaded; but in the course of the night the tower fell with a tremendous noise, and under its ruins concealed for ever the entrance to the mystic cavern. The conquest of Spain by the Saracens, and the death of the unfortunate Don Roderic, fulfilled the prophecy of the brazen statue." (Scott.)

141. him listed, it pleased him. *List* in this sense, and *listen*, are from two totally different roots. *Listen* is O. E. *hlystan*, from a root *hlus*, hear. *List* is O. E. *lystan*, from a Teutonic root signifying 'pleasure'; cf. Germ. *Lust*, English *lust* (in its older undepreciated sense): it remains in *listless*. The verb was originally impersonal.

141. magic wand. The wand is part of the equipment of conjurors to this day, as it was in the time of Moses.—Notice the inverted order of the words in this line.

142. Michael Scott "was chosen to go upon an embassy, to obtain from the King of France satisfaction for certain piracies committed by his subjects upon those of Scotland. Instead of preparing a new equipage and splendid retinue, the ambassador retreated to his study, opened his book, and evoked a fiend in the shape of a huge black horse, mounted upon his back, and forced him to fly through the air towards France. ... When he arrived at Paris, he tied his horse to the gate of the palace, entered, and boldly delivered his message. ... The king was about to return a contemptuous refusal to his demand, when Michael besought him to suspend his resolution till he had seen his horse stamp three times. The first stamp shook every steeple in Paris, and caused all the bells to ring;

the second threw down three of the towers of the palace; and the infernal steed had lifted his hoof to give the third stamp, when the king rather chose to dismiss Michael with the most ample concessions, than to stand to the probable consequences." (Scott.)

142. Notre Dame, the ancient and beautiful cathedral of Paris dedicated to the Virgin Mary, 'Our Lady.' *Dame* and *fame* rime to the eye, but not to the ear.

145, 146. "Michael Scott was once upon a time much embarrassed by a spirit, for whom he was under the necessity of finding constant employment. He commanded him to build a cauld, or dam-head, across the Tweed at Kelso; it was accomplished in one night, and still does honour to the infernal architect. Michael next ordered that Eildon Hills, which was then a uniform cone, should be divided into three. Another night was sufficient to part its summit into the three picturesque peaks which it now bears. At length the enchanter conquered this indefatigable demon by employing him in the hopeless and endless task of making ropes out of sea-sand." (Scott.)

In many countries, bridges and ramparts in wild places, either natural or constructed so long ago that their origin is forgotten, are traditionally ascribed to diabolical or magical agency. Such are the Devil's Dyke in Cambridgeshire, the Pont-y-Mynach in Cardiganshire, and the bridge over the Reuss in the Swiss canton of Uri.— **Eildon Hills** extend south of Melrose.

146. bridled the Tweed. The river is here compared to a horse, who is held back from running by a curb.

147. were, the old past subjunctive of 'to be'=would be.

152. bethought him of, remembered, took thought with himself about.

153. he gave me a sign, *i.e.* some magical indication.

155. evening close, the close, end, of the evening: *evening* is here an adjective.

157. laid of course refers to *he*, not to *me*.

158. massy, the same word as *massive*; huge.

158, 159. See note on line 142.

160. Mighty Book, the book containing his charms; referred to in note on line 142.

166. St. Michael's night, September 29th.

169. stained red, by the light from the stained window.

170. his patron's. Michael Scott naturally took St. Michael as his patron saint. In olden times nations and families believed them-selves to be under the special fatherly protection of a saint. St. George is the patron saint of England, St. Andrew of Scotland, St. Patrick of Ireland. (Lat. *pater*, father.)

175. without a blast. This suggests that the banners were moved by the spirits as they passed.

184–186. "Authors who treat of natural magic talk much of eternal lamps, pretended to have been found burning in ancient sepulchres.... One of these perpetual lamps is said to have been discovered in the tomb of Tulliola, the daughter of Cicero. The wick was supposed to be composed of asbestos." (Scott.)

185. chase, *i.e.* chase away, put to flight.

187. eternal doom, the Last Judgment. (O. E. *dóm*, judgment.)

188. flag-stone, paving-stone. (Icel. *flaga*, a slab of stone. *Flag* is a weak form of *flake*.)

193. portal. The large stone, covering the grave, is here called the gate or door of the grave. (Lat. *porta*, gate.)

193. expand, open. The usual meaning is 'spread out' (Lat. *expandere*).

196. amain. The word has two senses: (1) 'with force', as here and in v. 27; (2) more commonly 'with speed', as in ii. 393 and iv. 185. The word is from *a*, the preposition *on* (cf. note on *aloof*, line 96); O. E. *mægn*, strength.

197. toil-drops, drops of sweat produced by his labour.

198. by dint of, by the force of. *Dint* (O. E. *dynt*) originally meant 'stroke', 'blow', as in canto iii. line 53. The secondary meaning is the 'impression' made by the blow: in this sense also spelt *dent*. The third meaning is, generally, 'influence', 'force', as here.

198. passing = *surpassing*, extraordinary, very great.

203. galleries, passages along the walls, above the aisles and looking into the nave. See line 257.

207. cowl, hood. (O. E. *cufle* from Lat. *cucullus*.)

207. visage, face. (Lat. *videre, visum*, to see. The eyes are the most important feature.)

208. mail, armour, consisting of fine steel network. (Lat. *macula*, a hole, through Fr. *maille*.)

212. The Wizard's long beard had the appearance of rolling ripples on a silvery river. We commonly speak of '*flowing* hair'.

213. some, about (maybe more, maybe less).

213. seventy winters, 70 years. *Winters* is put for *years* because the great age of the wizard is called attention to: cf. "age's frost" in Introduction, line 95. The age of a child is often expressed by so many *summers*.

214. palmer, "one who bore a palm-branch in memory of having been to the Holy Land". (Skeat.) He placed palm-branches on the altar of his parish church. For an account of a palmer's wanderings see *Marmion*, canto i. stanza xxiii. (Church Latin *palmarius*.)

214. amice, a hood lined with gray fur, worn by pilgrims and friars. The word often occurs in company with the adjective *gray*, to distinguish it from the white amice, a square linen shoulder-cloth worn by priests.—The two words have different origins; the first being from O. F. *aumuce*, the Provençal form of which was *almussa*, which is probably the Arabic article *al* prefixed to German *mütse*, cap. The second is from Lat. *amictus*, thrown around (*am=ambi*, around; *ictus* from *iacere*, to throw), through Fr. *amict*.

215. wrought, ornamented, embroidered. We now say *worked*. *Wrought* is past part. from O. E. *weorcan*, to work, and is now used mainly poetically, and in such phrases as "wrought iron".

215. baldric, a leathern belt worn transversely from the right shoulder, and having the sword, &c., suspended from it. It was often richly ornamented. Cf. Tennyson, *Lady of Shalott*, 87, "And from his blazon'd baldric slung A mighty silver bugle hung". See also canto iii. lines 222, 223. The derivation of the word is uncertain.

216. pilgrim, one who travels to a distant land in order to visit a holy place. Such men bore some distinguishing mark on their dress. (O. F. *pelerin*, Lat. *peregrinus*, a traveller through a strange land.)

217. Book of Might, the mighty book containing the spells by which the wizard worked his magic.

221. fellest, most cruel. (O. F. *fel*, fierce, cruel.)

221. shook: the true past part. is *shaken*; cf. *rode*, line 225. Such participles occur often in Shakespeare, and Scott is loose in his use of the forms.

223. gotten grace, received pardon, favour. *Gotten* is an old, now disused, form of the past participle.

227. remorse, tenderness of heart, considerateness, pity; a meaning now lost except in 'remorseless' and 'without remorse'. Cf. *Waverley*, ch. xxxix., "Waverley's rest was sorely interrupted by the revellers hallooing forth their Jacobite songs, without remorse or mitigation of voice".

234. might, could. (O. E. *mægon* meant 'to be strong, able', and was used where we now use 'can'.)

235. brotherly; usually an adjective, here an adverb.

236. death-prayer, prayer for the dead.

238. speed thee, hasten. It is a kind of reflexive use, *thee* being an old dative.

239. dearly rue, have cause for bitter repentance.

240. those, thou may'st not look upon, the fiends whom Michael Scott had made his instruments.

245. "William of Deloraine might be strengthened in this belief by the well-known story of the Cid Ruy Diaz. When the body of that famous Christian champion was sitting in state by the high altar of the cathedral church of Toledo, where it remained for ten years, a certain malicious Jew attempted to pull him by the beard; but he had no sooner touched the formidable whiskers, than the corpse started up, and half unsheathed his sword. The Israelite fled; and so permanent was the effect of his terror, that he became Christian." (Scott.)

253. hardly might the postern gain, could scarcely reach the postern, the small door by which they had come. (Lit. back door, Lat. *posterus*, behind.)

257. Go through the chancel wall midway between floor and roof. See line 203. *Thread* implies the narrowness of the galleries.

260. fiends kept holiday. The spells being no longer secret, the spirits by whose aid the wizard performed his magical feats would be released from their bondage to him.

261. brought to day: 'brought to *light*' is the usual expression.

264. hie, hasten. (O. E. *higian*.)

268. return'd him. *Return* is here transitive, or used with *him* reflexively; *him = himself*.

269. sped, offered up in haste. See note on *speed*, line 69.

270. convent, the monks. The word is now used rather of the dwelling-place (especially of nuns) than of the inmates. (O. F. *covent*, Lat. *conventus*, assembly, from *convenire*.)

274. free = *freely*, adj. for adverb.

275. his hardihood to find, to recover his usual boldness.

280. nerves, muscles, sinews. (Lat. *nervus*.)

281. A favourite simile with all our poets. The *asp* is a tree of the poplar family, whose leaves quiver at the slightest breath of wind. —*Aspen*, properly an adjective like *birchen* (Introduction to canto i. line 28), is also used as a noun; cf. *Marmion*, canto vi. stanza xxx., "variable as the shade, By the light quivering aspen made", (O. E. *æps*; for similar instances of such transposition—*metathesis*—cf. *ask* and O. E. *acsian*, and *whit* for *wiht*; so *wrought* from *weorcan* : see i. 6, note.)

282. Full fain, very glad. *Full* is often thus used to strengthen an adjective or adverb. *Fain* is O. E. *fægen*, glad.

283. Cheviot, about 30 miles east of Branksome.: the hill giving its name to the whole chain.

284. joy'd, rejoiced. So in *2 Corinthians* vii. 13, "yea, and exceedingly more joyed we".

285. might = could, as before.

286. Notice how Scott, in leaving the subject of the rough Borderer for his description of the bright morning and the beauty of Margaret, changes his metre so as to suit his new subject.

287. Carter, "a mountain on the border of England, above Jedburgh". (Scott.) It is about 20 miles south-west of Cheviot. The sun, rising in the east, would naturally light up *Cheviot* before *Carter*, and that before *Branksome Towers*.

291. The subject is **flower**. Notice the unusual order. So in lines 292, 293, **violet** and **rose** are the subjects to **peeped** and **spread**.

291. blows, blooms. (O. E. *blówan* : cognate with Ger. *blühen*, Lat. *florere*.)

296. She is put beforehand for the true subject, **The fairest maid of Teviotdale**. This repetition of the subject serves two purposes: (1) it adds importance to the true subject, (2) it prevents the awkwardness of having a long compound subject before the verb, which would often make the sentence unrhythmical.

296. sleepless bed. This is an instance of transferred epithet, that is, an adjective which in meaning qualifies one thing, but is put in the sentence so as grammatically to qualify another. *Sleepless bed* means the bed on which *Margaret* was sleepless. So we speak of a 'sick bed'.

298. The questions are introduced in order to draw special attention to the incidents mentioned.

299. don = *do on*, put on. In O. E. *do* meant 'to place'. So *doff* = do off, put off; cf. *undo*.

299. kirtle. "Kirtle is not upper petticoat, but our modern gown, a waist and petticoat. A kirtle and mantle completed a woman's dress." (Furnivall.) The word is also used of a man's outer garment or tunic, as in canto iii. of this poem, line 226. (O.E. *cyrtel*, prob. a dim. of *skirt*.)

299. hastilie. The *e* is added to make the word look old-fashioned, and appear to rime with *tie*.

300. Notice that in this line there are twelve syllables instead of eight. The last seven, read rapidly, are very expressive of hurry.

301. to tie, *i.e.* in tying.

305. rouses him: reflexive: *him* = himself. *Self* was often omitted in early English, and in Shakespeare.

305. lair, the nook or kennel where he was lying. (Usually applied to the den of a wild beast, but it comes from O. E. *legan*, to lie.)

311. the castle round, *i.e.* the inmates of the castle who were lying asleep in their rooms around.

313. Romances contain many references to the strong and lasting affection between children and their foster-parents, *i.e.* those who have taken the place of their true parents in rearing them. Cf. *Fair Maid of Perth*, ch. xxvi., "Torquil ... entertained for his foster-child even a double portion of that passionate fondness which always attends that connection in the Highlands"; and ch. xxxi., where Torquil and his sons lose their lives in fighting for Eachin, their chief and Torquil's foster-son.

317. under the hawthorn's boughs. The *hawthorn*, like the aspen leaf, the evening-star, &c., is constantly referred to by poets. The hawthorn blooms in May (whence *may*, its popular name).

317. are set = have seated themselves. Cf. *Revelation* iii. 21, "I am set down with my Father".

322. she. Instead of making a direct statement, as in describing Cranstoun (lines 320, 321), the poet changes the construction, and in lines 328, 329 asks a rhetorical question. A predicate to *she* would have come awkwardly, separated by the subordinate clauses in lines 322–327.

322. scarce told, scarce hid. She did not quite express her love in words, nor could she quite hide it. *Scarce* is here an adverb.

328. peerless, matchless, without equal. (O. F. *pair*, Lat. *par*, equal.)

328. fair, a noun, often so used in poetry, especially in the 16th–18th centuries. Cf. the modern 'my *dear*'.

329. might compare; the nominative (*who*) is omitted.

330. methinks I see; not that he was blind, but that the ladies' interest was so great as to be almost visible. We talk of 'speaking eyes', and 'listening with eyes and ears', and 'to see pupils attend'.

330. methinks = it seems to me. *Me* is dative, and *thinks* is from the O. E. impersonal verb *thyncan*, to seem, which is distinct from *thencan*, the active verb. The former has now entirely given place to the latter, except in the poetical words *methinks*, *methought*.

331. minstrelsy, song, accompanied on the harp.

333. of snow, *i.e.* snow-white.

334. ween, think, expect.

334. melting, pathetic, affecting, drawing forth tender feelings and tears—another common poetical word, often used of the effect of music.

336. with tender fire, tenderly, yet earnestly.

338, 339. That is, his enemies might put an end to his life, but neither they nor the discouragement of Margaret's mother could put an end to his love.

341. denied, refused, *i.e.* refused to betroth herself to him.

342. might, *i.e. if* it might.

350. my veins are cold. The heat of the blood diminishes with age, and at the same time a man has less pleasure in the youthful occupations and thoughts that formerly pleased him.

351. may, can, as in i. 176; and elsewhere often.

352. mossed o'er, covered over with moss.

352. eld, old age. (O. E. *eldo*, which meant also 'time of life' generally.)

353. "The idea of Lord Cranstoun's Goblin Page is taken from a being called Gilpin Horner, who appeared, and made some stay, at a farm-house among the Border-mountains. A gentleman of that country has noted down the following particulars concerning his appearance:—

"'The only certain, at least most probable, account that ever I heard of Gilpin Horner was from an old man, of the name of Anderson, who was born, and lived all his life at Todshaw-hill, in Eskedale-muir, the place where Gilpin appeared and staid for some time. He said there were two men, late in the evening, when it was growing dark, employed in fastening the horses upon the uttermost part of their ground, when they heard a voice at some distance, crying, "*Tint! Tint! Tint!*" [lost]. One of the men,

named Moffat, called out, "What deil has tint you? Come here."
Immediately a creature of something like a human form appeared.
It was surprisingly little, distorted in features, and misshapen in
limbs. As soon as the two men could see it plainly, they ran home
in a great fright, imagining they had met with some goblin. By the
way, Moffat fell and it ran over him, and was home at the house as
soon as either of them, and staid there a long time; but I cannot say
how long. It was real flesh and blood, and ate and drank, was
fond of cream, and, when it could get at it, would destroy a great
deal. It seemed a mischievous creature; and any of the children
whom it could master, it would beat and scratch without mercy. It
was once abusing a child belonging to the same Moffat who had
been so frightened by its first appearance; and he, in a passion,
struck it so violent a blow upon the side of the head that it tumbled
upon the ground; but it was not stunned, for it set up its head
directly and exclaimed, "Ah, hah, Will o' Moffat, you strike sair!"
(viz. *sore*). After it had staid there long, one evening, when the
women were milking the cows in the loan, it was playing among the
children near by them, when suddenly they heard a loud shrill voice
cry three times, "*Gilpin Horner!*" It started, and said, "*That is me,
I must away*", and instantly disappeared, and was never heard of
more.'—As much has been objected to Gilpin Horner, on account of
his being supposed rather a device of the author than a popular
superstition, I can only say that no legend which I ever heard seemed
to be more universally credited; and that many persons of very good
rank, and considerable information, are well known to repose absolute
faith in the tradition." (Scott.)

353. **courser,** horse; often applied to the steeds used in tourna-
ments. (O. F. *corsier,* Lat. *cursus,* a running.)

354. **helm,** *i.e.* helmet.

358. **a-hunting.** "The *a*...used before verbal substantives be-
ginning with a consonant, is a shortened form of *an,* which was used
before vowels; *an* is merely a dialectal form of *on.*" (Morris, *Outlines,*
p. 178.) The *-ing* represents the O. E. suffix *-ung,* by which abstract
nouns were formed from verbs. Cf. *John's Gospel,* xxi. 3, "I go a-
fishing". Then the termination became confused with that of the
present participle, and the original force of the preposition was lost.

359. **trod** = trodden.

361. The thud caused by the goblin's leap was like the sound
of a racquet striking a tennis-ball.

365. **lighted** = alighted. (O. E. *alîhtan,* to spring down, dismount,
land on one's feet.)

366. **some whit,** somewhat. *Whit* is O.E. *wiht,* a person or thing.
We still use the expression 'not a whit', and *aught* and *naught* are
only contracted forms of *a wiht,* one whit, and *na wiht,* no whit.

367. rade, rode = *rád*, the O. E. past tense.

368. rid him = rid himself; see note on line 305.

371. Use, custom, familiarity. The meaning is that a marvellous thing ceases to be marvellous when one is accustomed to it. Our grandfathers were struck with amazement at the first steam-engines. There is a well-known proverb, " Familiarity breeds contempt".

374. menial flock, the troop of ordinary servants. (O. F. *meignal*, belonging to a *meisnee*, household.)

377. waspish, apt to resent affronts.

377. arch, slyly mischievous.

377. litherlie. In Scotch, *litherlie* is an adverb meaning 'lazily'. Here it is an adjective, and probably means 'mischievous' or 'ill-mannered', from O. E. *lythre*, bad.

379. full fain, very glad.

380. had been, would have been.

381. an, if; *and* is an old word meaning *if*, and the *d* was often omitted to avoid confusion with the copulative conjunction *and*.

381. ministry, service, aid. (Lat. *minister*, a servant.)

382. Home Castle is in Berwickshire, near the N. E. extremity of the Border. **Hermitage** Castle is almost due S. of Home, in Roxburghshire, near the S. W. extremity. Hence *All between Home and Hermitage* is another way of saying 'all the dwellers in the Border country'.

383. Goblin, from Greek *kobalos*, rogue, through dim. of L. Lat. *cobalus*; in O. F. *gobelin*.

386. Mary's Chapel of the Lowes, a chapel at the foot of a hill at the head of St. Mary's Loch, an expansion of the Yarrow. A small adjoining lake is called the Loch of the Lowes. The lake and the chapel are often mentioned in ballad and poem.

387. our Ladye's lake, St. Mary's Loch.

388. an offering, a present, probably of money, which he would lay before the altar as a thank-offering for his escape.

389. would pay his vows, meant, was determined to offer the prayers, &c., which it was his duty to offer.

390. On 25th'June 1557, Dame Janet Beaton, Lady Buccleuch, was accused in the Court of Justiciary of coming with two hundred armed men of the Scott clan to the kirk of St. Mary of the Lowes, " and breaking open the doors of the said kirk, in order to apprehend the laird of Cranstoune for his destruction. ... It is said that upon this rising the kirk of St. Mary was burned by the Scotts." (Scott.)

392. trysting-place, place appointed for meeting. The word *tryst* (= pledge) is the same as *trust*, but is used in poetry and romance for a promise between lovers. Cf. Burns, *Mary Morison*, "O Mary, at thy window be; It is the wish'd, the trysted hour".

392. Newark Lee, grassy plain at Newark. (Usually spelt *lea* : O. E. *leáh*, pasture.)

393. Wat of Harden, a Walter Scott, and an ancestor of the poet. *Harden* is a few miles N. of Branksome.

393. amain. See note on line 196.

394. John of Thirlestane, Sir John Scott, to whom was granted, by James V., a special coat-of-arms with the motto *Ready, aye Ready*. *Thirlestane* is between Harden and Buccleuch.

397. Douglas-burn, a stream flowing into the Yarrow below St. Mary's Loch.

398. prance ... gleam, present tenses, though the past tense is used in lines 396, 399. The present tense gives vividness to a narrative, but is here used probably for convenience of riming. Cf. lines 404, 405.

399. ere, before. (O. E. *ær.*)

400. void, empty.

401. very rage. *Very* is used to emphasise *rage*; it was just for rage that they burnt the chapel.

405. pricks, erects, points upward. (O. E. *prician*, from *prica*, a sharp point.) In the previous line the verb, *stood*, is in the past tense, and strictly *pricks* should also be past, 'pricked', and *hears* in line 406 should be 'heard'. Probably the only reason for the variation is that *hears* rimes with *ears*, while 'heard' does not.

411. cushat-dove, wood-pigeon. (O. E. *cusceote*, perhaps from *cucu*, quick, and *sceotan*, to shoot.)

414. pondering. We now usually say *ponder on* or *ponder over*, *ponder* being intransitive. But it used to be transitive; cf. *Luke's Gospel*, ii. 19, "But Mary kept all these things, and pondered them in her heart." (Lat. *ponderare*, to weigh.)

414. deep = *deeply*, adj. for adverb.

415. eastward. Melrose is almost due north of Branksome, but the road along which Deloraine had ridden to Melrose, and was now returning, led past Goldilands and Hawick (see canto i. 262–269), which are eastward from Branksome.

416. Notice how skilfully the Minstrel's age is turned to account by Scott. The pause for refreshment is quite natural in an old man, but Scott has brought his story to an interesting point, where his hearers are on tiptoe (as it were) with excitement to learn why it was that the Dwarf had parted the lovers. Hence a break here is very artistically managed.

416. pour'd expresses the rapid unbroken way in which the Minstrel sang his song.

419. of age = aged.

420. goblet. The *-et* is a diminutive ending; O. F. *gobel*, Lat. *cupellus*, a cup.

420. crown'd, filled to the brim, so that the goblet was topped with froth. Cf. *Marmion*, canto i. stanza xv.

421. blood. As "the blood is the life" of a human body, so the virtue of the grape is in its juice: hence the metaphor. A wine is produced near Basle called *Schweizerblut*, blood of the Swiss.

421. Velez' scorched vine. *Velez* is in Malaga, the best wine-producing province of Spain. *Scorched* expresses the intensity of the heat: it is a condensed and suggestive way of saying that the grapes of Velez ripen under a burning sun. Cf. "frozen brook", iii. 345, and note.

423. the big drop, *i.e.* tears. The Minstrel's feelings were touched by the generosity with which he was being treated.

425. son of song, *i.e.* minstrel. *Son* is thus poetically used for one whose life is devoted to any kind of work or duty; cf. "sons of labour".

428. quaff'd, drank in large draughts. (Scotch *quaich*, *queff*, a cup.)

431. cordial, heart-warming. (L. *cors*, heart.)

431. nectar in Greek fable was the drink of the gods. The word is applied to any delicious drink.

432. swell'd his old veins, by the increased flow of blood which the wine caused.

433. prelude, short strain of music played on his harp before he resumed his song. (Lat. *prae*, before; *ludere*, to play.)

433. ran. It was rapid, because the Minstrel was now refreshed and gay at heart. The prelude consisted no doubt of *runs* up and down the strings.

CANTO THIRD.

I.

AND said I that my limbs were old,
And said I that my blood was cold,
And that my kindly fire was fled,
And my poor wither'd heart was dead,
   And that I might not sing of love?—   5
How could I to the dearest theme,
That ever warm'd a minstrel's dream,
   So foul, so false a recreant prove!
How could I name Love's very name,
Nor wake my heart to notes of flame!   10

II.

In peace, Love tunes the shepherd's reed;
In war, he mounts the warrior's steed;
In halls, in gay attire is seen;
In hamlets, dances on the green.
Love rules the court, the camp, the grove,   15
And men below, and saints above;
For love is heaven, and heaven is love.

III.

So thought Lord Cranstoun, as I ween,
While, pondering deep the tender scene,
He rode through Branksome's hawthorn green.   20
   But the page shouted wild and shrill—
     And scarce his helmet could he don,
   When downward from the shady hill
     A stately knight came pricking on.
That warrior's steed, so dapple-gray,   25
Was dark with sweat, and splashed with clay;
   His armour red with many a stain:
He seem'd in such a weary plight,
As if he had ridden the livelong night;
   For it was William of Deloraine.   30

IV.

But no whit weary did he seem,
   When, dancing in the sunny beam,

He mark'd the crane on the Baron's cres.
For his ready spear was in his rest.
  Few were the words, and stern and high,   35
    That mark'd the foemen's feudal hate;
  For question fierce, and proud reply,
    Gave signal soon of dire debate.
Their very coursers seem'd to know
That each was other's mortal foe,   40
And snorted fire, when wheel'd around,
To give each foe his vantage-ground.

V.

In rapid round the Baron bent;
  He sigh'd a sigh, and pray'd a prayer;
The prayer was to his patron saint,   45
  The sigh was to his ladye fair.
Stout Deloraine nor sigh'd nor pray'd,
Nor saint, nor ladye, call'd to aid;
But he stoop'd his head, and couch'd his spear,
And spurred his steed to full career.   50
The meeting of these champions proud
Seem'd like the bursting thunder-cloud.

VI.

Stern was the dint the Borderer lent!
The stately Baron backwards bent;
Bent backwards to his horse's tail,   55
And his plumes went scattering on the gale;
The tough ash spear, so stout and true,
Into a thousand flinders flew.
But Cranstoun's lance, of more avail,
Pierced through, like silk, the Borderer's mail; 60
Through shield, and jack, and acton, past,
Deep in his bosom broke at last.—
Still sate the warrior saddle-fast,
Till, stumbling in the mortal shock,
Down went the steed, the girthing broke,   65
Hurl'd on a heap lay man and horse.
The Baron onward pass'd his course;
Nor knew—so giddy roll'd his brain—
His foe lay stretch'd upon the plain.

VII.

But when he rein'd his courser round,   70
And saw his foeman on the ground
　　Lie senseless as the bloody clay,
He bade his page to stanch the wound,
　　And there beside the warrior stay,
And tend him in his doubtful state,   75
And lead him to Branksome castle-gate:
His noble mind was inly moved
For the kinsman of the maid he loved.
" This shalt thou do without delay:
No longer here myself may stay;   80
Unless the swifter I speed away,
Short shrift will be at my dying day."

VIII.

Away in speed Lord Cranstoun rode;
The Goblin-Page behind abode;
His lord's command he ne'er withstood,   85
Though small his pleasure to do good.
As the corslet off he took,
The dwarf espied the Mighty Book!
Much he marvell'd a knight of pride,
Like a book-bosom'd priest should ride: 90
He thought not to search or stanch the wound
Until the secret he had found.

IX.

The iron band, the iron clasp,
Resisted long the elfin grasp:
For when the first he had undone,   95
It closed as he the next begun.
Those iron clasps, that iron band,
Would not yield to unchristen'd hand,
Till he smear'd the cover o'er
With the Borderer's curdled gore;   100
A moment then the volume spread,
And one short spell therein he read.
It had much of glamour might,
Could make a ladye seem a knight;
The cobwebs on a dungeon wall   105
Seem tapestry in lordly hall;

A nut-shell seem a gilded barge,
A sheeling seem a palace large,
And youth seem age, and age seem youth—
All was delusion. nought was truth.   110

X.

He had not read another spell,
When on his cheek a buffet fell,
So fierce, it stretch'd him on the plain,
Beside the wounded Deloraine.
From the ground he rose dismay'd,   115
And shook his huge and matted head;
One word he mutter'd, and no more,
" Man of age, thou smitest sore !"—
No more the Elfin Page durst try
Into the wondrous Book to pry;   120
The clasps, though smear'd with Christian gore,
Shut faster than they were before.
He hid it underneath his cloak.—
Now, if you ask who gave the stroke,
I cannot tell, so mot I thrive;   125
It was not given by man alive.

XI.

Unwillingly himself he address'd,
To do his master's high behest :
He lifted up the living corse,
And laid it on the weary horse;   130
He led him into Branksome Hall,
Before the beards of the warders all;
And each did after swear and say,
There only pass'd a wain of hay.
He took him to Lord David's tower,   135
Even to the Ladye's secret bower;
And, but that stronger spells were spread,
And the door might not be opened,
He had laid him on her very bed.
Whate'er he did of gramarye,   140
Was always done maliciously ;
He flung the warrior on the ground,
And the blood well'd freshly from the wound.

XII.

As he repass'd the outer court,
He spied the fair young child at sport :   145
He thought to train him to the wood ;
For, at a word, be it understood,
He was always for ill, and never for good.
Seem'd to the boy, some comrade gay
Led him forth to the woods to play ;   150
On the drawbridge the warders stout
Saw a terrier and lurcher passing out.

XIII.

He led the boy o'er bank and fell,
   Until they came to a woodland brook ;
The running stream dissolved the spell,   155
   And his own elvish shape he took.
Could he have had his pleasure vilde,
He had crippled the joints of the noble child ;
Or, with his fingers long and lean,
Had strangled him in fiendish spleen :   160
But his awful mother he had in dread,
And also his power was limited ;
So he but scowl'd on the startled child,
And darted through the forest wild ;
The woodland brook he bounding cross'd,   165
And laugh'd, and shouted, "Lost ! lost ! lost !"—

XIV.

Full sore amazed at the wondrous change,
   And frighten'd as a child might be,
At the wild yell and visage strange,
   And the dark words of gramarye,   170
The child, amidst the forest bower,
Stood rooted like a lily flower ;
   And when at length, with trembling pace,
     He sought to find where Branksome lay,
   He fear'd to see that grisly face   175
     Glare from some thicket on his way.
Thus, starting oft, he journey'd on,
And deeper in the wood is gone,—
For aye the more he sought his way,
The farther still he went astray,—   180

Until he heard the mountains round
Ring to the baying of a hound.

XV.

And hark! and hark! the deep-mouth'd bark
  Comes nigher still, and nigher:
Bursts on the path a dark blood-hound,   185
His tawny muzzle track'd the ground,
  And his red eye shot fire.
Soon as the wilder'd child saw he,
He flew at him right furiouslie.
I ween you would have seen with joy   190
The bearing of the gallant boy,
When, worthy of his noble sire,
His wet cheek glow'd 'twixt fear and ire!
He faced the blood-hound manfully,
And held his little bat on high;   195
So fierce he struck, the dog, afraid,
At cautious distance hoarsely bay'd,
  But still in act to spring;
When dash'd an archer through the glade,
And when he saw the hound was stay'd,   200
  He drew his tough bow-string;
But a rough voice cried, " Shoot not, hoy!
Ho! shoot not, Edward—'Tis a boy!"

XVI.

The speaker issued from the wood,
And check'd his fellow's surly mood,   205
  And quell'd the ban-dog's ire:
He was an English yeoman good,
  And born in Lancashire.
Well could he hit a fallow deer
  Five hundred feet him fro;   210
With hand more true, and eye more clear,
  No archer bended bow.
His coal-black hair, shorn round and close,
  Set off his sun-burnt face:
Old England's sign, St. George's cross,   215
  His barret-cap did grace;
His bugle-horn hung by his side,
  All in a wolf-skin baldric tied;
And his short falchion, sharp and clear,
Had pierced the throat of many a deer.   220

XVII.

His kirtle, made of forest green,
　Reach'd scantly to his knee;
And, at his belt, of arrows keen
　A furbish'd sheaf bore he;
His buckler scarce in breadth a span, 225
　No larger fence had he;
He never counted him a man,
　Would strike below the knee:
His slacken'd bow was in his hand,
And the leash, that was his blood-hound's band. 230

XVIII.

He would not do the fair child harm,
But held him with his powerful arm,
That he might neither fight nor flee;
For when the Red-Cross spied he,
The boy strove long and violently. 235
" Now, by St. George," the archer cries,
" Edward, methinks we have a prize!
This boy's fair face, and courage free,
Show he is come of high degree."—

XIX.

" Yes! I am come of high degree, 240
　For I am the heir of bold Buccleuch;
And, if thou dost not set me free,
　False Southron, thou shalt dearly rue!
For Walter of Harden shall come with speed,
And William of Deloraine, good at need, 245
And every Scott, from Esk to Tweed;
And, if thou dost not let me go,
Despite thy arrows, and thy bow,
I'll have thee hang'd to feed the crow!"—

XX.

" Gramercy, for thy good will, fair boy! 250
My mind was never set so high;
But if thou art chief of such a clan,
And art the son of such a man,
And ever comest to thy command,
　Our wardens had need to keep good order; 255

My bow of yew to a hazel wand,
　Thou 'lt make them work upon the Border.
Meantime, be pleased to come with me,
For good Lord Dacre shalt thou see;
I think our work is well begun,　　　　　　260
When we have taken thy father's son."

XXI.

Although the child was led away,
In Branksome still he seem'd to stay,
For so the Dwarf his part did play;
And, in the shape of that young boy,　　　265
He wrought the castle much annoy.
The comrades of the young Buccleuch
He pinch'd, and beat, and overthrew;
Nay, some of them he wellnigh slew.
He tore Dame Maudlin's silken tire,　　　270
And, as Sym Hall stood by the fire,
He lighted the match of his bandelier,
And wofully scorch'd the hackbuteer.
It may be hardly thought or said,
The mischief that the urchin made,　　　275
Till many of the castle guess'd,
That the young Baron was possess'd!

XXII.

Well I ween the charm he held
The noble Ladye had soon dispell'd;
But she was deeply busied then　　　　　280
To tend the wounded Deloraine.
　Much she wonder'd to find him lie,
　　On the stone threshold stretch'd along;
　She thought some spirit of the sky
　　Had done the bold moss-trooper wrong;　285
Because, despite her precept dread,
Perchance he in the Book had read;
But the broken lance in his bosom stood,
And it was earthly steel and wood.

XXIII.

She drew the splinter from the wound,　　290
　And with a charm she stanch'd the blood;
She bade the gash be cleansed and bound:
　No longer by his couch she stood;

But she has ta'en the broken lance,
   And wash'd it from the clotted gore,   295
   And salved the splinter o'er and o'er.
William of Deloraine, in trance,
   Whene'er she turn'd it round and round,
   Twisted as if she gall'd his wound.
     Then to her maidens she did say,   300
   That he should be whole man and sound,
     Within the course of a night and day.
Full long she toil'd; for she did rue
Mishap to friend so stout and true.

XXIV.

So pass'd the day—the evening fell,   305
'Twas near the time of curfew bell;
The air was mild, the wind was calm,
The stream was smooth, the dew was balm;
E'en the rude watchman, on the tower,
Enjoy'd and bless'd the lovely hour.   310
Far more fair Margaret loved and bless'd
The hour of silence and of rest.
On the high turret sitting lone,
She waked at times the lute's soft tone;
Touch'd a wild note, and all between   315
Thought of the bower of hawthorns green.
Her golden hair stream'd free from band,
Her fair cheek rested on her hand,
Her blue eyes sought the west afar,
For lovers love the western star.   320

XXV.

Is yon the star, o'er Penchryst Pen,
That rises slowly to her ken,
And, spreading broad its wavering light,
Shakes its loose tresses on the night?
Is yon red glare the western star?—   325
O, 'tis the beacon-blaze of war!
Scarce could she draw her tighten'd breath,
For well she knew the fire of death!

XXVI.

The Warder view'd it blazing strong,
And blew his war-note loud and long,   330

Till, at the high and haughty sound,
Rock, wood, and river, rang around.
The blast alarm'd the festal hall,
And startled forth the warriors all ;
Far downward in the castle-yard,   335
Full many a torch and cresset glared ;
And helms and plumes, confusedly toss'd,
Were in the blaze half-seen, half-lost ;
And spears in wild disorder shook,
Like reeds beside a frozen brook.   340

XXVII.

The Seneschal, whose silver hair
Was redden'd by the torches' glare,
Stood in the midst, with gesture proud,
And issued forth his mandates loud :—
"On Penchryst glows a bale of fire,   345
And three are kindling on Priesthaughswire ;
    Ride out, ride out,
    The foe to scout !
Mount, mount for Branksome, every man !
Thou, Todrig, warn the Johnstone clan,   350
    That ever are true and stout.—
Ye need not send to Liddesdale ;
For, when they see the blazing bale,
Elliots and Armstrongs never fail.—
Ride, Alton, ride, for death and life !   355
And warn the Warder of the strife.—
Young Gilbert, let our beacon blaze,
Our kin, and clan, and friends, to raise."

XXVIII.

Fair Margaret, from the turret head,
Heard, far below, the coursers' tread,   360
    While loud the harness rang,
As to their seats, with clamour dread,
    The ready horsemen sprang :
And trampling hoofs, and iron coats,
And leaders' voices, mingled notes,   365
    And out ! and out !
    In hasty rout,
    The horsemen gallop'd forth ;
Dispersing to the south to scout,
And east, and west, and north,   370

To view their coming enemies,
And warn their vassals and allies.

XXIX.

The ready page, with hurried hand,
Awaked the need-fire's slumbering brand,
   And ruddy blush'd the heaven :   375
For a sheet of flame, from the turret high,
Waved like a blood-flag on the sky,
   All flaring and uneven ;
And soon a score of fires, I ween,
From height, and hill, and cliff, were seen ;   380
Each with warlike tidings fraught ;
Each from each the signal caught ;
Each after each they glanced to sight,
As stars arise upon the night.
They gleam'd on many a dusky tarn,   385
Haunted by the lonely earn ;
On many a cairn's gray pyramid,
Where urns of mighty chiefs lie hid ;
Till high Dunedin the blazes saw,
From Soltra and Dumpender Law ;   390
And Lothian heard the Regent's order,
That all should bowne them for the Border.

XXX.

The livelong night in Branksome rang
   The ceaseless sound of steel ;
The castle-bell, with backward clang,   395
   Sent forth the 'larum peal ;
Was frequent heard the heavy jar,
Where massy stone and iron bar
Were piled on echoing keep and tower,
To whelm the foe with deadly shower ;   400
Was frequent heard the changing guard,
And watch-word from the sleepless ward ;
While, wearied by the endless din,
Blood-hound and ban-dog yell'd within.

XXXI.

The noble Dame, amid the broil,   405
Shared the gray Seneschal's high toil
And spoke of danger with a smile ;

Cheer'd the young knights, and council sage
Held with the chiefs of riper age.
No tidings of the foe were brought,   410
Nor of his numbers knew they aught,
Nor what in time of truce he sought.
　　Some said, that there were thousands ten ;
And others ween'd that it was nought
　　But Leven Clans, or Tynedale men,   415
Who came to gather in black-mail ;
And Liddesdale, with small avail,
　　Might drive them lightly back agen.
So pass'd the anxious night away,
And welcome was the peep of day.   420

CEASED the high sound—the listening throng
Applaud the Master of the Song ;
And marvel much, in helpless age,
So hard should be his pilgrimage.
Had he no friend—no daughter dear,   425
His wandering toil to share and cheer ;
No son to be his father's stay,
And guide him on the rugged way ?
"Ay, once he had—but he was dead !"—
Upon the harp he stoop'd his head,   430
And busied himself the strings withal,
To hide the tear that fain would fall.
In solemn measure, soft and slow,
Arose a father's notes of woe.

NOTES.

CANTO THIRD.

1. And said I. This refers back to ii. 346-351. The *and* is introduced by the Minstrel, for the purpose of reminding his hearers of his former declaration, and of preparing them for some modification of it. In this use *and* is common in ballads.

3. kindly fire, natural enthusiasm.

5. might, could.

6. theme, subject.

7. warm'd a minstrel's dream, made his dream pleasant.

8. recreant, traitor. (F. *recroire*, L. Lat. *recredere*, to change one's belief.)

10. Nor=and not.

10. notes of flame, song of passion, love. See quotation in next note.

11-17. The meaning of these lines is, that people of all classes, rich and poor, and of all kinds of different occupations, are all influenced by love. Cf. Coleridge, *Love*, a poem which Scott admired—

> "All thoughts, all passions, all delights,
> Whatever stirs this mortal frame,
> All are but ministers of Love,
> And feed his sacred flame."

Love is personified, and so is said to perform the actions of persons under the influence of love.

11. tunes the shepherd's reed, causes the shepherd to play love-songs on his pipe. In poetry, shepherds are represented as playing on reeds or stalks which they have made into musical instruments; several stalks of different lengths being joined together by means of wax.

12. That is, the warrior goes off to fight for his lady-love, or encouraged by her.

13. In halls, for example, at balls or parties. *Halls*, of the rich, contrasted with *hamlets* in the next line, of the poor.

14. Lovers among the poorer classes dance together at the village merrymakings on the green.

15. the grove, poets, students, learned people. From the shady walks of the Academy (public pleasure-ground) at Athens, where Plato and other philosophers used to talk with their disciples.

17. In this line *heaven* is used in two senses. **Love is heaven** means that human love brings with it pleasures and blessings so great as to deserve to be called 'heavenly'. **Heaven is love** means that heaven, God, is the very fount of love, *Love* itself.

19. pondering, here used transitively, as in ii. 414. *Ponder* is now usually intransitive, and joined with *on* or *over*.

19. deep, deeply: adjective for adverb.

21. wild and shrill, adjectives for adverbs.

22. The knight, when not in action, rode with his helmet off. Cf. *Marmion*, i. 60, "His helm hung at his saddle-bow".

22. scarce, *i.e.* scarcely.

22. don, put on. Literally *do on*; so *doff, do off*, to put off.

22. There were two reasons why Cranstoun was almost taken unawares: (1) he was lost in thought; (2) Deloraine had been riding under the shade of trees (see *shady hill* in next line), and so had not been seen except by the Dwarf.

24. pricking on. *Pricking* = spurring, and was originally used transitively. It is more common intransitively.

25. dapple, spotted.

28, 29. There is some confusion in the construction here. The complete sense is: 'he was in such a weary plight that it seemed as if...'.

29. the livelong night, all night long. Livelong properly means 'as long as life lasts'.

31. no whit, not at all. (*Whit* is O. E. *wiht*, person, thing. *Not* and *naught* (or *nought*) are both contractions of O. E. *ná whit*.)

33. mark'd, observed.

33. "The crest of the Cranstouns, in allusion to their name, is a crane dormant, holding a stone in his foot, with an emphatic Border motto, *Thou shalt want ere I want*." (Scott.)

34. his ready spear. *Ready* is a proleptic epithet, *i.e.* it anticipates what is stated in the words *in his rest*. It also implies that Deloraine himself, as a tried Border knight, was ready to welcome an occasion to use his spear.

34. in his rest. The *rest* was a loop or hook in which the heavy spear was supported when couched ready for the charge. The word was also written *arest*.

35. **high.** Scott constantly uses *high* in a variety of senses, not always definite: cf. i. 79, 176, 189, 209; ii. 220; iii. 128, 240, 331, 406. 'High words' is a common phrase for threats and words said in anger.

36. **mark'd,** showed, were a sign of.

36. **feudal hate,** the hatred which they bore one another because of the *feud* or quarrel between the two families to which they belonged. *Feudal* may have also the same meaning as in "feudal system", *feudal hate* thus meaning hatred in which every dependant of the noble families shared, simply because he *was* a dependant. It was not a *personal* hatred.

38. **dire,** dreadful.

38. **debate,** strife. This meaning has now disappeared, 'debate' being applied only to a contest in words. But the old meaning is found in the phrase of Queen Elizabeth, when she called Mary Stuart "the daughter of debate". (O. F. *debatre*, from L. Lat. *de-*, intensive prefix, *batuere*, to beat. Mod. F. *se débattre* has the meaning 'to struggle'.)

39. **coursers,** horses. (O. F. *corsier*, Lat. *cursus*, a running.)

40. **other's.** '*The* other's' would be more usual.

40. **mortal,** deadly. (Lat. *mortalis*, from *mors*, death.)

42. **vantage-ground,** the space between the combatants necessary in order to enable the horses to charge at "full career".

47, 48. In canto II. stanza vi. Deloraine expressed his contempt for prayers, &c.

49. **couch'd,** lowered in readiness to charge.

50. **to full career,** until he ran at full speed. *Career* means properly a 'road'. (O. F. *cariere*, L. Lat. *carraria*, i.e. *carraria via*, a way for the *carrus*, car.) It was a term used in Norman chivalry for the 'course' in the lists.

53. **dint,** blow.

53. **lent,** gave.

58. **flinders,** splinters, small pieces. (Norwegian *flindra*.)

59. **avail,** strength. See note on line 417 below.

60. **mail,** the fine steel network which formed his armour. (O.F. *maille*, Lat. *macula*, a small hole.)

61. **jack,** a leathern coat worn over the hauberk (coat of mail). It usually had no sleeves, and was sometimes padded with metal. (O. F. *jaque*: cf. *jacket*.)

61. acton, a wadded or quilted tunic worn under the hauberk. (O. F. *auqueton,* from Sp. *alcoton,* from Arabic *al-qūtun,* the cotton.) The manner in which these pieces of armour were worn may be seen from Chaucer, *Rime of Sir Thopas,* 148, "next his sherte an aketoun, And over that an habergeoun ... And over that a fyn hauberk". The terrific effect of Cranstoun's blow is paralleled in an old romance called *Eger and Grine,* 124 ff.:—

> " I gaue my horsse what head he wold,
> our steeds brought us together soone:
> alas, that meeting I may mone !
> ffor through coate armour & acton,
> through brest plate & Habergion,
> through all my armour lesse & more
> Cleane through the body he me bore;
> & I still in my sadle sate."

63. sate; the *e* makes the *a* long, and so makes the word more like the O. E. original *sǽt.*

63. saddle-fast, firm in saddle. A word coined in the same way as *stedfast* ('firm in place'), *soothfast* ('firm in truth'), *shamefast* (= 'shamefaced', a corrupt form). O. E. *fæst* meant 'firm': we retain this meaning in "fast bind, safe find", "fast shut", &c., but the more common meaning nowadays is 'quick'.

64. mortal. The shock did not actually cause death, but it was so terrific that it seemed likely to.

65. girthing, strap which passed round the body of the horse, keeping the saddle in place.

66. on a heap. The more common expression would be 'in a heap'. But cf. Psalm lxxix. 1, "they have laid Jerusalem on heaps". *On* and *in* are closely related words, and were often used one for the other.

67. onward pass'd his course = passed onward *on* his course. It appears that we have to supply the preposition *on* from the adverb *onward. Pass* is not as a rule used transitively in this sense.

68. giddy, used as an adverb.

70. rein'd his courser round, turned his horse round by means of the reins.

73, 74. bade his page to stanch...stay. Both verbs, or neither, should have *to,* the sign of the infinitive. In O. E. the present infinitive was marked by the termination *-an,* which became successively *-en* and *-e,* and then disappeared entirely, *to* being used instead. Auxiliary verbs were followed by the infinitive without *to;* and the distinction between auxiliary and non-auxiliary verbs not being as yet clearly made, many verbs commonly used with other verbs kept or omitted *to* indifferently.

75. doubtful state. It was doubtful whether he was very severely hurt or not.

77. inly, within.

80. myself, emphatic pronoun.

81. the swifter. Such a comparative as this usually has a corresponding comparative, as in lines 179, 180, "the more...the farther", or an explanatory clause. The comparative appears to have little force here. We might understand, 'unless I speed away more swiftly (than I should otherwise), for the reason that (*the*) I have overthrown one of the Branksome knights so near the Tower'.

82. short shrift will be, there will be little time for confession and absolution, for I shall be killed. In the Roman Catholic church great importance is attached to a dying man's confessing and receiving absolution immediately before death, in order that he may have an assured entrance into Paradise. To kill a man without allowing shriving-time was therefore to endanger his immortal soul. (*Shrift* is O. E. *scrift*, from *scrifan*, to prescribe penance; Lat. *scribere*, to write.)

82. dying day, *i.e.* the day for my dying. So "washing day", the day for washing.

87. corslet, small piece of armour for protecting the body; cuirass. (-*let* is the diminutive ending: O. F. *cors*, Lat. *corpus* the body.)

88. Mighty Book, the book containing the magician's spells, which Deloraine had brought from Melrose.

90. "At Unthank, two miles N.E. from the church (of Ewes), there are the ruins of a chapel for divine service, in time of Popery. There is a tradition, that friars were wont to come from Melrose or Jedburgh, to baptise and marry in this parish; and from being in use to carry the mass-book in their bosoms, they were called by the inhabitants, *Book-a-bosomes.*" (Quoted by Scott.)

The page's amazement was natural. Learning was almost entirely confined to the clergy. Deloraine knew not enough Latin to save his neck at Hairibee. Cf. *Quentin Durward*, ch. v., where Le Balafré, of Louis XI.'s Scottish body-guard, is amazed at his nephew's ability to read and write: "'To read and write!' exclaimed Le Balafré, who was one of those sort of people who think all knowledge is miraculous which chances to exceed their own—'To write, sayst thou, and to read! I cannot believe it—never Durward could write his name that ever I heard of, nor Lesly either. I can answer for one of them—I can no more write than I can fly.'"

There is also implied here the contempt in which the lower clergy were held by men of action—a contempt that long survived. In Elizabeth's day, Nathan Drake tells us, the nobleman had his chaplain, but treated him only as a higher domestic. So in *Esmond*, Dr.

Tusher occasionally dined with the Earl of Castlewood, but showed his sense of his inferiority by always leaving the table when the pudding came in.

91. He thought not to does not mean only 'did not intend to'. The goblin was so eager to find out the secret that he *forgot* his master's command.

93–101. Christening was believed to protect persons and things— bells were christened, and are still in the Roman Catholic church— from receiving harm from evil spirits.

101. A = one. (*A* is a shortened form of O. E. *án*, one.)

101. spread, lay open. Cf. *expand*, ii. 193.

102. spell, form of words supposed to have a magical power.

103–110. " *Glamour*, in the legends of Scottish superstition, means the magic power of imposing on the eyesight of the spectators, so that the appearance of an object shall be totally different from the reality. ...To a similar charm the ballad of Johnny Fa' imputes the fascina- tion of the lovely Countess, who eloped with that gipsy leader :—

> ' Sae soon as they saw her weel-far'd face,
> They cast the glamour o'er her.'

The art of glamour, or other fascination, was anciently a princi- pal part of the skill of the *jongleur*, or juggler, whose tricks formed much of the amusement of a Gothic castle." (Scott.)

Scott goes on to tell a story from Froissart of a magician who caused the garrison of a besieged castle to surrender, by deceiving them with the illusion of the sea breaking over the wall; and who afterwards offered to put the same castle into the hands of a second assailant by deluding the defenders with the appearance of a bridge on the sea. He quotes also, from a poem written in 1452–3, account of the juggling tricks of a jay in an assembly of birds—

> " He could wirk windaris [wonders], quhat way that he wald,
> Mak a gray gus [goose] a gold garland,
> A lang spere of a bittile [mallet], for a berne bald [baron bold],
> Nobilis of nutschelles, and silver of sand."

In his second note on the ballad of *Christie's Will* in the *Border Minstrelsy*, Scott refers to Chaucer's *Frankeleines Tale*: cf. line 395 :—

> " He him remembred, that upon a day
> At Orleaunce in studie a book he say [saw]
> Of magike naturel...
>
> .   .   .   .
>
> Anon for joye his herte [heart] gan to dance,
> And to himself he saied prively;
>
> .   .   .   .

For I am siker [sure] that ther be sciences,
By which men maken divers apparences,
Swiche [such] as thise subtil tragetoures [jugglers] play.
For oft at festes have I wel herd say,
That tragetoures, within an halle large,
Have made come in a water and a barge,
And in the halle rowen up and doun.
Somtime hath semed come a grim leoun [lion],
And somtime floures spring as in a mede,
Somtime a vine, and grapes white and rede,
Somtime a castel al of lime and ston."

Aurelius went to the magician's house—
" Tho saw he knightes justen in a plain.
And after this he did him swiche plesaunce,
That he him showed his lady on a dance,
On which himselven danced, as him thought.
And whan this maister, that this magike wrought,
Saw it was time, he clapped his hondes [hands] two,
And farewel, al the revel is ago [gone]."

103. **glamour might,** magic power. (*Glamour* is probably only a variation of *gramarye* (see note on that word, line 140 below), the *l* having replaced the *r* by confusion with *glimmer*.)

108. **sheeling,** a shepherd's hut. (Dim. of *sheel*, a Scotch word connected with Icel. *skali*, a hut, from a Sanskrit root *sku*, cover.)

112. **buffet,** blow. (Diminutive of O. F. *bufe*, a blow, slap.)

113. Supply *that* between *fierce* and *it*.

116. **matted,** with his thick hair twisted and tangled like a mat.

117. **One word,** a single expression.

118. This was the expression said to have been used by Gilpin Horner, the strange dwarfish creature who was said to have stayed some time at a farm-house among the Border mountains, and who was the original of Scott's goblin-page.

118. **sore** = sorely.

124-126. Scott quotes an anecdote told him by Dr. Henry More, about an eccentric old gentleman, who, said Dr. More, "told me he had used all the magical ceremonies of conjuration he could, to raise the devil or a spirit, and had a most earnest desire to meet with one, but never could do it. But this he told me, when he did not so much as think of it, while his servant was pulling off his boots in the hall, some invisible hand gave him such a clap upon the back that it made all ring again; 'so,' thought he now, ' I am invited to the converse of my spirit,' and therefore, so soon as his boots were off, and his shoes on, out he goes into the yard and next field, to find out the spirit that had given him this familiar clap on the back, but found none neither in the yard nor field next to it".

125. so mot I thrive, so may I prosper—a phrase of the nature of an oath, used to strengthen affirmations. (*Mot* is an O. E. present tense *môt*, may. The *o* is long: consequently the word is often spelt *mote*. The past tense was *moste*, which we have in *must*, but with a different meaning.)

127. himself he address'd, he prepared, set about. (O. F. *adressier*, L. Lat. *addrictiare*, Lat. *directum*, straight.)

128. high, stern, peremptory.

128. behest, command. (O. E. *behæs*. The original form was *hǽs*, from *hátan*, to command. The final *t* has been added, as in *amongst, whilst*, &c.)

129. living corse. *Corse* is in modern English a poetical word only applied to a dead body, as always in Shakespeare; hence *living corse* must mean a living body which yet appeared to be a corpse. But up to the 17th century even *corpse*, of which *corse* is a shortened form, might be used for a living body. (O. F. *corps*, Lat. *corpus*, a body.)

132. before the beards. This phrase implies daring and impudent defiance. *Beards* may be used for "faces": this is then an instance of *synecdoche*, putting a part for the whole. But daring is certainly implied: cf. *1 Samuel* xvii. 35, where David says of his adventure with the lion, "I caught him by the beard, and smote him, and slew him". And as the beard was an emblem of dignity, 'to beard a man' was to insult him deeply. In the classical story the Roman senators remained motionless until the Gauls pulled their beards. Prince John provoked the Irish chiefs by pulling their beards.

132. warders, guards, those who were always 'on the watch'.

134. wain, wagon. (O. E. *wægn*.) Scott mentions, in his note on *glamour* partially quoted in note on lines 103–110 above, an instance in which a gipsy exhibited a fowl trailing what appeared to be the huge trunk of an oak, but what was really a bulrush.

137. but that, &c., *i.e.* if they had not been spread.

137. spread. Probably the metaphor is from spreading a net to catch a bird.

139. had laid, *i.e.* would have laid.

139. on her very bed, actually on her bed. *Very* calls attention to the impudence of the page's intention.

140. gramarye, magic, enchantment (O. F. *gramare, grimoire,* conjuring-book), from *gramaire,* grammar, the 'grammar' having been regarded as a book of secret science from which one could learn how to confound the devil.

143. well'd, flowed like water from a spring. (O. E. *weallan,* to boil.)

145. the fair young child, the Ladye's son; see i. 89.

146. to train, to draw away enticingly (an obsolete sense). (F. *trainer,* L. Lat. *trahinare,* Lat. *trahere,* to draw.)

147. at a word, in short. In this case *a* is used in the original sense 'one'; see note on line 101. Cf. Scotch *ae.*

149. The full sentence would be '(it) seem'd...(that) some comrade'. Such words were and are often omitted where the omission gave rise to no doubt of the meaning. *It* is really unnecessary; it merely anticipates the subject of the verb, which is the sentence beginning "Some comrade". *That* is often omitted in ordinary speech, and many instances occur in this poem.

151. drawbridge, a bridge over the moat at the entrance to the castle, which could be let out or drawn back at will.

152. lurcher, a kind of hunting-dog, a dog that *lurks,* lies in wait.

153. fell, rock.

155. "It is a firm article of popular faith, that no enchantment can subsist in a living stream. Nay, if you can interpose a brook betwixt you and witches, spectres, or even fiends, you are in perfect safety. Burns's inimitable *Tam o' Shanter* turns entirely upon such a circumstance. The belief seems to be of antiquity. Brompton informs us, that certain Irish wizards could, by spells, convert earthen clods, or stones, into fat pigs, which they sold in the market, but which always reassumed their proper form when driven by the deceived purchasers across a running stream." (Scott.)

157. vilde, a corruption of *vile,* due perhaps to confusion with *wild.*

158. had = would have; so in line 160, &c.

161. had in dread, considered a person always to be feared.

163. but, only.

169. visage, countenance, face.

171. bower. Properly a building (O. E. *búr*). Often used for a lady's private room. Here used for the kind of room formed by the over-arching trees in the forest. See line 28 of the Introduction of the poem.

175. grisly, horrible. (O. E. *grislic*, formed with suffix *-lic* from the past participle of a verb *greósan*, to afflict with horror.)

179. aye, always.

182. Ring to, *i.e.* in response to; echoing. See ii. 105 and the note there.

188. Soon as, *i.e. as* soon as.

188. wilder'd, gone astray.

189. furiouslie. The *e* is added to give an old-fashioned appearance: cf. *ladye*, &c. But the O. E. adverbial termination was *-lice*; *-lic* was adjectival.

190. ween, think, believe.

191. bearing, manner, conduct.

192. his noble sire, his noble father, the Sir Walter Scott who had been killed in the fight with the Carrs. See i. 58.

197. at cautious distance, at such a distance as caution told him it would be prudent to remain at: a condensed phrase.

198. in act to spring, crouching in readiness to spring.

205. fellow, companion.

206. quell'd, put an end to, subdued.

206. ban-dog, mastiff. Originally *band-dog*; so called because it was fastened up by a band to keep guard of the house. The word is used here as if it were the same as *bloodhound*, a dog used in hunting.

207. yeoman, small land-owner. See note on i. 20.

208. Lancashire, being one of the northern counties, suffered from the attacks of the Scots and naturally supplied men for the border warfare. The men of Lancashire and Cheshire played a conspicuous if not heroic part in the battle of Flodden Field.

209. fallow, of a brownish colour. (O.E. *fealo*, pale red.)

210. fro, now only used in the phrase 'to and fro'. (*Fro* is a Scandinavian form (O. Norse *frá*): cf. Scotch *frae*; the *m* in *from* is a superlative ending.)

216. barret-cap, a small flat cap. (F. *barrette*, L. Lat. *birretum*, cap, from *birrus*, cloak: cf. *biretta*, the cap worn by Roman Catholic clergy.)

217. bugle-horn, usually abbreviated to *bugle*. So called because originally made from the horn of an ox. (O. F. *bugle*, a wild ox, Lat. *buculum*.)

218. All, used as meaning 'altogether', or poetically without any definite meaning.

218. baldric, belt.

219. falchion, short curved sword.

219. clear, in its old sense of 'bright'. (O. F. *cler*, Lat. *clarus*.)

221-228. Imitated, Scott tells us, from Drayton's *Polyolbion*, Song 26—

> "A hundred valiant men had this brave Robin Hood,
> Still ready at his call, that bowmen were right good;
> All clad in Lincoln green, with caps of red and blue,
> His fellow's winded horn not one of them but knew.
> When setting to their lips their bugles shrill,
> The warbling echoes waked from every dale and hill;
> Their bauldrics set with studs athwart their shoulders cast,
> To which under their arms their sheafs were buckled fast,
> A short sword at their belt, a buckler scarce a span,
> Who struck below the knee not counted then a man.
> All made of Spanish yew, their bows were wondrous strong,
> They not an arrow drew but was a cloth-yard long.
> Of archery they had the very perfect craft,
> With broad arrow, or but, or prick, or roving shaft."

221. kirtle, tunic. See note on ii. 299.

221. forest green, green-coloured buckram such as foresters used to wear. It is also called 'Lincoln green' and 'Kendal green'. About the middle of the 14th century, Flemish cloth-weavers settled, by leave of Edward III., in several towns in the north and east of England, among them Carlisle and Lincoln.

224. furbish'd, polished. (O. F. *fourbir*, from O. Germ. *furpjan*.)

225. buckler, small round shield. So called from the knob in its centre. (O. F. *boucler*, Lat. *buculla*, a little cheek.)

226. fence, protection.

227, 228. See the extract from Drayton, above. Scott adds: "To wound an antagonist in the thigh, or leg, was reckoned contrary to the law of arms"; and quotes from Froissart an account of a tilt between an English squire and a Frenchman: "they met at the speare poyntes rudely; the French squyer justed right pleasantly; the Englishman ran too lowe, for he strak the Frenchman depe into the thigh. Wherewith the Erle of Buckingham was right sore displeased, and so were all the other lords, and sayde how it was shamefully done." So nowadays hitting 'below the belt' is forbidden by the code of schoolboy honour.

227, 228. him ... Would, that person who would.

230. leash, a thong to hold in a dog. (O. F. *lesse* Lat. *laxus* slack.)

239. of high degree, of noble birth, high rank.

243. Southron, a form of *Southern*· a name then applied in contempt by Scots to English.

243. dearly rue, bitterly repent.

244. Walter of Harden, one of the Scott clan. He took his name from *Harden*, a few miles N. of Branksome.

245. good at need. `This was the common description of Deloraine.

248. despite, in spite of.

249. to feed the crow, *i.e.* he would have him hanged on a tree in the forest, where the birds would find his dead body and feed on it.

250. Gramercy, thanks. Often used mockingly. It was formerly spelt *graunt* or *grand mercy*. (O. F. *grand merci*, much thanks.)

254. And ever become lord in fact, as you are in name, of Buccleuch. **command**, in the same sense as in 'command of an army', or 'of a fleet'.

255. wardens. The marches or borders between England and Scotland were divided into parts, each under the charge of a governor called a warden. *Warden* is a doublet of *guardian*; at the Tower of London there are *warders*, at St. James's Palace *guards*. *Warden* is still used as the name of a president or governor in 'Warden of the Cinque Ports', 'Warden of Merton College,' &c.

255. had, would have.

256. *i.e.* I will wager my bow to a hazel wand.

259. good Lord Dacre, Lord Dacre of the North, one of the English commanders at the battle of Pinkie, 1547.

266. annoy, here a noun. *Annoy*, and its equivalent *annoyance*, once meant serious harm, rather than mere vexation.

270. Maudlin, shortened form of *Magdalene*, representing popular pronunciation. Magdalen College at Oxford is spoken of as *Maudlin*. Cf. *Chumley*, the pronunciation of 'Cholmondeley'.

270. tire, headdress. From *attire*. (O. F. *atirier*, to arrange.)

271. Sym, short for *Symon*.

272. bandelier, a belt worn across the breast, used to support the musket and hold cartridges. (O. F. *bandouillere*, from an Ital. dim. of *banda*, a sash.)

273. **hackbuteer**, musketeer. (Dutch *haak*, hook; *bus*, gun-barrel.)

274. **may**, can.

275. **urchin.** The original meaning, hedgehog (O. F. *eriçon*, Lat. *ericius*), is found in *The Tempest*, i. 2. 326, where Prospero threatens Caliban that urchins shall prick him and pinch him all night long. Goblins were supposed sometimes to take a hedgehog's shape.

277. **possess'd**, *i.e.* with an evil spirit.

280, 281. **busied...To tend.** The usual phrase is 'in tending', *in* with a verbal noun being used rather than the infinitive, which is here used in what would be called a *gerundial* sense.

284. **some spirit of the sky**, one of the spirits supposed to be always hovering in the air. *Sky* was often used by the poets for *atmosphere*.

285. **moss-trooper**, the common name for the Border warriors. *Moss* = marsh.

286. **precept dread**, strict command.

287. **But Deloraine could not read.** Cf. i. 257, "Letter nor line know I never a one, Were 't my neck-verse at Hairibee".

291. Scott quotes:

> "Tom Potts was but a serving man,
> But yet he was a doctor good;
> He bound his handkerchief on the wound,
> And with some kinds of words he stanched the blood".

> *Pieces of Ancient Popular Poetry*, Lond. 1791, p. 131.

The following charm for stanching blood, from a 15th century MS., is given in Brand's *Popular Antiquities*, p. 729:—

"Jesus that was in Bethleem born, and baptyzed was in the flumen Jordane, as stente the water at hys comyng, so stente the blood of thys Man N. thy Servvaunt, thorw the vertu of thy holy Name ✚ Jesu ✚ and of thy cosyn swete Sent Jon. And sey thys charme fyve tymes with fyve Pater Nosters, in the worschep of the fyve woundys."

292. **bade the gash be**, i.e. bade (*that*) the gash (*should*) be. The cleansing and binding was done by the maidens mentioned in line 300.

294–296. Scott quotes from a "discourse upon the cure by sympathy", pronounced by Sir Kenelm Digby, and published in 1658. "Mr. James Howel...coming by chance as two of his best friends were fighting in duel, he did endeavour to part them; and, putting himselfe between them, seized, with his left hand, upon the

hilt of the sword of one of the combatants, while with his right
hand he laid hold of the blade of the other.   They, being trans-
ported with fury one against the other, struggled to rid themselves
of the hindrance their friend made that they should not kill one
another; and one of them roughly drawing the blade of his sword,
cuts to the very bone the nerves and muscles of Mr. Howel's hand;
and then the other disengaged his hilts, and gave a crosse blow on
his adversarie's head, which glanced towards his friend, who heaving
up his sore hand to save the blow, he was wounded on the back of
his hand as he had been before within. ... Having searched his hurts,
they bound up his hand with one of his garters, to close the veins
which were cut and bled abundantly."   Finding that his wounds did
not heal, Mr. Howel went to Sir Kenelm Digby, who was renowned
as having effected some marvellous cures.   Sir Kenelm says: " I
asked him then for any thing that had the blood upon it: so he
presently sent for his garter, wherewith his hand was first bound:
and as I called for a bason of water, as if I would wash my hands,
I took a handful of powder of vitriol and presently dissolved it.   As
soon as the bloudy garter was brought me, I put it within the bason,
observing in the interim what Mr. Howel did, who stood talking
with a gentleman in a corner of my chamber, not regarding at all
what I was doing; but he started suddenly, as if he had found some
strange alteration in himself.   I asked him what he ailed.   'I know
not what ailes me; but I finde that I feel no more pain.'"   Sir
Kenelm then advised him to give up plasters, and only keep the
wound clean.   Shortly after, Sir Kenelm took the garter out of the
water; immediately Mr. Howel felt a renewal of the pain and fever,
which again disappeared when the garter was replaced in the basin.
King James I. took a great interest in this matter, and to him Sir
Kenelm confessed that he had learnt the secret from a Carmelite
friar, who had learnt it in Armenia.   Scott adds: " I presume that
the success ascribed to the sympathetic mode of treatment might
arise from the pains bestowed in washing the wound and excluding
the air, thus bringing on a cure by the first intention".

296. salved, anointed with healing ointment.

297. trance, fit of unconsciousness.

299. gall'd, rubbed.

305–340. Such pictures as are here given show how greatly Scott
improved on the rough ballads which he took as his model.   Stanza
xxiv. makes us realize the beautiful evening scene from Margaret's
turret window.   Then in stanzas xxv. and xxvi. the style has quite
changed, and we feel ourselves in the midst of the clang of arms and
the glare of signal fires.

306. curfew bell, the bell originally rung as a signal for all lights
and fires to be put out.   (O. F. *covre-feu*, cover fire.)   The time of
ringing it varied: it was in some places eight o'clock, in Scotland
often 9 and 10 o'clock.

308. dew was balm, the evening dew was as pleasant as heal-
ing ointment to a wound. (*Balm* is short for *balsam*, a kind of
sweet-scented gum.)

309. rude, unrefined, rough.

313. lone, *i.e.* alone.

314. waked. *Wake* is often thus poetically used for beginning
a strain of music on a harp or other stringed instrument.

315. all between; see note on line 218.

316. bower; see note on line **171.** Margaret had met Lord
Cranstoun among the hawthorns in the morning.

320. Poets ancient and modern associate the Evening-star, Hes-
perus, with love. Campbell and Byron afford instances: so Long-
fellow, *The Evening Star*—

> " Lo ! in the painted oriel of the west,
>
> Like a fair lady at her casement, shines
> The evening star, the star of love and rest !
>
> O my beloved, my sweet Hesperus !
> My morning and my evening star of love ! "

And Tennyson, *The Gardener's Daughter*, 160 ff.—

> " I, that whole day,
> Saw her no more, altho' I linger'd there
> Till every daisy slept, and Love's white star
> Beam'd thro' the thicken'd cedar in the dusk".

See also the last stanza of the Lady Isabel's song in *Quentin Dur-
ward*, ch. iv.—

> " The village maid steals through the shade,
>   Her shepherd's suit to hear;
> To beauty shy, by lattice high,
>   Sings high-born cavalier.
> The star of love, all stars above,
>   Now reigns o'er earth and sky;
> And high and low its influence know—
>   But where is County Guy?"

321. Penchryst Pen, between Jedburgh and Branksome. (*Pen*,
Celtic word, meaning 'mountain'; in Gaelic *beinn*.)

322. ken, sight. The word is now little used except in Scotland
and in such phrases as " within his ken". (*Ken* is another form of
can, Icelandic *kenna*, to know.)

324. Shakes its loose tresses. This is a classical metaphor frequently imitated by modern poets. Cf. Spenser, *Virgils Gnat*, 68, "fayre Aurora, with her rosie heare, The hatefull darknes now had put to flight"; and *1 Henry VI*. i. 1. 2, "Comets, importing change of times and states, Brandish your crystal tresses in the sky". (The word *comet* itself is a Greek word meaning long-haired.)

327. tighten'd breath, an instance of transferred epithet. She felt a tightening of the *chest*, and her *breath* came shorter.

330. war-note, sound on the bugle, which told of the approach of an enemy.

333. festal hall, the hall where the warriors were spending the evening in jollity.

334. startled forth, startled so that they *rushed* forth: a condensed expression.

335. downward usually implies motion. Here it expresses two things: (1) the downward looking of the warder; (2) the fact that the glare of torches was far below him.

336. cresset, cup-shaped vessel for holding fire, either mounted on a pole, as here, or suspended from the roof as in *Marmion*, canto ii. stanza xviii. (O. F. *creuset*, a little cruse, Du. *kroes*.)

340. This is an instance of what would be called by the grammarians 'pregnant construction', *i.e.* a sentence implying much more than it actually states. A frozen brook implies cold, and cold weather implies rough winds. This line is therefore a suggestive word-picture. We see the brook, and the reeds, themselves stiffened with frost, swaying and clashing together under the furious blast.

341-392. For a lengthy description of a similar feudal call to arms cf. *Lady of the Lake*, canto iii. stanzas xi.-xxiv.

341. Seneschal, steward, officer who had charge of the domestic and ceremonial arrangements. (O. F. *seneschal*, from a Gothic *sins*, old; *skalks*, servant.)

344. mandates, commands.

345. bale, "beacon-fagot. The border beacons, from their number and position, formed a sort of telegraphic communication with Edinburgh.—The act of Parliament 1455, c. 48, directs, that one bale or fagot shall be warning of the approach of the English in any manner; two bales that they are *coming indeed*; four bales, blazing beside each other, that the enemy are in great force. 'The same taikenings to be watched and maid at Eggerhope (Eggerstand) Castell, fra they se the fire of Hume, that they fire right swa. And in like manner on Sowtra Edge, sall se the fire of Eggerhope Castell, and mak taikening in like manner: And then may all Louthaine be warned, and in special the Castell of Edinburgh; and their four fires to be made in like manner, that they in Fife, and fra Striveling east, and the east part of Louthaine, and to Dunbar, all may se them, and come to the defence of the realme.' These beacons (at least in latter times) were a 'long and strong tree set up, with a long iron pole across the head of it, and an iron brander fixed on a stalk in the middle of it, for holding a tar-barrel.'" (Scott.) (O. E. *bǽl*, blazing pile.)

346. Priesthaughswire, hill some miles s. e. of Branksome. (*Haugh*, Scotch *how*, Icel. *haugr*, a mound. *Swire*, or *sware*, the curve of a hill: Icel. *swyr*, a neck.)

348. to scout, to watch their movements.

349. "*Mount for Branksome* was the gathering word of the Scotts."

356. Warder=*warden*: see note on line 255 above.

361. harness, armour.

362. clamour dread. *Dread* (=dreadful, awe-inspiring) because it suggested the din of battle, and boded ill for the foes against whom the horsemen were setting forth.

364. coats, *i.e.* of armour.

367. rout, crowd. (F. *route*, from Lat. *rupta*, broken, from *rumpere*. "This L. *rupta* came to mean (1) a defeat, flying mass of broken troops; (2) a fragment of an army, a troop; (3) a way broken or cut through a forest, a way, route."

372. vassals, tenants, dependants.

372. allies, those who joined them on such occasions as these.

374. ready page and **slumbering brand** imply that the beacon-fire was never allowed to be completely extinguished, and suggest the suddenness of the Border forays.

374. need-fire, beacon. The word properly means *forced fire*, fire which, produced by friction with wood, was superstitiously supposed in the Scottish Highlands to possess certain virtues.

377. blood-flag, *i.e.* a flag *blood-red.*

381. fraught, filled, charged. (M. E. *fraught*, past part. of verb *fraghten*, of which no part but *fraught* was used. From Swedish *frakt*, a cargo. So modern *freight*, a spelling of O. F. *fret* due to confusion with *fraught*.)

383. glanced to sight, came suddenly into sight.

385. tarn, a mountain lake. (Icel. *tjörn*, pool.)

386. earn (or *erne*), eagle.

387. cairn. " The cairns, or piles of loose stones, which crown the summit of most of our Scottish hills, and are found in other re-markable situations, seem usually, though not universally, to have been sepulchral monuments. Six flat stones are commonly found in the centre, forming a cavity of greater or smaller dimensions, in which an urn is often placed. The author is possessed of one, dis-covered beneath an immense cairn at Roughlee, in Liddesdale. It is of the most barbarous construction; the middle of the substance alone having been subjected to the fire, over which, when hardened, the artist had laid an inner and outer coat of unbaked clay, etched with some very rude ornaments; his skill apparently being inade-quate to baking the vase, when completely finished. The contents were bones and ashes, and a quantity of beads made of coal. This seems to have been a barbarous imitation of the Roman fashion of sepulture." (Scott.) (Gael. *carn*, rock.)

388. urns, tombs.

389. Dunedin, Edinburgh, Edwin's fort; so called after Edwin, king of Northumbria.

390. Soltra, Dumpender Law, hills in N.W. Berwickshire. (*Law* = O. E. *hlœw*, hill), ground gradually rising; in Scotch it remains as *low*.)

391. Lothian, the county of Edinburgh.

391. the Regent, Mary of Guise, the mother of Mary, Queen of Scots, who was then in France.

392. bowne them, make themselves ready to go. In canto v. line 497 " bowning" means simply ' going '. The original meaning is simply ' make ready ', ' prepare '. *Bowne* is also an adjective, ' ready '. We have the word *bound*, the *d* of which is added (cf. above, line 128, note), from M. E. *boun*.

394. The sound was caused by the getting ready of arms and armour.

395. with backward clang. It was customary, for the purpose of raising an alarm, to ring a peal of bells beginning with the bass bell, and so producing an ascending instead of a descending scale. Cf. *Adam Bell*, 346, " There was many an out horne in Carlile was blowne, And the bells backward did ring". So in *The Fair Maid of Perth*, ch. xix., the enraged citizens ring the church bells " back-ward ". But ' backward ' in this sense cannot be applied to one bell, nor does *peal* in the next line seem a suitable term for the sound of one bell.

396. 'larum, shortened from *alarum*. A northern form of *alarm* due to the strong burr of the *r*. (F. *alarme*, Ital. *all' arme* = *alle arme*, ultimately from Lat. *ad illa arma*, to your arms!)

397. **frequent** = frequently.   So in line 401.

397. **jar**, harsh discordant sound.

398-400. In his note to *Auld Maitland*, in the *Border Minstrelsy*, Scott gives a lengthy account of the engines of war and the missiles used in assaulting and defending castles before the introduction of gunpowder. In a quotation from Henry the Minstrel's *History of Wallace*, recounting the defence of York by the English against Wallace, occur the following lines :

> " Many were hurt ere they from the walls went ;
> Stones on springalds they did cast out so fast,
> And goads of iron made many grone agast ".

" The *springalds* were *balistæ*, or large cross-bows, wrought by machinery, and capable of throwing stones, beams, and huge darts. They were numbered among the heavy artillery of the age. ... Goads, or sharpened bars of iron, were an obvious and formidable missile weapon.   Thus, at the assault of Rochemiglion, 'They within cast out great barres of iron, and pots with lyme, wherewith they hurt divers Englishmen, such as adventured themselves too far'. " (Scott.)

399. keep, stronghold.   The French name was *donjon*; hence in *Marmion*, i. 4, "donjon keep"; where Scott in his note says: "The *donjon*...means the strongest part of a feudal castle ; a high square tower, with walls of tremendous thickness, situated in the centre of the other buildings, from which, however, it was usually detached.   Here, in case of the outward defences being gained, the garrison retreated to make their last stand.   The donjon contained the great hall, and principal rooms of state for solemn occasions, and also the prison of the fortress ; from which last circumstance we derive the modern and restricted use of the word *dungeon*."

400. whelm, completely cover and destroy.

402. ward = warder, sentinel.

405. broil, turmoil, confusion.   The word is now used only in the sense of a noisy quarrel, brawl.   In former times it had a more dignified meaning.   (F. *brouiller*, to jumble, confuse.)

406. high, important, grave.

408. sage, wise.

412. in time of truce.   An agreement had apparently been made that for a certain time neither side would attack the other.

416. black-mail.   In former times the Lowlands and the border of the Highlands of Scotland were infested by bands of freebooters, under their own chiefs, who refrained from molesting farmers, or protected them against other bands, on condition of receiving an annual tribute. This was called *black-mail*. (O. E. *male*, Icel. *mala*, tribute. *Mail* is otherwise derived by some from O. F. *mail*, a small coin. *Black*, because immoral, as in 'black-leg', &c. Jamieson (*Scottish Dictionary*) derives from Germ. *placken*, to vex.)

417. with small avail, with a small force. *Avail* is properly an abstract noun, and is not now used in this sense. So we use 'force' for a body of soldiers; cf. "powers" in i. 49. (O. F. *a*, and *vaille*, Lat. *valere*, to be strong.)

418. lightly, easily.

418. agen represents the pronunciation and a former spelling of *again*. (O. E. *on-gean*.)

421. high sound, spirited song.

426. his wandering toil, transferred epithet; the toil of him wandering.

427. stay, support.

431. withal, the emphatic form of 'with', is used for *with* after the object at the end of a sentence.

432, 433. Notice the alliteration: "*f*ain would *f*all"; "*s*olemn measure, *s*oft and *s*lo " and the effect of the soft *s* sound in the latter line.

CANTO FOURTH.

I.

Sweet Teviot! on thy silver tide
　　The glaring bale-fires blaze no more;
No longer steel-clad warriors ride
　　Along thy wild and willow'd shore;
Where'er thou wind'st, by dale or hill,　　5
All, all is peaceful, all is still,
　　As if thy waves, since Time was born,
Since first they roll'd upon the Tweed,
Had only heard the shepherd's reed,
　　Nor started at the bugle-horn.　　10

II.

Unlike the tide of human time,
　　Which, though it change in ceaseless flow,
Retains each grief, retains each crime
　　Its earliest course was doom'd to know;
And, darker as it downward bears,　　15
Is stain'd with past and present tears.
　　Low as that tide has ebb'd with me,
It still reflects to Memory's eye
The hour my brave, my only boy,
　　Fell by the side of great Dundee.　　20
Why, when the volleying musket play'd
Against the bloody Highland blade,
Why was not I beside him laid!—
Enough—he died the death of fame;
Enough—he died with conquering Græme.　　25

III.

Now over Border, dale and fell,
　　Full wide and far was terror spread;
For pathless marsh, and mountain cell,
　　The peasant left his lowly shed.
The frighten'd flocks and herds were pent　　30
Beneath the peel's rude battlement;
And maids and matrons dropp'd the tear,
While ready warriors seized the spear.
From Branksome's towers, the watchman's eye
Dun wreaths of distant smoke gan spy,　　35

Which, curling in the rising sun,
Show'd southern ravage was begun.

IV.

Now loud the heedful gate-ward cried—
  " Prepare ye all for blows and blood !
Watt Tinlinn, from the Liddel-side,   40
  Comes wading through the flood.
Full oft the Tynedale snatchers knock
  At his lone gate, and prove the lock ;
It was but last St. Barnabright
They sieged him a whole summer night,   45
But fled at morning ; well they knew,
In vain he never twang'd the yew.
Right sharp has been the evening shower,
That drove him from his Liddel tower ;
And, by my faith," the gate-ward said,   50
" I think 'twill prove a Warden-raid."

V.

While thus he spoke, the bold yeoman
Enter'd the echoing barbican.
He led a small and shaggy nag,
That through a bog, from hag to hag,   55
Could bound like any Billhope stag.
It bore his wife and children twain ;
A half-clothed serf was all their train ;
His wife, stout, ruddy, and dark-brow'd,
Of silver brooch and bracelet proud,   60
Laugh'd to her friends among the crowd.
He was of stature passing tall,
But sparely form'd, and lean withal ;
A batter'd morion on his brow ;
A leather jack, as fence enow,   65
On his broad shoulders loosely hung ;
A Border axe behind was slung ;
His spear, six Scottish ells in length,
  Seem'd newly dyed with gore ;
His shafts and bow, of wondrous strength,   70
  His hardy partner bore.

VI.

Thus to the Ladye did Tinlinn show
The tidings of the English foe :—

" Belted Will Howard is marching here,
And hot Lord Dacre, with many a spear,   75
And all the German hackbut-men,
Who have long lain at Askerten :
They cross'd the Liddel at curfew hour,
And burn'd my little lonely tower :
The fiend receive their souls therefor!   80
It had not been burnt this year and more.
Barn-yard and dwelling, blazing bright,
Served to guide me on my flight ;
But I was chased the livelong night.
Black John of Akeshaw, and Fergus Græme,   85
Fast upon my traces came,
Until I turn'd at Priesthaugh Scrogg,
And shot their horses in the bog,
Slew Fergus with my lance outright—
I had him long at high despite :   9c
He drove my cows last Fastern's night."

VII.

Now weary scouts from Liddesdale,
Fast hurrying in, confirm'd the tale ;
    As far as they could judge by ken,
        Three hours would bring to Teviot's strand 95
    Three thousand arméd Englishmen—
        Meanwhile, full many a warlike band,
From Teviot, Aill, and Ettrick shade,
Came in, their Chief's defence to aid.
    There was saddling and mounting in haste,   10c
        There was pricking o'er moor and lea ;
    He that was last at the trysting-place
    Was but lightly held of his gaye ladye.

VIII.

From fair St. Mary's silver wave,
    From dreary Gamescleugh's dusky height,   105
His ready lances Thirlestane brave
    Array'd beneath a banner bright.
The tressured fleur-de-luce he claims
To wreathe his shield, since royal James,
Encamp'd by Fala's mossy wave,   :10
The proud distinction grateful gave,
    For faith 'mid feudal jars ;

What time, save Thirlestane alone,
Of Scotland's stubborn barons none
  Would march to southern wars;   115
And hence, in fair remembrance worn,
Yon sheaf of spears his crest has borne;
Hence his high motto shines reveal'd—
" Ready, aye ready," for the field.

IX.

An aged Knight, to danger steel'd,   120
  With many a moss-trooper, came on;
And, azure in a golden field,
The stars and crescent graced his shield,
  Without the bend of Murdieston.
Wide lay his lands round Oakwood tower,   125
And wide round haunted Castle-Ower;
High over Borthwick's mountain flood,
His wood-embosom'd mansion stood;
In the dark glen, so deep below,
The herds of plunder'd England low;   130
His bold retainers' daily food,
And bought with danger, blows, and blood.
Marauding chief! his sole delight
The moonlight raid, the morning fight;
Not even the Flower of Yarrow's charms,   135
In youth, might tame his rage for arms;
And still, in age, he spurn'd at rest,
And still his brows the helmet press'd,
Albeit the blanchèd locks below
Were white as Dinlay's spotless snow;   140
  Five stately warriors drew the sword
    Before their father's band;
  A braver knight than Harden's lord
    Ne'er belted on a brand.

X.

Scotts of Eskdale, a stalwart band,   145
  Came trooping down the Todshawhill;
By the sword they won their land,
  And by the sword they hold it still.
Hearken, Ladye, to the tale,
How thy sires won fair Eskdale.—   150
Earl Morton was lord of that valley fair,
The Beattisons were his vassals there.

The Earl was gentle, and mild of mood,
The vassals were warlike, and fierce, and rude;
High of heart, and haughty of word, 155
Little they reck'd of a tame liege lord.
The Earl into fair Eskdale came,
Homage and seignory to claim:
Of Gilbert the Galliard a heriot he sought,
Saying, " Give thy best steed, as a vassal ought." 160
—" Dear to me is my bonny white steed,
Oft has he help'd me at pinch of need;
Lord and Earl though thou be, I trow,
I can rein Bucksfoot better than thou."—
Word on word gave fuel to fire, 165
Till so highly blazed the Beattison's ire,
But that the Earl the flight had ta'en,
The vassals there their lord had slain.
Sore he plied both whip and spur,
As he urged his steed through Eskdale muir; 170
And it fell down a weary weight,
Just on the threshold of Branksome gate.

XI.

The Earl was a wrathful man to see,
Full fain avengèd would he be.
In haste to Branksome's Lord he spoke, 175
Saying—" Take these traitors to thy yoke;
For a cast of hawks, and a purse of gold,
All Eskdale I'll sell thee, to have and hold:
Beshrew thy heart, of the Beattisons' clan
If thou leavest on Eske a landed man; 180
But spare Woodkerrick's lands alone,
For he lent me his horse to escape upon."
A glad man then was Branksome bold,
Down he flung him the purse of gold;
To Eskdale soon he spurr'd amain, 185
And with him five hundred riders has ta'en.
He left his merrymen in the mist of the hill,
And bade them hold them close and still;
And alone he wended to the plain,
To meet with the Galliard and all his train. 190
To Gilbert the Galliard thus he said:—
" Know thou me for thy liege-lord and head;
Deal not with me as with Morton tame,
For Scotts play best at the roughest game.

(814) D 2

Give me in peace my heriot due,   195
Thy bonny white steed, or thou shalt rue.
If my horn I three times wind,
Eskdale shall long have the sound in mind."—

XII.

Loudly the Beattison laugh'd in scorn;
" Little care we for thy winded horn.   200
Ne'er shall it be the Galliard's lot,
To yield his steed to a haughty Scott.
Wend thou to Branksome back on foot,
With rusty spur and miry boot."—
He blew his bugle so loud and hoarse,   205
That the dun deer started at fair Craikcross;
He blew again so loud and clear,
Through the grey mountain-mist there did lances appear;
And the third blast rang with such a din,
That the echoes answer'd from Pentoun-linn,   210
And all his riders came lightly in.
Then had you seen a gallant shock,
When saddles were emptied, and lances broke!
For each scornful word the Galliard had said,
A Beattison on the field was laid.   215
His own good sword the chieftain drew,
And he bore the Galliard through and through;
Where the Beattisons' blood mix'd with the rill,
The Galliard's-haugh men call it still.
The Scotts have scatter'd the Beattison clan,   220
In Eskdale they left but one landed man.
The valley of Eske, from the mouth to the source,
Was lost and won for that bonny white horse.

XIII.

Whitslade the Hawk, and Headshaw came,
And warriors more than I may name;   225
From Yarrow-cleugh to Hindhaugh-swair,
    From Woodhouselie to Chester-glen.
Troop'd man and horse, and bow and spear;
    Their gathering word was Bellenden.
And better hearts o'er Border sod   230
To siege or rescue never rode.
    The Ladye mark'd the aids come in,
        And high her heart of pride arose:

She bade her youthful son attend,
That he might know his father's friend,   235
  And learn to face his foes.
"The boy is ripe to look on war;
  I saw him draw a cross-bow stiff,
And his true arrow struck afar
  The raven's nest upon the cliff;   240
The red cross, on a southern breast,
Is broader than the raven's nest:
Thou, Whitslade, shalt teach him his weapon to wield,
And o'er him hold his father's shield."

XIV.

Well may you think, the wily page   245
Cared not to face the Ladye sage.
He counterfeited childish fear,
And shriek'd, and shed full many a tear,
  And moan'd and plain'd in manner wild.
    The attendants to the Ladye told,   250
  Some fairy, sure, had changed the child,
    That wont to be so free and bold.
Then wrathful was the noble dame;
She blush'd blood-red for very shame:—
"Hence! ere the clan his faintness view;   255
Hence with the weakling to Buccleuch!—
Watt Tinlinn, thou shalt be his guide
To Rangleburn's lonely side.—
Sure some fell fiend has cursed our line,
That coward should e'er be son of mine!"—   260

XV.

A heavy task Watt Tinlinn had,
To guide the counterfeited lad.
Soon as the palfrey felt the weight
Of that ill-omen'd elfish freight,
He bolted, sprung, and rear'd amain,   265
Nor heeded bit, nor curb, nor rein.
  It cost Watt Tinlinn mickle toil
  To drive him but a Scottish mile;
    But as a shallow brook they cross'd,
  The elf, amid the running stream,   270
  His figure changed, like form in dream,
    And fled, and shouted, "Lost! lost! lost!"

Full fast the urchin ran and laugh'd,
But faster still a cloth-yard shaft
Whistled from startled Tinlinn's yew,   275
And pierced his shoulder through and through.
Although the imp might not be slain,
And though the wound soon heal'd again,
Yet, as he ran, he yell'd for pain ;
And Wat of Tinlinn, much aghast,   280
Rode back to Branksome fiery fast.

XVI.

Soon on the hill's steep verge he stood,
That looks o'er Branksome's towers and wood ;   ·
And martial murmurs, from below,
Proclaim'd the approaching southern foe.   285
Through the dark wood, in mingled tone,
Were Border pipes and bugles blown ;
The coursers' neighing he could ken,
A measured tread of marching men ;
While broke at times the solemn hum,   290
The Almayn's sullen kettle-drum ;
 And banners tall, of crimson sheen,
  Above the copse appear ;
 And, glistening through the hawthorn green,
  Shine helm, and shield, and spear.   295

XVII.

Light forayers, first, to view the ground,
Spurr'd their fleet coursers loosely round ;
 Behind, in close array, and fast,
  The Kendal archers, all in green,
 Obedient to the bugle blast,   300
  Advancing from the wood were seen.
To back and guard the archer band,
Lord Dacre's bill-men were at hand :
A hardy race, on Irthing bred,
With kirtles white, and crosses red,   305
Array'd beneath the banner tall,
That stream'd o'er Acre's conquer'd wall ;
And minstrels, as they march'd in order,
Played, " Noble Lord Dacre, he dwells on the Border."

XVIII.

Behind the English bill and bow,   310
The mercenaries, firm and slow,

Moved on to fight, in dark array,
By Conrad led of Wolfenstein,
Who brought the band from distant Rhine,
And sold their blood for foreign pay.　315
The camp their home, their law the sword,
They knew no country, own'd no lord:
They were not arm'd like England's sons,
But bore the levin-darting guns;
Buff coats, all frounced and 'broider'd o'er,　320
And morsing-horns and scarfs they wore;
Each better knee was bared, to aid
The warriors in the escalade;
All, as they march'd, in rugged tongue,
Songs of Teutonic feuds they sung.　325

XIX.

But louder still the clamour grew,
And louder still the minstrels blew,
When, from beneath the greenwood tree,
Rode forth Lord Howard's chivalry;
His men-at-arms, with glaive and spear,　330
Brought up the battle's glittering rear,
There many a youthful knight, full keen
To gain his spurs, in arms was seen;
With favour in his crest, or glove,
Memorial of his ladye-love.　335
So rode they forth in fair array,
Till full their lengthen'd lines display;
Then call'd a halt, and made a stand,
And cried, " St. George, for merry England!"

XX.

Now every English eye, intent　340
On Branksome's armèd towers was bent;
So near they were, that they might know
The straining harsh of each cross-bow;
On battlement and bartizan
Gleam'd axe, and spear, and partisan;　345
Falcon and culver, on each tower,
Stood prompt their deadly hail to shower;
And flashing armour frequent broke
From eddying whirls of sable smoke,
Where upon tower and turret head,　350
The seething pitch and molten lead
Reek'd, like a witch's caldron red.

While yet they gaze, the bridges fall,
The wicket opes, and from the wall
Rides forth the hoary Seneschal.   355

XXI.

Armèd he rode, all save the head,
His white beard o'er his breast-plate spread;
Unbroke by age, erect his seat,
He ruled his eager courser's gait;
Forced him, with chasten'd fire, to prance,   360
And, high curvetting, slow advance:
In sign of truce, his better hand
Display'd a peelèd willow wand;
His squire, attending in the rear,
Bore high a gauntlet on a spear.   365
When they espied him riding out,
Lord Howard and Lord Dacre stout
Sped to the front of their array,
To hear what this old knight should say.

XXII.

"Ye English warden lords, of you   370
Demands the Ladye of Buccleuch,
Why, 'gainst the truce of Border tide,
In hostile guise ye dare to ride,
With Kendal bow and Gilsland brand,
And all yon mercenary band,   375
Upon the bounds of fair Scotland?
My Ladye reads you swith return;
And, if but one poor straw you burn,
Or do our towers so much molest,
As scare one swallow from her nest,   380
St. Mary! but we'll light a brand
Shall warm your hearths in Cumberland."

XXIII.

A wrathful man was Dacre's lord,
But calmer Howard took the word:
"May't please thy Dame, Sir Seneschal,   385
To seek the castle's outward wall,
Our pursuivant-at-arms shall show
Both why we came, and when we go."—
The message sped, the noble Dame
To the wall's outward circle came;   390

Each chief around lean'd on his spear,
To see the pursuivant appear.
All in Lord Howard's livery dress'd,
The lion argent deck'd his breast;
He led a boy of blooming hue—   395
O sight to meet a mother's view!
It was the heir of great Buccleuch.
Obeisance meet the herald made,
And thus his master's will he said :—

XXIV.

" It irks, high Dame, my noble Lords   400
'Gainst ladye fair to draw their swords;
But yet they may not tamely see,
All through the Western Wardenry,
Your law-contemning kinsmen ride,
And burn and spoil the Border-side;   405
And ill beseems your rank and birth
To make your towers a flemens-firth.
We claim from thee William of Deloraine,
That he may suffer march-treason pain.
It was but last St. Cuthbert's even   410
He prick'd to Stapleton on Leven,
Harried the lands of Richard Musgrave,
And slew his brother by dint of glaive.
Then, since a lone and widow'd Dame
These restless riders may not tame,   415
Either receive within thy towers
Two hundred of my master's powers,
Or straight they sound their warrison,
And storm and spoil thy garrison:
And this fair boy, to London led,   420
Shall good King Edward's page be bred."

XXV.

He ceased—and loud the boy did cry,
And stretch'd his little arms on high;
Implored for aid each well-known face,
And strove to seek the Dame's embrace.   425
A moment changed that Ladye's cheer,
Gush'd to her eye the unbidden tear;
She gazed upon the leaders round,
And dark and sad each warrior frown'd;
Then, deep within her sobbing breast   430
She lock'd the struggling sigh to rest;

Unalter'd and collected stood,
And thus replied, in dauntless mood :—

XXVI.

" Say to your Lords of high emprize,
Who war on women and on boys,   435
That either William of Deloraine
Will cleanse him, by oath, of march-treason stain,
Or else he will the combat take
'Gainst Musgrave, for his honour's sake.
No knight in Cumberland so good,   440
But William may count with him kin and blood.
Knighthood he took of Douglas' sword,
When English blood swell'd Ancram's ford ;
And but Lord Dacre's steed was wight,
And bare him ably in the flight,   445
Himself had seen him dubb'd a knight.
For the young heir of Branksome's line,
God be his aid, and God be mine ;
Through me no friend shall meet his doom ;
Here, while I live, no foe finds room.   450
    Then, if thy Lords their purpose urge,
        Take our defiance loud and high ;
    Our slogan is their lyke-wake dirge,
        Our moat, the grave where they shall lie."

XXVII.

Proud she look'd round, applause to claim   455
Then lighten'd Thirlestane's eye of flame ;
    His bugle Wat of Harden blew ;
Pensils and pennons wide were flung,
To heaven the Border slogan rung,
    " St. Mary for the young Buccleuch !"   460
The English war-cry answer'd wide,
    And forward bent each southern spear ;
Each Kendal archer made a stride,
    And drew the bowstring to his ear ;
Each minstrel's war-note loud was blown ;—   465
But, ere a grey goose-shaft had flown,
    A horseman gallop'd from the rear.

XXVIII.

" Ah ! noble Lords !" he breathless said,
" What treason has your march betray'd ?

What make you here, from aid so far,   47~
Before you walls, around you war?
Your foemen triumph in the thought
That in the toils the lion's caught.
Already on dark Ruberslaw
The Douglas holds his weapon-schaw;   475
The lances, waving in his train,
Clothe the dun heath like autumn grain;
And on the Liddel's northern strand,
To bar retreat to Cumberland,
Lord Maxwell ranks his merry-men good,   480
Beneath the eagle and the rood;
   And Jedwood, Eske, and Teviotdale,
      Have to proud Angus come;
   And all the Merse and Lauderdale
      Have risen with haughty Home.   485
   An exile from Northumberland,
      In Liddesdale I've wander'd long;
   But still my heart was with merry England,
      And cannot brook my country's wrong;
And hard I've spurr'd all night, to show   490
The mustering of the coming foe."

XXIX.

"And let them come!" fierce Dacre cried,
"For soon yon crest, my father's pride,
That swept the shores of Judah's sea,
And waved in gales of Galilee,   495
From Branksome's highest towers display'd,
Shall mock the rescue's lingering aid!—
Level each harquebuss on row;
Draw, merry archers, draw the bow;
Up, bill-men, to the walls, and cry,   500
Dacre for England, win or die!"—

XXX.

"Yet hear," quoth Howard, "calmly hear,
Nor deem my words the words of fear:
For who, in field or foray slack,
Saw the blanche lion e'er fall back?   505
But thus to risk our Border flower
In strife against a kingdom's power,
Ten thousand Scots 'gainst thousands three,
Certes, were desperate policy.

Nay, take the terms the Ladye made,   510
Ere conscious of the advancing aid :
Let Musgrave meet fierce Deloraine
In single fight, and, if he gain,
He gains for us ; but if he's cross'd,
'Tis but a single warrior lost :   515
The rest, retreating as they came,
Avoid defeat, and death, and shame."

XXXI.

Ill could the haughty Dacre brook
His brother Warden's sage rebuke ;
And yet his forward step he staid,   520
And slow and sullenly obey'd.
But ne'er again the Border side
Did these two lords in friendship ride ;
And this slight discontent, men say,
Cost blood upon another day.   525

XXXII.

The pursuivant-at-arms again
    Before the castle took his stand ;
His trumpet call'd, with parleying strain,
    The leaders of the Scottish band ;
And he defied, in Musgrave's right,   530
Stout Deloraine to single fight ;
A gauntlet at their feet he laid,
And thus the terms of fight he said :—
" If in the lists good Musgrave's sword
    Vanquish the Knight of Deloraine,   535
Your youthful chieftain, Branksome's Lord,
    Shall hostage for his clan remain :
If Deloraine foil good Musgrave,
The boy his liberty shall have.
    Howe'er it falls, the English band,   540
Unharming Scots, by Scots unharm'd,
In peaceful march, like men unarm'd,
    Shall straight retreat to Cumberland."

XXXIII.

Unconscious of the near relief,
The proffer pleased each Scottish chief,   545
    Though much the Ladye sage gainsay'd ;

For though their hearts were brave and true,
From Jedwood's recent sack they knew,
   How tardy was the Regent's aid :
And you may guess the noble Dame   550
   Durst not the secret prescience own,
Sprung from the art she might not name,
   By which the coming help was known.
Closed was the compact, and agreed
   That lists should be enclosed with speed,   555
Beneath the castle, on a lawn :
They fix'd the morrow for the strife,
On foot, with Scottish axe and knife,
   At the fourth hour from peep of dawn ;
When Deloraine, from sickness freed,   560
Or else a champion in his stead,
Should for himself and chieftain stand,
Against stout Musgrave, hand to hand.

XXXIV.

I know right well, that, in their lay,
Full many minstrels sing and say,   565
   Such combat should be made on horse,
On foaming steed, in full career,
With brand to aid, when as the spear
   Should shiver in the course :
But he, the jovial Harper, taught   570
Me, yet a youth, how it was fought,
   In guise which now I say ;
He knew each ordinance and clause
Of Black Lord Archibald's battle-laws,
   In the old Douglas' day.   575
He brook'd not, he, that scoffing tongue
Should tax his minstrelsy with wrong,
   Or call his song untrue :
For this, when they the goblet plied,
And such rude taunt had chafed his pride,   580
   The Bard of Reull he slew.
On Teviot's side, in fight they stood,
And tuneful hands were stain'd with blood ;
Where still the thorn's white branches wave,
Memorial o'er his rival's grave.   585

XXXV.

Why should I tell the rigid doom,
That dragg'd my master to his tomb,

How Ousenam's maidens tore their hair,
Wept till their eyes were dead and dim,
And wrung their hands for love of him,   590
   Who died at Jedwood Air?
He died!—his scholars, one by one,
To the cold silent grave are gone;
And I, alas! survive alone,
To muse o'er rivalries of yore,   595
And grieve that I shall hear no more
The strains, with envy heard before;
For, with my minstrel brethren fled,
My jealousy of song is dead.

HE paused: the listening dames again   600
Applaud the hoary Minstrel's strain.
With many a word of kindly cheer,—
In pity half, and half sincere,—
Marvell'd the Duchess how so well
His legendary song could tell—   605
Of ancient deeds, so long forgot;
Of feuds, whose memory was not;
Of forests, now laid waste and bare;
Of towers, which harbour now the hare;
Of manners, long since changed and gone;   610
Of chiefs, who under their gray stone
So long had slept, that fickle Fame
Had blotted from her rolls their name,
And twined round some new minion's head
The fading wreath for which they bled;   615
In sooth, 'twas strange, this old man's verse
Could call them from their marble hearse.

The Harper smiled, well-pleased; for ne'er
Was flattery lost on poet's ear:
A simple race! they waste their toil   620
For the vain tribute of a smile;
E'en when in age their flame expires,
Her dulcet breath can fan its fires:
Their drooping fancy wakes at praise,
And strives to trim the short-lived blaze.   625

Smiled then, well-pleased, the Aged Man,
And thus his tale continued ran.

NOTES.

CANTO FOURTH.

The third canto concluded with a description of the night preparations at Branksome Castle. Then the Minstrel made a pause, and being asked by his admiring listeners whether he had no children to comfort his old age, he is overcome with grief at the remembrance of his dead son, and tries to hide his tears by bending over his harp, and feigning to busy himself with its strings. Then he resumes his song; and the first two stanzas of the fourth canto consist of a touching and beautiful reference to the contrast between the troubled time when his son was killed, and the peaceful time that has succeeded.

1. **on thy silver tide.** This gives us a picture of the reflection of the red fires in the clear surface of the stream.

2. **bale-fires,** "beacon-fagots. The Border beacons, from their number and position, formed a sort of telegraphic communication with Edinburgh." (O.E. *bǽl*, a blazing pile.)

3. **steel-clad warriors,** such as Deloraine, who had ridden by the Teviot's side on his way to Melrose: cf. i. 262, "And soon the Teviot side he won".

4. **willow'd,** fringed with willows. The mention of the 'willow' is here appropriate, for the willow is often associated with grief. See the 'willow song' in *Othello*, iv. 3. 41—

> "The poor soul sat sighing by a sycamore tree,
>   Sing all a green willow;
> Her hand on her bosom, her head on her knee,
>   Sing willow, willow, willow.
> The fresh stream ran by her and murmur'd her moans;
>   Sing willow, willow, willow;
> Her salt tears fell from her, and softened the stones;
>   Sing willow, willow, willow."

7. **Time** is personified.

8. **roll'd upon,** rolled down to. The Teviot is a tributary of the Tweed.

9. **the shepherd's reed.** In poetry shepherds are represented as living an ideally peaceful life, passing their leisure in playing on flute-like instruments, made of 'reeds', or stalks. Several hollow stalks of different lengths were bound together with wax, and so formed the Pan-pipe, an instrument like that of the Punch-and-Judy man.

10. bugle-horn, usually abbreviated to *bugle.* So called because originally made from the horn of an ox. (O. F. *bugle*, a wild ox, Lat. *buculum.*) The bugle-horn is here representative of warfare.

11. Unlike the tide..., *i.e.* the tide...is unlike. **The tide of human time** means the course of man's life, which is often compared to a stream. But a stream flows on ever peacefully, giving no sign of the events that have taken place upon its banks; while the griefs and crimes which have entered into a man's life are retained long in his memory.

15. bears, tends, moves. The verb is here intransitive, as in such phrases as 'bear to the left'.

17. The Minstrel compares the closing years of his life to the lowness of the ebbing tide (O. E. *ebba*, the fall, back-flow of the tide), which nevertheless reflects images.

20. great Dundee, Graham of Claverhouse (called *conquering Græme* in line 25), Viscount Dundee, who was killed at the battle of Killiecrankie in 1689. He was fighting on behalf of James II. at the head of the Scots, and was killed at the moment of victory. See *Old Mortality.*

21. the volleying musket. The muskets of William III.'s troops were useless against the claymores of the impetuous Highlanders. (*Volley* means a 'flight' or discharge of shot from many guns fired together: Fr. *volée*, from Lat. *volare*, to fly.)

24, 25. The father is consoled when he remembers that his son died in a famous fight, and with a famous leader.

26. The Minstrel here resumes his story.

26. fell, rocky ground.

27. Full, very. *Full* is often thus used to strengthen an adjective or adverb.

28. For, to go to. Cf. such phrases as 'passenger for London', 'he left home for school'.

28, 29. Scott tells us that "the morasses were the usual refuge of the Border herdsmen on the approach of an English army. Caves, hewed in the most dangerous and difficult-to-be-got-at places, also afforded an occasional retreat."

31. peel, small square tower. There were formerly many of these towers on the Borders, and some are still to be seen.

35. Dun, brown, dark, dusky.

35. distant smoke, the smoke from the 'lowly sheds' which had been left by the terrified peasantry.

37. southern ravage, the ravage (laying waste, burning, slaying) committed by *southrons*, as the English were contemptuously called by the Scots.

38. gate-ward, gate-keeper. *Ward* is really the same word as 'guard'.

40. Watt Tinlinn. "This person was, in my younger days, the theme of many a fireside tale. He was a retainer of the Buccleuch family, and held for his Border service a small tower on the frontiers of Liddesdale. Watt was by profession a *sutor* [*i.e.* a shoemaker], but by inclination and practice an archer and warrior." (Scott.) *Watt* is an abbreviation of 'Walter'.

40. Liddel, a tributary of the river Esk, which flows into the Solway Firth.

42. snatchers, robbers who rob secretly and suddenly. The word is applied particularly to robbers of cattle.

43. lone gate. Notice how much Scott often expresses in few words. Tinlinn lived alone in a solitary tower, situated on the outskirts of the Borders.

43. prove, test and find out its strength. So David refused to wear Saul's armour because he had not 'proved' it.

44. St. Barnabright, St. Barnabas' day, June 11th, which before 1752 was regarded as the longest day in the year; hence the termination *bright*. The day was also called *Barnaby bright*. *Barnaby* is from *Barnabé*, an O.F. form of Lat. *Barnabas*, the name of Paul's companion on his missionary journeys. There is an old saying—

> " Barnaby Bright,
> The longest day and the shortest night ".

45. sieged, shortened from 'besieged'. (O.F. *siege*: connected with Lat. *sedere*, to sit down.)

47. In vain qualifies *twang'd*.

47. twang'd the yew, *i.e.* shot with his bow made of yew, the string of which made a twang when let go. (*Twang*, another form of *tang*, is a word made in imitation of the sound.)

48. The sudden onset of the English is compared to a sudden shower which compels people caught in it to run for shelter. Watt Tinlinn was not a man to run from a slight danger.

51. a Warden-raid, an inroad commanded by the Warden, or governor of the Border country, in person, and therefore more serious than an ordinary raid. (*Raid* is connected with *ride*, and originally meant a 'riding'.)

52. yeoman, accented on the second syllable here. The title *yeoman* was given to a servant next above a groom, and below a sergeant. It was also given to a bailiff's attendant. In a secondary sense the word was applied "to people of middling rank not in service; and in more modern times it came to signify a small landholder" (Morris). The *yeomen* formed part of the army.—Much conjecture has been exercised in deriving the word. Tyrwhitt and Morris refer it (most probably) to *yeongeman,* a young man. "The A.S. *geongra*=a vassal, and *geongorscipe*=service. It is the latter etymology that explains the modern form *yeoman.*" (Morris.)

53. barbican, "generally a small round tower for the station of an advanced guard placed just before the outward gate of the castle-yard" (Nares' *Glossary*). It was properly a watch-tower. But Scott appears to use the word indifferently for a tower and an extensive outwork—more often the latter. Cf. *Ivanhoe,* ch. xxi.: "The access, as usual in castles of the period, lay through an arched barbican, or outwork, which was terminated and defended by a small turret at each corner"; *id.* ch. xxvii.: "Passing the moat on a single plank, they reached a small barbican, or exterior defence, which communicated with the open field by a well-defended sally-port".—Cf. canto i. 261, "sounding barbican".

54. nag, a little horse. Properly, one who neighs (O. E. *hnægan*).

55. hag, broken ground in a bog, firm enough to afford a foothold.

56. Billhope, in Liddesdale. Scott says: "There is an old rhyme, which thus celebrates the places in Liddesdale remarkable for game:

> 'Billhope braes for bucks and raes,
>   And Carit haugh for swine,
> And Tarras for the good bull-trout,
>   If he be ta'en in time'".

57. twain, an old form of *two* (O. E. *twegen*).

58. serf, bondsman. (Lat. *servus,* a slave.)

58. all their train, *i.e.* was the only attendant they had. (Lat. *trahere,* to draw along.)

60. The Borderers were careless about their houses and furniture, because they were so likely to be destroyed. But they made up for it by decking their women with splendid ornaments.

62. passing, *i.e.* surpassing; adj. for adverb.

63. withal, besides, in addition.

64. morion, helmet without a visor, *i.e.* the piece of metal protecting the face. (Perhaps from Span. *morra,* crown of the head.)

65. jack, a leathern coat usually worn over the hauberk (coat of mail). It usually had no sleeves, and was sometimes padded with metal. (O. F. *jaque*; cf. *jacket*.)

65. fence, protection; shortened from 'defence'.

65. enow, old form of *enough*, often used in poetry. (O. E. *genóh*.)

68. six Scottish ells. A Scottish ell is about 37 inches. (O. E. *eln*, the length of the arm from the elbow to the tip of the middle finger.)

70. shafts, *i.e.* arrows.

71. His hardy partner. The wives of the rough Borderers were as used to the dangers and toils of the Border warfare as their husbands. Tinlinn's wife could laugh at the matter: see line 61.

72. show, *i.e.* describe.

74. Belted Will Howard, Lord William Howard, son of the Duke of Norfolk. His wife brought him Naworth Castle in Cumberland, and he became Warden of the Western Marches, and won a terrible reputation by the severity with which he put down Border excesses. He really lived a few years after the date of the events of this poem. *Belted* implies, as was indeed the fact, that the belt was the most conspicuous part of his dress; cf. v. 264—

> "His Bilboa blade, by Marchmen felt,
> Hung in a broad and studded belt".

75. Lord Dacre, a name derived from the exploits of one of the ancestors of the family at the siege of *Acre*, or Ptolemais, under Richard Cœur de Lion. (*Dacre=d'Acre*, of Acre.) There were two families of the name, the Dacres of the South and the Dacres of the North. "A chieftain of the latter branch was warden of the West Marches during the reign of Edward VI. He was a man of hot and obstinate character."

75. spear=spearman. So we speak of a good batsman in cricket as a 'good bat'.

76. German hackbut men, German musketeers (Dutch *haak*, hook; *bus*, gun-barrel). In the wars with Scotland, Henry VIII. and his successors hired a large number of foreign troops. At the battle of Pinkie in 1547 there were 800 hackbuteers in the English army, most of them foreigners.

77. lain, been stationed. Askerten was an old castle, now in ruins, in the north of Cumberland.

78. curfew hour, the time of ringing the evening bell. The Normans introduced into England the practice of ringing a bell as a signal for lights and fires to be put out—a beneficial practice, for the houses were made of wood. The time of ringing was usually eight o'clock, but the custom varied, nine and even ten o'clock being common for a long time in Scotland. (*Curfew* is from O. F. *couvre-feu*, cover fire.)

80. **fiend, the devil.** (O. E. *feond*, a hating one, an enemy. Satan is the chief *enemy* of God and man; hence Milton in *Paradise Lost* often calls him "the Enemy".)

80. **receive,** *i.e.* may he receive; subjunctive mood.

81. A little humorous touch. For the "little lonely tower" to escape burning for a whole year was a wonderful event.

84. **livelong night,** all night long. *Livelong* properly means 'as long as life lasts'.

85. Scott has been blamed for introducing names like these into his poem, but they make the story seem more real. *Fergus Graeme*, a Scotch name, seems out of place as applied to a member of the southern force; but there was a Border family of Grahams who seem to have plundered Scotch and English indifferently. See vi. 181–186.

87. **Priesthaugh Scrogg,** a hill shaded with trees, some miles S.E. of Branksome. (*Haugh*, Scotch *how*, a mound. *Scrogg*, the same as *shaw*, a shady wood.)

90. 'I held him long in fierce hatred.'

91. **drove,** carried off, drove away. Cf. the word 'drover'.

91. **Fastern's night,** more often called *Fastern's e'en* (so *Hallow e'en*, all saints' evening); also called Fastingham Tuesday and Shrove Tuesday. It is the day before Ash Wednesday, which begins the fast of Lent, and it used to be the custom to spend it in all sorts of revelry and feasting. The Borderer was, perhaps, superstitious enough to fear stealing during the fast, and doubtless he could drive off the cattle with more secrecy while the owners were engaged in their jollity.

94. **ken,** sight. The word is now little used except in Scotland and in such phrases as "within his ken", where it means 'knowledge'. (*Ken* is another form of *can*, Icelandic *kenna*, to know.)

95. **strand,** shore. Hence *Strand*, the name of the street in London, because it runs along parallel with and near to the shore of the Thames.

98. **Aill,** stream rising on high ground in Selkirkshire, flowing into the Teviot.

98. **Ettrick shade,** a well-wooded district in Selkirkshire, where the Buccleuchs had one of their earliest estates.

100. Notice the change of metre here, producing a galloping effect in accord with the sense.

101. pricking, spurring. Properly a transitive verb, 'to prick' (a horse); here intransitive.

101. lea, grassy meadow or plain.

102. trysting-place, place appointed for meeting. The word *tryst* (= pledge) is the same as *trust*, but is used in poetry and romance for a promise between lovers. Cf. Burns, *Mary Morison*, "O Mary, at thy window be; It is the wish'd, the trysted hour".

103. lightly held of, little esteemed by. *Of* was frequently used thus for *by*.

103. gaye ladye. The *e* is added in each case to give the word an old-fashioned appearance. *Ladye* must be pronounced with accent on the second syllable. *Gaye ladye* means 'lady-love', and *gaye* is what is called an ornamental epithet, like 'good' in 'good man' meaning 'husband'.

104. St. Mary's silver wave, St. Mary's Loch, an expansion of the river Yarrow. *Wave* is put for 'lake', just as *tide* is put for 'river' in line 1.

105. Gamescleugh; see note on *Thirlestane*, line 106. *Cleugh* means a hollow or glen in a hill-side: it is connected with *cleft*.

106. lances, men bearing lances; see note on line 75 above.

106. Thirlestane. "Sir John Scott of Thirlestane flourished in the reign of James V., and possessed the estates of Thirlestane, Gamescleugh, &c., lying upon the river of Ettrick, and extending to St. Mary's Loch, at the head of Yarrow. It appears, that when James had assembled his nobility, and their feudal followers, at Fala, with the purpose of invading England, and was, as is well known, disappointed by the obstinate refusal of his peers, this baron alone declared himself ready to follow the King wherever he should lead. In memory of his fidelity, James granted to his family a charter of arms, entitling them to bear a border of fleur-de-luce, similar to the tressure in the royal arms, with a bundle of spears for the crest; motto, *Ready, aye ready*." (Scott.)

108. tressured, bordered with a kind of plaited lacing. (*Tressure* is connected with *tress*, a plait, from a Greek word meaning 'threefold'.)

108. fleur-de-luce, a lily-shaped ornament consisting of three leaves. *Luce* is another form of *lys* or *lis*, lily.

108, 109. he claims To wreathe, *i.e.* he claims the right to put that border, like a wreath, upon his shield.

110. Fala's mossy wave, a marshy district in the s.e. of Edinburghshire. *Moss* = marsh.

111. grateful, adjective qualifying or in apposition to *royal James*.

112. faith, fidelity.

112. feudal jars. *Feudal* here has two senses combined: (1) the ordinary sense, as in 'feudal system': *feudal jars* meaning the struggles in which the dependants of the noble family were involved because they held their lands on condition of doing service in war this *feud* is from O.H.G. *fihu*, property, through O.F. *fieu* and L. Lat. *feudum*: (2) belonging to a *feud*, a strife between families This *feud* is from O.E. *fæhth*, enmity.—In this case probably the second meaning is the stronger. Cf. iii. 36, "feudal hate".—*Jar* means 'quarrel'; it is properly a musical term meaning 'discord'.

113. What time, at the time when: in imitation of the Latin phrase *quo tempore*.

113. Thirlestane; pronounce as three syllables.

117. crest, a device placed on a shield. Formerly it was an ornamental addition to the helmet. (Lat. *crista*, tuft on a bird's head.)

118. high, famous, noble.

120. An aged Knight. This was Walter Scott of Harden, who lived in the reign of Queen Mary, and was a noted freebooter. Many stories are told about him. He married a Mary Scott, who was called the Flower of Yarrow, and Sir Walter Scott was descended from him.

120. to danger steel'd, used, hardened to danger, as though with a coating of steel.

121. moss-trooper, the usual name for the robber-warriors of the Borders. The name arises from the fact that the Border-lands are marshy: see note on line 110 above.

122-124. These lines give the 'arms' of the Harden family. All noble families have what are called 'coats of arms' or armorial bearings, which consist of various devices painted on shields, and mottoes.

122. azure qualifies *stars* and *crescent*. The stars and crescent were painted blue on a golden field, or 'ground' as we should ordinarily say, meaning the surface of the shield. All these are technical terms belonging to heraldry, *i.e.* the science of armorial bearings.

124. Wat of Harden, as the "aged Knight" was usually called, was descended from a younger son of a Laird of Buccleuch, who lived before one of his family got the estate of Murdieston by his marriage with its heiress in 1296. Hence he was only entitled to bear the arms of the Scott family, and not those of the Murdieston family. The *bend* is a straight-lined figure drawn crosswise on the shield.

125, 126. Oakwood tower ... **Castle-Ower,** names of towers on Harden's estate.

127. Borthwick, a rapid stream flowing into the Teviot between Branksome and Hawick.

128. wood-embosom'd mansion, house snugly placed amidst trees. *Mansion,* which means literally 'an abiding-place' (Lat. *manere,* to remain), is usually applied to a house of considerable size, and is, perhaps, not appropriate to the dwelling of Harden : see note on line 60 above.

131. retainers, armed servants, wearing the livery of their master, but of higher rank than the domestic servants.

133. Marauding, plundering.

135. Flower of Yarrow; see note on line 120.

136. might tame ... **arms,** could subdue his passion for fighting.

137. spurn'd at, despised. (O.E. *speornan,* to kick against: cf. *spur.*)

139. Albeit, although.

140. Dinlay, a mountain in Liddesdale. In the ballad of *Jamie Telfer* it is said—

> "The Dinlay snaw was ne'er mair white
> Nor the lyart [gray] locks of Harden's hair".

144. brand, sword, so called probably from its flashing in light. (O.E. *brand;* *beornan,* to burn.)

Stanzas x.-xii. were not in the first edition, and are not so good in style as the rest of the poem.

145. stalwart, strong, stout. (O.E. *stælweorth,* 'steal-worthy'. "The original sense seems to have been 'good at stealing'.")

146. Todshaw means 'fox-wood'; see note on line 87.

150. sires, ancestors. (Lat. *senior,* elder, through F. *sire.*)

152. vassals, dependants. (From a Cornish word, through Latin.)

154. rude, rough, uncultivated.

156. Little they reck'd of, they little cared for. (O.E. *recan,* to care.)

156. liege lord, lord to whom they owed allegiance or loyalty.

158. Homage, the service of a vassal to his lord. (Through F. from Lat. *homaticum,* service of a *homo,* man.)

158. seignory, lordship. (F. *seigneur,* lord; Lat. *senior.*)

159. galliard, gay. The word is also the name of a lively dance.

159. heriot, a fine or present which the owner of a property exacted from the family of a tenant who had died. It was usually the best thing he had; often his best horse. (O. E. *heregeatu*, literally 'military dress'.)

161. bonny, pretty. Quite a common word in Scotland. (Perhaps from F. *bonne*, good.)

162. at pinch of need, at a time of great necessity. (Cf. the phrases 'at a pinch', 'the pinch of poverty'.)

163. trow, believe. (Connected with *true*, *truth*, &c.)

164. rein, *i.e.* manage with the reins.

164. Bucksfoot, the name of the horse.

165. gave fuel to fire, increased their angry mood, just as added fuel increases the heat of a fire.

166. ire, anger.

167. But that, that unless.

168. had = would have.

169. Sore he plied, he made frequent and hard use of.

174. Full fain, quite determined.

176. to thy yoke, under your authority. The *yoke* is properly the piece of wood placed across the backs of oxen to couple them together at the plough. Hence the word came to be metaphorically used as a sign of submission. When an army had been defeated by the Romans, the conquered soldiers had to pass 'under the yoke', which in this case was formed of a spear laid across two other spears placed upright in the ground.

177. cast, the number cast or let go at once. Hawks were once used in hunting.

178. to have and hold, *i.e.* for you to keep possession of. It is an old legal phrase.

179. Beshrew, may a curse light on. (O. E. *screawa*, a shrew-mouse, supposed to have a very venomous bite.)

179. of the Beattisons' clan. These words must be understood as coming after *landed man*.

180. landed, holding property in land. A participle formed from a noun. Cf. the phrases "belted knight" (Burns), "towered cities" (Milton).

185. amain. The word has two senses: (1) 'with force', as in ii. 196, and v. 27; (2) more commonly 'with speed', as here and in ii. 393. (From *a*, a form of the preposition *on*; O. E. *mægn*, strength.)

186. has ta'en, took. The perfect tense is used instead of the past simply for the sake of the rime.

187. merrymen, a word often used for the followers of an outlaw chief: cf. 'Robin Hood and his merrymen'. They were called *merry* probably because they were believed to live a gay life quite free from care; so *merry* became what is called a permanent epithet, *i.e.* an adjective which is so frequently attached to a noun as to make with it a common phrase: cf. "merry Carlisle" in canto i. line 51.

188. hold them, keep themselves; reflexive.

189. wended, made his way, went. (*Went* is the past tense of the O.E. *wendan*, and has taken the place of the old past tense of *go*, which was *yode*.)

192. Know me for, recognize me as.

196. rue, repent, be sorry.

197. wind, sound, blow (by sending wind into it).

206. Craikcross, a hill near the bank of the Teviot.

208. This line contains four extra syllables.

210. Pentoun-linn. *Linn* is a hollow or deep pool: cf. *Linlithgow*.

212. had you, would you have.

217. bore, pierced.

219. Haugh here means 'low-lying flat ground', not 'hill', as in line 87.

It was quite natural that the Minstrel should wish to please the Lady to whom he was singing by an account of this famous deed of her ancestors. But his proper story is rather awkwardly interrupted.

226. swair, or *swire*, is the descent of a hill.

228. bow and spear, bowman and spearman.

229. gathering word, word passed among the clan as a signal for meeting.

229. Bellenden, a place in the centre of the Scotts' estates, near the head of the Borthwick.

230. sod, ground, soil.

232. mark'd, observed.

232. aids, those who came to aid her.

235. his father's friend; not any particular friend: the meaning is, 'learn to recognize those who were friendly to the family'.

239. true, that was proved to be true by striking the mark at which it was aimed. *True* means sure, certain.

241. The red cross, St. George's cross, borne on their coats by the English soldiers.

245. the wily page. The young heir having been sent for, the goblin page, who was pretending to be the boy, did not wish to face the Ladye, because he knew that she was skilled in magic and might detect the trick. *Wily,* cunning, tricky.

246. sage, wise.

247. counterfeited childish fear, acted in pretence of being afraid.

249. plain'd, lamented, made a wailing noise. (Lat. *plangere,* to beat the breast.)

252. wont, used; properly the past participle of O.E. *won,* to dwell or be used to: sometimes used as a past tense, as here; more often as an adjective, 'was wont'.

255. Hence! *i.e.* go hence.

255. faintness, *i.e.* faintheartedness, cowardice.

256. weakling. *-ling* is a diminutive ending, as in 'duckling', 'gosling': here it implies contempt.

258. Rangleburn, a hill. The word must be lengthened to four syllables by a strong burr of the *r*: cf. "Unicorn", i. 207.

259. fell, cruel, spiteful.

260. Notice that the Ladye does not say, 'that a son of mine should ever be a coward'. What she says is stronger.

262. counterfeited, pretended. *Counterfeit* would be the more usual and correct word.

263. Soon as, *i.e.* as soon as.

263. palfrey, a riding-horse. The word is generally applied to a lady's horse: cf. *Marmion,* vi. 7, "The Ancient Earl, with stately grace, Would Clara on her palfrey place".

264. ill-omen'd, containing a prophecy of evil. The meaning is that mishap of some kind was sure to result from the riding of such a mischievous urchin.

264. elfish, elf-like. *Elves* were supernatural beings of dwarfish shape, having magical powers which they usually exercised mischievously.

264. freight, burden. The word is scarcely ever now used except for the cargo of a ship, or the sum paid for the carriage of the cargo.

267. mickle, much. (O.E. *mycel*, great; now only used in Scotland.)

268. a Scottish mile, about one eighth longer than an English mile.

270, 271. "It is a firm article of popular faith, that no enchantment can subsist in a living stream. Nay, if you can interpose a brook betwixt you and witches, spectres, or even fiends, you are in perfect safety. Burns's inimitable *Tam o' Shanter* turns entirely upon such a circumstance. The belief seems to be of antiquity. Brompton informs us, that certain Irish wizards could, by spells, convert earthen clods, or stones, into fat pigs, which they sold in the market, but which always re-assumed their proper form when driven by the deceived purchasers across a running stream." (Scott.)

272. "Lost! lost! lost!" This was the goblin's only cry; see canto ii. line 376.

273. urchin. The original meaning was 'hedgehog' (O.F. *eriçon*, Lat. *ericius*). Cf. *The Tempest*, i. 2. 326, where Prospero threatens Caliban that urchins shall prick him and pinch him all night long. Goblins were supposed sometimes to take a hedgehog's shape; so in *Macbeth* evil spirits are referred to as toads and rats.

274. cloth-yard shaft, an arrow the length of a yard for measuring cloth.

275. whistled. The arrow whizzed through the air.

277. imp, little demon. (The original meaning was simply 'offspring', from a word meaning a 'graft' on a tree.)

277. might, could.

280. aghast, horror-struck. (O.E. *agǽstan*, to terrify.) The rough Borderers were bold enough before enemies of flesh and blood, but were superstitiously afraid of the spirits of the air. Tinlinn thought the lad must be a spirit in human shape.

282. verge, edge.

284. martial murmurs, the far-off sounds of soldiers marching, bugles blowing and armour clashing. (*Martial* is from *Mars*, the Roman god of War.)

288. ken, recognize. (Properly 'know': O.E. *cunnan*.)

289. measured tread, stepping in time; not walking anyhow, but with a regular even step. (Cf. the use of *measure* as applied to poetry.)

290. Notice the order of the words.

291. Almayn, German. See lines 76, 77 and stanza xviii. (Lat. *Allemanni*, a German tribe; Fr. *Allemand*.)

291. **sullen.** Words like this, properly applicable only to persons, are often applied to things to express some similarity between their qualities and those of persons, or the effect they have on the mind. So Shakespeare speaks of an "angry trumpet"; Milton of "merry bells" and "jocund rebecks" (a kind of fiddle); Spenser speaks of the "builder oak", the "warlike beech", &c.

291. **kettle-drum,** so called because it is made of a copper-vessel, something like the bowl of a kettle, covered with parchment.

292. **crimson sheen.** *Sheen* may here be either a noun or an adjective. In the former case *crimson sheen* would be a very poetical phrase, *sheen* meaning 'fairness' or 'brilliance'. In the latter case the expression is not so poetical, meaning 'brilliant crimson cloth'. The thing meant in both cases is practically the same. Scott else-where uses *sheen* as an adjective: cf. *Lady of the Lake*, i. 208, "All twinkling with the dew-drops sheen".

293. **copse,** a wood of small trees; the word is contracted from *coppice.*

295. **helm,** *i.e.* helmet.

296. **Light,** *i.e.* lightly armed, or perhaps 'light-footed'.

296. **forayers,** properly, men who are sent out on a foray, in search of forage or food. The meaning here appears to be 'scouts'.

297. **loosely,** scattered, not in close array like the archers.

298. **fast** probably means here 'firm', not 'swift'.

299. **Kendal,** a small town in Westmoreland, once famous for its manufacture of a green-coloured cloth. Westmoreland would natu-rally supply men for the Border warfare, and the archers of Kendal would naturally be dressed in the 'Kendal green'.

299. **all;** not 'all the archers', but 'entirely': *all* is an adverb.

302. **back,** support. Cf. the phrase 'back up'.

303. **bill-men,** men armed with 'bills', *i.e.* axes mounted on long handles. The *bill* was a weapon commonly used by the in-fantry in the middle ages.

304. **Irthing,** a small tributary of the Eden. *on Irthing bred* im-plies that, being born and brought up so near the Border, they had been long accustomed to the Border raids and so had become "a hardy race".

305. **kirtles.** The kirtle was properly a part of a woman's dress: here it means 'tunic', or 'upper garment'.

305. **crosses red,** the St. George's cross stitched on their tunics.

307. See note on line 75 above.

310. **bill and bow,** billmen and bowmen.

311. mercenaries, soldiers hired for money. (Lat. *merces,* pay, wages.) As soldiers were so often hired to fight for a bad cause, the word *mercenary* has now a bad meaning.

313. Notice the order.

316, 317. Scott quotes from Froissart an anecdote of some mercenaries who called themselves "frendes to God, and enemyes to alle the worlde; for without we make ourselfe to be feared, we gete nothynge".

319. levin-darting, fire-flashing. (*Levin* is from an old word meaning 'lightning'.)

320. Buff, a kind of leather made from the skin of the buffalo. The word is now used chiefly for the colour of the leather, a dull yellow.

320. frounced, decked with fringes or plaits. (O. F. *froncer,* to wrinkle.)

321. morsing-horns, powder-flasks, made of horn. (Fr. *amorce,* priming.)

321. scarfs. The plural in use now is *scarves.*

322. better, right.

323. escalade, the surmounting of the walls of a fort or town, by means of ladders. (Fr. *escalade,* Lat. *scala,* a ladder.)

324. All belongs to *they* in the next line = 'they all'

324. in rugged tongue, in German, which contains many rough guttural consonant sounds.

325. Teutonic. The Germans, like the English, belong to the Teutonic branch of the European races. The *Teutones* were an ancient German tribe.

325. sung. *Sang* is the correct past tense.

328. the greenwood tree, a general term that often occurs in old ballads.

329. chivalry, horse-soldiers, cavalry. (O. F. *chevalerie,* horsemanship, from *cheval,* a horse.)

330. glaive, sword. (Lat. *gladius.*)

331. battle, army. So Psalm lxxvi. 3, "There brake he...the shield, the sword, and the battle".

333. To gain his spurs. A squire, on being made a knight, was presented with a pair of gold spurs. Hence 'to win one's spurs' was originally a phrase meaning 'to gain the honour of knighthood'; then it came to mean generally 'to win honour', and could be used of knights, as here.

334. favour, a love-token. In the middle ages a knight often rode to battle wearing some little token given him either by his lady-love, or by some lady whom for the occasion he had chosen for his patroness.

337. display, spread out, extend; its literal meaning. (Lat. *dis*, apart; *plicare*, to fold; through Fr. *despleier*, another form of which is *desploier*, whence the military term *deploy*.)

339. In order to make the rime with *stand*, *England* must be accented on the second syllable.

340. intent, intently, fixedly; adj. for adverb.

342. The first *they* refers to the armed towers, the second to the Englishmen.

342. might know, could recognize, hear. See *ken* in line 288.

343. The straining harsh, the harsh sound made as the bow-string was pulled back. It must be remembered that the cross-bow was a weapon so strong that the string had to be fitted to the notch of the bolt by some mechanical contrivance, and the bolt was let fly by means of a trigger. It was the creaking of this machinery that the English heard.

344. battlement, a wall behind which soldiers might walk, and having openings through which they could shoot.

344. bartizan, a small overhanging turret projecting from the angles of a wall.

345. partisan, a kind of halbert, or long staff with a sharp piercing weapon at the end. (The origin of the word is doubtful.)

346. Falcon and culver, small cannon formerly used. The former was so called from the bird of prey, by a kind of metaphor; the latter, also called *caliver* and *culverin*, from a resemblance to the snake (O. F. *coleuvrin*, Lat. *colubra*, an adder).

347. prompt, ready. (Lat. *promptus*, brought forward.)

347. hail. The comparison of shot from guns to rain or hail is very common.

348. frequent broke, frequently showed through.

349. eddying whirls. *Eddy* and *whirl* have much the same meaning, 'to move in a circular way'.

349. sable, black. The smoke was that of the "seething pitch", not of the cannon.

351. seething, boiling.

352. Reek'd, smoked.

352. a witch's caldron, a vessel in which witches were supposed to boil together all kinds of horrible things in order to manufacture charms. (Lat. *calere*, to be hot.)

353. bridges, drawbridges over the moat surrounding the castle.

354. wicket, a small gate or door in a large one, capable of being opened independently.

355. Seneschal, steward, officer who had charge of the domestic and ceremonial arrangements.

358. seat, position as he sat.

360. with chasten'd fire, with spirit, but somewhat subdued.

361. curvetting, leaping; raising both fore-legs at once, then letting them fall and raising the hind-legs. (Lat. *curvare*, to bend.)

364. squire, attendant; literally a shield-bearer (O. F. *escuyer*, Lat. *scutarius*; *scutum*, a shield.)

365. "A glove upon a lance was the emblem of faith among the ancient Borderers, who were wont, when anyone broke his word, to expose this emblem, and proclaim him a faithless villain at the first Border meeting. This ceremony was much dreaded." (Scott.)

372. The phrase *against the truce of Border tide* occurs in the ballad of *Kinmont Willie* in Scott's *Minstrelsy*. In his Introduction to that poem Scott quotes a long account of the capture of a Scotsman, the hero of the ballad, by a band of Englishmen in time of truce, and of his rescue by Scotts under Buccleuch.

373. In hostile guise, in the manner of an enemy.

376. Scotland, accented on second syllable: cf. line 339.

377. reads, advises. (O. E. *rǽdan*, to advise; *rǽd*, counsel. Richard II. was called "Richard the Redeles", *i.e.* the wanting in counsel.)

377. swith, quickly. (O. E. *swith*, strong.)

380. scare, *i.e.* to scare.

381. St. Mary! but. *But* means 'if not': the seneschal makes a kind of vow to St. Mary.

382. shall, that shall; the nominative relative is omitted.

383. Dacre's lord, Lord Dacre; as though there were a place *Dacre* from which the lord took his title: see note on line 75.

384. took the word, spoke up. Dacre was too angry to speak.

387. pursuivant, messenger or herald. (F. *poursuivant*, Lat. *pro*, forward; *sequi*, to follow.)

389. sped, *i.e.* being sped, delivered.

394. **The lion argent**, a figure of a lion woven in silver thread upon his coat. The lion is the crest of the Howards. (Lat. *argentum*, silver.)

398. **Obeisance meet**, the low bow that it was proper to make to the Ladye.

400. **It irks**, it distresses, vexes; impersonal verb.

402. **may**, can.

403. **Wardenry**, the part of the country under the rule of the warden.

404. **contemning**, despising, setting at naught.

406. **beseems**, *i.e.* it beseems, becomes.

407. **flemens-firth**, refuge for outlaws. (O.E. *flœmingr*, outlaw; *firth*, a sheltered place.)

409. **march-treason** was the name given to several offences peculiar to the Border, among which was riding against the opposite party in time of truce.

409. **pain**, penalty, punishment.

410. **St. Cuthbert's even**, the day before the festival of St. Cuthbert, March 20th.   St. Cuthbert, once prior of Melrose, became bishop of Lindisfarne, and died in 687.

411. **prick'd**, spurred his horse.

412. **Harried**, plundered, ravaged. (O.E. *hergian*.)

413. **dint**, blow.

417. **powers**, forces, soldiers.

418. **straight**, at once.

418. **warrison**, war-sound.   The word is wrongly used, as it means properly 'reward'.

421. **King Edward**, Edward VI.

426. **A moment**, for one moment.

426. **cheer**, countenance. (O. F. *chere*.)

428. The Ladye as a mother longed to receive her son back in safety, but looking round on the warriors, she remembers that she, until her son is grown up, is their head, and she stifles her personal feelings.

434. **of high emprize**, *i.e.* who undertake important enterprises. This is ironical, *i.e.* the Ladye means the opposite of what she says. A war "on women and on boys" could not be considered a "high emprize". *Emprize* is a bad rime to *boys*.

437. **cleanse him**, purge, free himself.

437. by oath. In doubtful cases, Border criminals were allowed to state on their oath whether they were or were not guilty.

440, 441. *I.e.* 'there is no knight in Cumberland so high-born that Deloraine cannot reckon an equal number of famous and well-born ancestors and connections'.

442. The dignity of knighthood was not originally dependent on royalty, but could be conferred by anyone who was himself a knight. It was conferred by striking with the sword the shoulder of the kneeling man.

443. "The Battle of Ancram Moor, or Penielheuch, was fought A.D. 1545. The English, commanded by Sir Ralph Evers and Sir Brian Latoun, were totally routed, and both their leaders slain in the action. The Scottish army was commanded by Archibald Douglas, Earl of Angus, assisted by the Laird of Buccleuch and Norman Lesley." (Scott.)

444. but, had it not been that.

444. wight, swift, strong. (Icelandic *vigr*, in fighting condition.)

446. Himself had seen, Lord Dacre himself would have seen.

446. dubb'd, tapped with the sword. See note on line 442 above.

447. For, as for.

451. their purpose urge, persevere in their intention.

453. slogan, war-cry. (Gaelic *sluagh*, army; *gairm*, outcry.)

453. lyke-wake, the watching of a dead body before its burial. (O.E. *lic*, corpse: cf. *lych-gate*, the gate at which a pause is made by those carrying the bier while the first part of the burial service is read; *wacan*, to watch: cf. Hereward the *Wake*, *i.e.* the watchful.)

453. dirge, mournful song. (Contracted from *dirige*, the first word of a solemn Latin hymn, *Dirige, Domine, deus meus, in conspectu tuo vitam meam*, 'Direct, O Lord my God, my life in Thy sight'.)

456. lighten'd, flashed like lightning.

458. Pensils, small pennons. (Contracted from *pennoncel.*)

458. pennons, long narrow flags. (Lat. *penna*, a feather.)

464. to his ear, up to his ear, and on a level with his eye, so as to take good aim.

470. What make you? What are you doing? A French idiom.

473. toils, net, snare. (Lat. *tela*, web, through F. *toile.*)

474. Ruberslaw, a hill in Teviotdale. *Law* means 'a mound'.

475. The Douglas, *i.e.* the head of the Douglas clan.

475. weapon-schaw, a muster or show of military forces. *Wappen-schaw* is, perhaps, the more usual form of the word: cf. *Old Mortality*, ch. i., "The sheriff of the county of Lanark was holding the wappen-schaw of a wild district...When the musters had been made, the young men, as was usual, were to mix in various sports." *Schaw* = show.

479. bar retreat, prevent retreat.

481. the eagle and the rood, the arms of Lord Maxwell. (O.E. *ród*, cross; the *rood* being a crucifix: cf. *Holyrood*.)

482. Jedwood, *i.e.* the people of Jedwood or Jedburgh, a town some miles N.E. of Branksome.

482. Eske, river flowing into the Solway Firth.

482. Teviotdale, the valley of the Teviot, a tributary of the Tweed.

484. Merse, part of Berwickshire, along the left bank of the Tweed.

484. Lauderdale, the western district of Berwickshire.

485. Home, name of the head of a family whose seat was Home Castle, in Berwickshire.

486. exile, one compelled to live away from his own country.

487. Liddesdale, the valley of the Liddel.

489. brook, bear, endure.

493. father, *i.e.* forefather, ancestor.

494. 495. See note to line 75.

494. Judah's sea, the Sea of Galilee.

498. harquebuss, musket. (*Arquebus* is the more common spelling.)

498. on row, in a row.

500. Notice that Dacre again is wrathful, while Howard (line 502) is more calm and able to give the matter due consideration.

505. the blanche lion, the "lion argent" of line 394. Scott notes that "the crest of a warrior was often used as a *nomme de guerre*" (war-name), and mentions that Richard III. was known as the "Boar of York". (F. *blanc*, white.)

506. flower, best troops. Cf. the phrases 'flower of the flock', 'in the flower of his age'.

509. certes, certainly.

509. were desperate policy, *i.e.* to set 3000 English against 10,000 Scots would be a course of action only to be justified in a desperate or hopeless case.

510. made. Terms had been *offered* by the Ladye, but not *made*, *i.e.* agreed to on both sides.

511. Ere conscious of, before she knew. Howard did not know that the Ladye had secret means of intelligence: see lines 551-553.

512. Scott notes that trial by combat, common in feudal times, continued to be practised on the Borders up to the 17th century.

514. cross'd, defeated.

521. slow, slowly.

528. parleying strain, notes sounding a parley, *i.e.* a meeting for the purpose of talking about the matter. (F. *parler*, to speak: cf. *parliament*.)

530. in Musgrave's right, on behalf of Musgrave.

532. The throwing down of a glove was the mark of defiance in the middle ages, and of a challenge to fight. The challenged knight showed his acceptance of the challenge by picking up the glove.

534. lists, spaces marked out for the fight, enclosed by barriers.

538. foil, defeat.

538. Notice that *Musgrave* here is accented on the second syllable.

540. Howe'er it falls, whatever the result may be.

545. proffer, offer, the plan suggested.

546. gainsay'd, opposed it.

548. Jedwood's recent sack, the plunder of Jedburgh by the English that had lately taken place, namely in 1545, under the Earl of Hertford, afterwards the Protector Somerset.

549. tardy, slow, behindhand.

549. the Regent. On the death of James V. in 1542, leaving an infant daughter, Mary Queen of Scots, only seven days old, the Earl of Arran made himself regent, and held that office till 1554.

551. prescience, foreknowledge. (Lat. *prae*, before; *scire*, to know.)

552. the art, *i.e.* the black art or magic. The fact that the Ladye dared not confess her magic power prevented her from using it: hence the events of the story follow one another as though she had no such power.

556. lawn, open grassy space; properly a cleared place in a wood.

561. stead, literally place. (O.E. *stede*, a place. Cf. *1 Chronicles*, v. 22, "And they dwelt in their steads until the captivity".)

562. chieftain, *i.e.* his chieftain, the young heir.

564. The discussion introduced here brings into prominence again the personality of the old Minstrel, and prepares the way for his lines on the old Harper, his master.

567. in full career, running at full speed. *Career* means properly a 'road'. (O. F. *cariere,* Lat. *carraria,* a way for the *carrus,* car.)   It was a term used for the 'course' in the lists. —Scott, in his note on line 512, quotes an account of a single combat on horseback that took place in 1558.   "When they were in readiness, the trumpets sounded, the heralds cried, and the judges let them go.   They then encountered very fiercely."

568. when as, when.   The *as* was formerly added because *when* was properly an interrogative adverb.

569. shiver, break, snap.   When the spears broke, swords were used.

570. the jovial Harper. "One of our ancient Border minstrels, called Rattling Roaring Willie.   This name was probably derived from his bullying disposition; being, it would seem, such a roaring boy as is frequently mentioned in old plays."   Scott gives an account of a quarrel he had with a brother minstrel, whom he killed, Willie then suffering execution at Jedburgh.   The murdered minstrel was known by the name of Sweet Milk, from a place on Rule Water (a tributary of the Teviot), so called.

571. yet a youth, while I was still young.

572. guise, manner.

572. say, describe, tell.

573. ordinance and clause, rule and sentence.

573. Black Lord Archibald's battle-laws, a collection of regulations for the conduct of Border warfare, made by a Lord Archibald Douglas, called *Black* because of his ferocity, in the 14th century.

576. The repetition of *he* emphasises the jealous pride of the Harper.

577. tax...with wrong, find fault with his song.   Cf. the phrase 'take to task'.

579. the goblet plied, passed the wine-cup merrily round, *i.e.* drank freely.   (*Ply* means 'to pass to and fro': cf. the phrase 'to ply for hire'.)

580. chafed, irritated, galled.   (Lit. warmed; F. *chauffer.*)

581. The Bard of Reull; see note on line 570.

583. tuneful.   This is an epithet fittingly applied to hands that played the harp.

584. thorn's white branches. "A thorn tree marks the scene of the murder, which is still called Sweet Milk Thorn." (Scott.)

586. rigid doom, unalterable fate; or perhaps 'unmerciful judgment'. The Harper, having committed a murder, justly suffered; but his pupil thinks of him not as a criminal, but as his master, and a fine minstrel.

587. dragg'd. Willie was taken as he lay sleeping in the meadow by Ousenam Water; his hands were tied behind him, and he was carried off to Jedburgh.

588. Scott quotes from the ballad of *Rattling Roaring Willie*. named after the Harper—

> " The lasses of Ousenam water
> Are rugging and riving their hair,
> And a' for the sake of Willie,
> His beauty was so fair ".

Ousenam or Oxnam is between Jedburgh and Branksome.

591. at Jedwood Air, at the time of the Jedwood assizes, *i.e.* the periodical trials. (*Air* is from O. F. *erre*, Lat. *iter*, a journey, and is the Scotch form of the English *eyre*. 'Justices in eyre' are judges travelling on circuit. Jamieson in his *Scottish Dictionary* quotes: " About this time the king went to the south land to the *Airs*, and held justice in Jedburgh ".)

595. muse, ponder on, think about.

595. yore, former times; a common poetical word. (O. E. *geára*, of years; the genitive plural of *geár*.)

598. with my minstrel brethren fled, *i.e.* now that my minstrel brethren are gone. Or *fled* may be taken with *jealousy of song*: 'having fled, it is now dead'.

599. jealousy of song, pride in my own powers of singing, or perhaps pride in the whole brotherhood of minstrels, and jealousy for their fame.

605. legendary song, old story in the form of a song. The word *legend* is usually applied to a story containing something marvellous. (Lat. *legenda*, things to be read.)

605. could, *i.e.* he could.

607. whose memory was not, the recollection of which was gone. Cf. "because they are not", *i.e.* no longer exist, are dead, in *S. Matthew*, ii. 18, " Rachel weeping for her children, and would not be comforted, because they are not ".

609. harbour, give shelter to. (A Scandinavian word, meaning literally 'army-shelter'.) The word is very appropriate here: the towers were once filled with noisy soldiers, now they are inhabited by quiet timid hares—a very great contrast.

612. fickle, changeable, not favouring anyone long.

612. Fame is personified, and is represented as keeping rolls of parchment in which the names of her favourites (*i.e.* those who for a time were famous) are written.

614. minion, favourite. (F. *mignon,* dainty, pleasing (cf. *mignonette*), from O. Germ. *minna,* love.)

615. The fading wreath. A man's fame is here compared to the wreath placed on the head of a hero or victor.

616. In sooth, truly.

616. 't was strange, because he was so old, and old people as a rule do not have very clear recollections.

617. call them, *i.e.* bring them to mind almost as clearly as if the very men were present before them.

617. hearse, tomb. (Properly a carriage for a dead body, but many poets, as Ben Jonson, Shakespeare, Milton, use the word as it is used here.—The O. F. *herce* meant a harrow.)

618, 619. ne'er ... ear, never was a flattering word spoken without pleasing a poet.

620. waste, *i.e.* spend.

621. vain tribute, useless reward.—Shelley says : " Poets' food is fame and love ".

622. flame, poetic enthusiasm, spirit, or imagination.

623. Her dulcet breath, the sweet breath of flattery. The poet's power of song is compared to a flame, which sinks lower and lower as he grows older, but can be fanned up into brightness again by flattery. But only for a time : the "blaze" is "short-lived".

CANTO FIFTH.

I.

CALL it not vain :—they do not err,
  Who say, that when the Poet dies,
Mute Nature mourns her worshipper,
  And celebrates his obsequies :
Who say, tall cliff, and cavern lone,   5
For the departed Bard make moan ;
That mountains weep in crystal rill ;
That flowers in tears of balm distil ;
Through his loved groves that breezes sigh,
And oaks, in deeper groan, reply ;   10
And rivers teach their rushing wave
To murmur dirges round his grave.

II.

Not that, in sooth, o'er mortal urn
Those things inanimate can mourn ;
But that the stream, the wood, the gale   15
Is vocal with the plaintive wail
Of those, who, else forgotten long,
Lived in the poet's faithful song,
And, with the poet's parting breath,
Whose memory feels a second death.   20
The Maid's pale shade, who wails her lot,
That love, true love, should be forgot,
From rose and hawthorn shakes the tear
Upon the gentle Minstrel's bier :
The phantom Knight, his glory fled,   25
Mourns o'er the field he heap'd with dead ;
Mounts the wild blast that sweeps amain,
And shrieks along the battle-plain.
The Chief, whose antique crownlet long
Still sparkled in the feudal song,   30
Now, from the mountain's misty throne,
Sees, in the thanedom once his own,
His ashes undistinguish'd lie,
His place, his power, his memory die :
His groans the lonely caverns fill,   35
His tears of rage impel the rill :

All mourn the Minstrel's harp unstrung,
Their name unknown, their praise unsung.

III.

Scarcely the hot assault was staid,
The terms of truce were scarcely made,   40
When they could spy, from Branksome's towers,
The advancing march of martial powers.
Thick clouds of dust afar appear'd,
And trampling steeds were faintly heard;
Bright spears, above the columns dun,   45
Glanced momentary to the sun;
And feudal banners fair display'd
The bands that moved to Branksome's aid.

IV.

Vails not to tell each hardy clan,
   From the fair Middle Marches came;   50
The Bloody Heart blazed in the van,
   Announcing Douglas, dreaded name!
Vails not to tell what steeds did spurn,
Where the Seven Spears of Wedderburne
   Their men in battle-order set;   55
And Swinton laid the lance in rest,
That tamed of yore the sparkling crest
   Of Clarence's Plantagenet.
Nor list I say what hundreds more,
From the rich Merse and Lammermore,   60
And Tweed's fair borders, to the war,
Beneath the crest of Old Dunbar,
   And Hepburn's mingled banners come,
Down the steep mountain glittering far,
   And shouting still, "A Home! a Home!"   65

V.

Now squire and knight, from Branksome sent,
On many a courteous message went;
To every chief and lord they paid
Meet thanks for prompt and powerful aid;
And told them,—how a truce was made,   70
   And how a day of fight was ta'en
'Twixt Musgrave and stout Deloraine;
   And how the Ladye pray'd them dear,

That all would stay the fight to see,
And deign, in love and courtesy, 75
　To taste of Branksome cheer.
Nor, while they bade to feast each Scot,
Were England's noble Lords forgot.
Himself, the hoary Seneschal
Rode forth, in seemly terms to call 80
Those gallant foes to Branksome Hall.
Accepted Howard, than whom knight
Was never dubb'd, more bold in fight;
Nor, when from war and armour free,
More famed for stately courtesy: 85
But angry Dacre rather chose
In his pavilion to repose.

VI.

Now, noble Dame, perchance you ask,
　How these two hostile armies met?
Deeming it were no easy task 90
　To keep the truce which here was set;
Where martial spirits, all on fire,
Breathed only blood and mortal ire.—
By mutual inroads, mutual blows,
By habit, and by nation, foes, 95
　They met on Teviot's strand;
They met and sate them mingled down,
Without a threat, without a frown,
　As brothers meet in foreign land:
The hands, the spear that lately grasp'd, 100
Still in the mailèd gauntlet clasp'd,
　Were interchanged in greeting dear;
Visors were raised, and faces shown,
And many a friend, to friend made known,
　Partook of social cheer. 105
Some drove the jolly bowl about;
　With dice and draughts some chased the day;
And some, with many a merry shout,
In riot, revelry, and rout,
　Pursued the foot-ball play. 110

VII

Yet, be it known, had bugles blown,
　Or sign of war been seen,
Those bands so fair together ranged,
Those hands, so frankly interchanged,

Had dyed with gore the green :   115
The merry shout by Teviot-side
Had sunk in war-cries wild and wide,
    And in the groan of death ;
And whingers, now in friendship bare,
The social meal to part and share,   120
    Had found a bloody sheath.
'Twixt truce and war, such sudden change
Was not infrequent, nor held strange,
    In the old Border-day :
But yet on Branksome's towers and town,   125
In peaceful merriment, sunk down
    The sun's declining ray.

VIII.

The blithsome signs of wassel gay
Decay'd not with the dying day ;
Soon through the latticed windows tall   130
Of lofty Branksome's lordly hall,
Divided square by shafts of stone,
Huge flakes of ruddy lustre shone ;
Nor less the gilded rafters rang
With merry harp and beakers' clang :   135
    And frequent, on the darkening plain,
        Loud hollo, whoop, or whistle ran,
    As bands, their stragglers to regain,
        Give the shrill watchword of their clan ;
And revellers, o'er their bowls, proclaim   140
Douglas or Dacre's conquering name.

IX.

Less frequent heard, and fainter still,
    At length the various clamours died :
And you might hear, from Branksome hill,
    No sound but Teviot's rushing tide ;   145
Save when the changing sentinel
The challenge of his watch could tell ;
And save, where, through the dark profound,
The clanging axe and hammer's sound
    Rung from the nether lawn ;   150
For many a busy hand toil'd there,
Strong pales to shape, and beams to square,
The lists' dread barriers to prepare
    Against the morrow's dawn.

X.

Margaret from hall did soon retreat,   155
    Despite the Dame's reproving eye;
Nor mark'd she, as she left her seat,
    Full many a stifled sigh;
For many a noble warrior strove
To win the Flower of Teviot's love,   160
    And many a bold ally.—
With throbbing head and anxious heart,
All in her lonely bower apart,
    In broken sleep she lay:
By times, from silken couch she rose;   165
While yet the banner'd hosts repose,
    She view'd the dawning day:
Of all the hundreds sunk to rest,
First woke the loveliest and the best.

XI.

She gazed upon the inner court,   170
    Which in the tower's tall shadow lay;
Where coursers' clang, and stamp, and snort,
    Had rung the livelong yesterday;
Now still as death; till stalking slow,—
    The jingling spurs announced his tread,—   175
A stately warrior pass'd below;
    But when he raised his plumed head—
        Blessed Mary! can it be?—
Secure, as if in Ousenam bowers,
He walks through Branksome's hostile towers,   180
    With fearless step and free.
She dared not sign, she dared not speak—
Oh! if one page's slumbers break,
    His blood the price must pay!
Not all the pearls Queen Mary wears,   185
Not Margaret's yet more precious tears,
    Shall buy his life a day.

XII.

Yet was his hazard small; for well
You may bethink you of the spell
    Of that sly urchin page;   190
This to his lord he did impart,
And made him seem, by glamour art,
    A knight from Hermitage.

Unchallenged thus, the warder's post,
The court, unchallenged, thus he cross'd,   195
   For all the vassalage:
But O! what magic's quaint disguise
Could blind fair Margaret's azure eyes!
   She started from her seat;
While with surprise and fear she strove,   200
And both could scarcely master love—
   Lord Henry's at her feet.

XIII.

Oft have I mused, what purpose bad
That foul malicious urchin had
   To bring this meeting round;   205
For happy love's a heavenly sight,
And by a vile malignant sprite
   In such no joy is found;
And oft I've deem'd, perchance he thought
Their erring passion might have wrought   210
   Sorrow, and sin, and shame;
And death to Cranstoun's gallant Knight,
And to the gentle ladye bright,
   Disgrace and loss of fame.
But earthly spirit could not tell   215
The heart of them that loved so well.
True love's the gift which God has given
To man alone beneath the heaven:
   It is not fantasy's hot fire,
     Whose wishes, soon as granted, fly;   220
   It liveth not in fierce desire,
     With dead desire it doth not die;
It is the secret sympathy,
The silver link, the silken tie,
Which heart to heart, and mind to mind,   225
In body and in soul can bind.—
Now leave we Margaret and her knight,
To tell you of the approaching fight.

XIV.

Their warning blasts the bugles blew,
   The pipe's shrill port aroused each clan;   230
In haste, the deadly strife to view,
   The trooping warriors eager ran:
Thick round the lists their lances stood,

Like blasted pines in Ettrick wood;
To Branksome many a look they threw, 235
The combatants' approach to view,
And bandied many a word of boast,
About the knight each favour'd most.

XV.

Meantime full anxious was the Dame;
For now arose disputed claim, 240
Of who should fight for Deloraine,
'Twixt Harden and 'twixt Thirlestane:
They 'gan to reckon kin and rent,
And frowning brow on brow was bent;
But yet not long the strife—for, lo! 245
Himself, the Knight of Deloraine,
Strong, as it seem'd, and free from pain,
In armour sheath'd from top to toe,
Appear'd, and craved the combat due.
The Dame her charm successful knew, 250
And the fierce chiefs their claims withdrew.

XVI.

When for the lists they sought the plain,
The stately Ladye's silken rein
Did noble Howard hold;
Unarmèd by her side he walk'd, 255
And much, in courteous phrase, they talk'd
Of feats of arms of old.
Costly his garb—his Flemish ruff
Fell o'er his doublet, shaped of buff,
With satin slash'd and lined; 260
Tawny his boot, and gold his spur,
His cloak was all of Poland fur,
His hose with silver twined;
His Bilboa blade, by Marchmen felt,
Hung in a broad and studded belt; 265
Hence, in rude phrase, the Borderers still
Call'd noble Howard, Belted Will.

XVII.

Behind Lord Howard and the Dame,
Fair Margaret on her palfrey came,
Whose foot-cloth swept the ground: 270

White was her wimple, and her veil,
And her loose locks a chaplet pale
　　Of whitest roses bound;
The lordly Angus, by her side,
In courtesy to cheer her tried;　　　　　　275
Without his aid, her hand in vain
Had strove to guide her broider'd rein.
He deem'd, she shudder'd at the sight
Of warriors met for mortal fight;
But cause of terror, all unguess'd,　　　　280
Was fluttering in her gentle breast,
When, in their chairs of crimson placed,
The Dame and she the barriers graced.

XVIII.

Prize of the field, the young Buccleuch,
An English knight led forth to view;　　　285
Scarce rued the boy his present plight,
So much he long'd to see the fight.
Within the lists, in knightly pride,
High Home and haughty Dacre ride;
Their leading-staffs of steel they wield,　　290
As marshals of the mortal field;
While to each knight their care assign'd
Like vantage of the sun and wind.
Then heralds hoarse did loud proclaim,
In King and Queen, and Warden's name,　　295
　　That none, while lasts the strife,
Should dare, by look, or sign, or word,
Aid to a champion to afford,
　　On peril of his life;
And not a breath the silence broke,　　　300
Till thus the alternate Heralds spoke:—

XIX.

ENGLISH HERALD.

"Here standeth Richard of Musgrave,
　　Good knight and true, and freely born,
Amends from Deloraine to crave,
　　For foul despiteous scathe and scorn.　　305
He sayeth, that William of Deloraine
　　Is traitor false by Border laws;
This with his sword he will maintain,
　　So help him God, and his good cause!"

XX.

SCOTTISH HERALD.

" Here standeth William of Deloraine,   310
Good knight and true, of noble strain,
Who sayeth, that foul treason's stain,
     Since he bore arms, ne'er soil'd his coat;
     And that, so help him God above!
He will on Musgrave's body prove,   315
He lies most foully in his throat."

LORD DACRE.

" Forward, brave champions, to the fight!
Sound trumpets!"——

LORD HOME.

——" God defend the right!"—
Then, Teviot! how thine echoes rang,
When bugle-sound and trumpet-clang   320
     Let loose the martial foes,
And in mid-list, with shield poised high,
And measured step and wary eye,
     The combatants did close.

XXI.

Ill would it suit your gentle ear,   325
Ye lovely listeners, to hear
How to the axe the helms did sound,
And blood pour'd down from many a wound;
For desperate was the strife and long,
And either warrior fierce and strong.   330
But, were each dame a listening knight,
I well could tell how warriors fight!
For I have seen war's lightning flashing,
Seen the claymore with bayonet clashing,
Seen through red blood the war-horse dashing, 335
And scorn'd, amid the reeling strife,
To yield a step for death or life.—

XXII.

'T is done, 't is done! that fatal blow
     Has stretch'd him on the bloody plain;
He strives to rise—Brave Musgrave, no!   340
     Thence never shalt thou rise again!

He chokes in blood—some friendly hand
Undo the visor's barred band,
Unfix the gorget's iron clasp,
And give him room for life to gasp!—   345
O, bootless aid!—haste, holy Friar,
Haste, ere the sinner shall expire!
Of all his guilt let him be shriven,
And smooth his path from earth to heaven!

XXIII.

In haste the holy Friar sped;—   350
His naked foot was dyed with red,
    As through the lists he ran;
Unmindful of the shouts on high,
That hail'd the conqueror's victory,
    He raised the dying man;   355
Loose waved his silver beard and hair,
As o'er him he kneel'd down in prayer;
And still the crucifix on high
He holds before his darkening eye;
And still he bends an anxious ear,   360
His faltering penitence to hear;
    Still props him from the bloody sod,
Still, even when soul and body part,
Pours ghostly comfort on his heart,
    And bids him trust in God!   365
Unheard he prays;—the death-pang 's o'er!
Richard of Musgrave breathes no more.

XXIV.

As if exhausted in the fight,
Or musing o'er the piteous sight,
    The silent victor stands;   370
His beaver did he not unclasp,
Mark'd not the shouts, felt not the grasp
    Of gratulating hands.
When lo! strange cries of wild surprise,
Mingled with seeming terror, rise   375
    Among the Scottish bands;
And all, amid the throng'd array,
In panic haste gave open way
To a half-naked ghastly man,
Who downward from the castle ran: 380

He cross'd the barriers at a bound,
And wild and haggard look'd around,
  As dizzy, and in pain;
And all, upon the armèd ground,
  Knew William of Deloraine!   385
Each ladye sprung from seat with speed;
Vaulted each marshal from his steed;
  "And who art thou", they cried,
"Who hast this battle fought and won?"—
His plumèd helm was soon undone—   390
  "Cranstoun of Teviot-side!
For this fair prize I've fought and won",—
And to the Ladye led her son.

XXV.

Full oft the rescued boy she kiss'd,
And often press'd him to her breast;   395
  For, under all her dauntless show,
Her heart had throbb'd at every blow;
Yet not Lord Cranstoun deign'd she greet,
Though low he kneelèd at her feet.
Me lists not tell what words were made,   400
What Douglas, Home, and Howard, said—
  —For Howard was a generous foe—
And how the clan united pray'd
  The Ladye would the feud forgo,
And deign to bless the nuptial hour   405
Of Cranstoun's Lord and Teviot's Flower.

XXVI.

She look'd to river, look'd to hill,
  Thought on the Spirit's prophecy,
Then broke her silence stern and still,—
  "Not you, but Fate, has vanquish'd me.   410
Their influence kindly stars may shower
On Teviot's tide and Branksome's tower,
  For pride is quell'd, and love is free."—
She took fair Margaret by the hand,
Who, breathless, trembling, scarce might stand; 415
  That hand to Cranstoun's lord gave she:—
"As I am true to thee and thine,
Do thou be true to me and mine!
  This clasp of love our bond shall be;

For this is your betrothing day,   420
And all these noble lords shall stay,
To grace it with their company."—

XXVII.

All as they left the listed plain,
Much of the story she did gain;
How Cranstoun fought with Deloraine,   425
And of his page, and of the Book
Which from the wounded knight he took;
And how he sought her castle high,
That morn, by help of gramarye;
How, in Sir William's armour dight,   430
Stolen by his page, while slept the knight,
He took on him the single fight.
But half his tale he left unsaid,
And linger'd till he joined the maid.—
Cared not the Ladye to betray   435
Her mystic arts in view of day;
But well she thought, ere midnight came,
Of that strange page the pride to tame,
From his foul hands the Book to save,
And send it back to Michael's grave.—   440
Needs not to tell each tender word
'Twixt Margaret and 'twixt Cranstoun's lord;
Nor how she told of former woes,
And how her bosom fell and rose,
While he and Musgrave bandied blows.—   445
Needs not these lovers' joys to tell:
One day, fair maids, you 'll know them well.

XXVIII.

William of Deloraine, some chance
Had waken'd from his deathlike trance;
And taught that, in the listed plain,   450
Another, in his arms and shield,
Against fierce Musgrave axe did wield,
    Under the name of Deloraine.
Hence, to the field, unarm'd, he ran,
And hence his presence scared the clan,   455
Who held him for some fleeting wraith,
And not a man of blood and breath.
    Not much this new ally he loved,
    Yet, when he saw what hap had proved,

He greeted him right heartilie :   460
He would not waken old debate,
For he was void of rancorous hate,
   Though rude, and scant of courtesy;
In raids he spilt but seldom blood,
Unless when men-at-arms withstood,   465
Or, as was meet, for deadly feud.
He ne'er bore grudge for stalwart blow,
Ta'en in fair fight from gallant foe :
   And so 't was seen of him, e'en now,
     When on dead Musgrave he look'd down ; 470
   Grief darken'd on his rugged brow,
     Though half disguisèd with a frown ;
And thus, while sorrow bent his head,
His foeman's epitaph he made.

XXIX.

" Now, Richard Musgrave, liest thou here !   475
   I ween, my deadly enemy ;
For, if I slew thy brother dear,
   Thou slew'st a sister's son to me ;
And when I lay in dungeon dark,
   Of Naworth Castle, long months three,   480
Till ransom'd for a thousand mark,
   Dark Musgrave, it was long of thee.
And, Musgrave, could our fight be tried,
   And thou wert now alive, as I,
No mortal man should us divide,   485
   Till one, or both of us, did die :
Yet rest thee God ! for well I know
I ne'er shall find a nobler foe.
In all the northern counties here,
Whose word is Snaffle, spur, and spear,   490
Thou wert the best to follow gear !
'T was pleasure, as we look'd behind,
To see how thou the chase could'st wind,
Cheer the dark blood-hound on his way,
And with the bugle rouse the fray !   495
I 'd give the lands of Deloraine,
Dark Musgrave were alive again."—

XXX.

So mourn'd he, till Lord Dacre's band
Were bowning back to Cumberland.

They raised brave Musgrave from the field,   500
And laid him on his bloody shield;
On levell'd lances, four and four,
By turns, the noble burden bore.
Before, at times, upon the gale,
Was heard the Minstrel's plaintive wail   505
Behind, four priests, in sable stole,
Sung requiem for the warrior's soul:
Around, the horsemen slowly rode;
With trailing pikes the spearmen trode;
And thus the gallant knight they bore,   510
Through Liddesdale to Leven's shore;
Thence to Holme Coltrame's lofty nave,
And laid him in his father's grave.

THE harp's wild notes, though hush'd the song,
The mimic march of death prolong;   515
Now seems it far, and now a-near,
Now meets, and now eludes the ear;
Now seems some mountain side to sweep,
Now faintly dies in valley deep;
Seems now as if the Minstrel's wail,   520
Now the sad requiem, loads the gale;
Last, o'er the warrior's closing grave,
Rung the full choir in choral stave.

After due pause, they bade him tell,
Why he, who touch'd the harp so well,   525
Should thus, with ill-rewarded toil,
Wander a poor and thankless soil,
When the more generous Southern Land
Would well requite his skilful hand.

The Aged Harper, howsoe'er   530
His only friend, his harp, was dear,
Liked not to hear it rank'd so high
Above his flowing poesy:
Less liked he still, that scornful jeer
Misprised the land he loved so dear;   535
High was the sound, as thus again
The Bard resumed his minstrel strain.

NOTES.

CANTO FIFTH.

Towards the end of the fourth canto, the Minstrel was led to mention the old Harper who had taught him the manner of the combat between Musgrave and the supposed Deloraine. This occasions a lament for his old master and for all his brother minstrels who have died, leaving him the only representative of their order. At the opening of the fifth canto he pictures Nature as sharing in this lamentation.

The first two stanzas are very different from the greater part of the poem. They belong to the poetry of feeling and fancy, not to the poetry of incident, and as such they raise the *Lay* far above the level of ordinary ballad poetry.

1. Call it not vain. The Minstrel knows that the fancy *is* vain, unreal and impossible; but he appeals to his hearers to allow him to cherish the fancy.

1. they do not err. Poets often represent Nature as mourning for the poets who have sung of her. So Virgil in one of his *Eclogues* speaks of pines and fountains and groves calling for the absent one: in *Lycidas*, the elegy for his friend Edward King, Milton says—

"Thee, Shepherd, thee the woods, and desert caves
 With wild thyme and the gadding vine o'ergrown
 And all their echoes mourn";

in *Adonais*, the elegy for his friend John Keats, Shelley speaks of the winds sobbing and the flowers shedding tears of sorrow at his loss.

2. Poet. Ben Jonson says, "A poet is that which by the Greeks is called a maker, or a feigner; his art, an art of imitation; expressing the life of man in fit measure, numbers, and harmony: from the word *poiein*, which signifies to make or feign". The same idiom is found in other languages. O. E. *scóp* meant a poet, literally, a shaper, maker. The word *maker* was actually used for poet by Elizabethan authors, and in Scotland: cf. Dunbar's *Lament for the Makaris*.

4. obsequies, funeral ceremonies. (Lat. *obsequias*; *ob*, near; *sequi*, to follow.)

6. make moan, a poetical phrase for 'lament'.

8. tears of balm, *i.e.* balmy tears, a poetic name for the dew-drops that fall from the flowers and are supposed to contain some of their perfume. *Balm*, a contraction of *balsam*, a sweet-smelling herb.

8. distil, fall in single drops. (Lat. *stillare*; from *stilla*, a drop.)

9. Notice the order of the words. The natural order is, 'that breezes sigh through his loved groves'.

12. dirges, mournful songs. (Contracted from *dirige*, the first word of a solemn Latin hymn, *Dirige, Domine, deus meus, in conspectu tuo vitam meam*, 'Direct, O Lord my God, my life in Thy sight'.)

13. Scott now gives up the 'vain' fancy that cliffs and caverns, mountains and flowers, oaks and rivers mourn for the poet; and indulges in another fancy, that the mountains, and cliffs, and groves, &c., are haunted by spirits of those about whom the poet has sung —spirits that mourn because there is now no longer a poet to keep their memory alive.

13. in sooth, in truth.

13. mortal urn, the tomb. Urns were in old times used to enclose the ashes of dead bodies, which were burnt instead of being buried; hence the general poetic use of the word as meaning 'tomb'.

14. inanimate, lifeless. (Lat. *anima*, breath, life.)

16. vocal, as if possessing voice. (Lat. *vocalis*; *vox*, voice.)

17. else, otherwise.

20. The antecedent of whose is those in line 17. The clause "with the poet's parting breath" is adverbial to *feels*; the meaning is that when the poet dies, the persons who, though dead, have lived in the poet's song, now die again, since they cease to be commemorated.

21. shade, spirit.

23. rose and hawthorn, often mentioned in connection with lovers: see note on canto ii. 317.

24. gentle is fittingly applied to the Minstrel as the poet of love: it would not be fitting in connection with the "phantom Knight" or the "feudal song".

25. phantom, ghostly, spectral. (Gk. *phantasma*, something shown.)

27. Mounts. The phantom knight is spoken of as riding on the wind as on a horse.

27. amain, with force. (*a*, O. E. prefix; *mægn*, strength.)

29. antique. Since this word must be accented on the first syllable in order to preserve the rhythm, it is probably used as Shakespeare and Milton use it, namely as 'ornamented', 'quaintly carved'. Cf. *Hamlet*, ii. 2. 491, "his antique (*i.e.* decorated) sword"; *Il Penseroso*, 158, "antick (*i.e.* ornamented) pillars". The derivation is from Lat. *antiquus*, old.

29. crownlet, small crown, coronet. The word is used only by Scott. (-*let*, the diminutive ending: cf. 'corslet', 'rivulet', 'goblet', &c.)

30. feudal song, song composed by the poet as a feudal servant of the chief. See note on *feudal*, canto i. 76.

32. thanedom, the lands which he ruled as thane. *Thane*, or *thegn*, was an O. E. title of nobility. The E. suffix -*dom* marks power or state.

37. unstrung; either (1) deprived altogether of strings; cf. the "unstringed viol" in *Richard II.* i. 3. 162; or (2) with the strings loosened, not strung up. The second alternative is perhaps the better here, because the harp would naturally be neglected, but not necessarily destroyed, at the Minstrel's death.

39. The Minstrel's story is here resumed.

42. martial powers, warlike forces. *Martial* is from *Mars*, the Roman god of war.

45. columns dun, the columns of advancing soldiers, which the clouds of dust caused to appear dun-colour'd.

46. 'Flashed moment by moment in reflection of the sun's rays.' **Momentary** = 'momentarily', and expresses the fact that the spears of each line of soldiers came for a moment into a position from which they flashed a reflection towards the onlookers, then passed on, making way for the next line; and so on.

47. fair. This may be (1) an adjective qualifying *banners*, "feudal banners fair" being quite in Milton's manner; cf. "native woodnotes wild", *L'Allegro*, 134; or (2) a predicative adjective referring to *bands*. This depends on whether *banners* or *bands* is the subject of *display'd*. If *banners*, then *display'd* must mean 'revealed', 'showed who they were'. If *bands*, then *display'd* has the usual meaning, 'raised and held unfurled'.

49. Vails, it avails; **vails not**, it is of no use.

50. The relative *that*, subject of *came*, is omitted.

50. Middle Marches, one of the three parts into which the Border lands were divided.

51. **The Bloody Heart** was blazoned on the banner of the Douglases. ·It was chosen because it was to a Lord James Douglas that Robert Bruce committed his heart to be carried to the Holy Land.

52. **Douglas, Archibald Douglas,** 7th earl of Angus.

53. **spurn,** kick up their heels; an active verb used intransitively.

54. **Seven Spears of Wedderburne,** the seven sons of Sir David Home of Wedderburn, slain at Flodden.

56. **Swinton.** "At the battle of Beaugé, in France, the Duke of Clarence, brother of Henry V., was unhorsed by Sir John Swinton, who distinguished him by a coronet of precious stones which he wore round his crest." (Scott.)

56. **in rest.** The 'rest' was a loop or hook in which the spear was supported when couched ready for the charge.

59. **Nor** list I, nor does it please me. *List* (O. E. *hlystan*) is properly an impersonal verb, requiring a dative case. See "him listed", canto ii. 141.

60. **Merse,** one of the three divisions of Berwickshire.

60. **Lammermore,** a ridge of rough ground in Berwick and Haddington shires.

62. **the crest of Old Dunbar.** "The Earls of Home, descendants of the Dunbars, carried a lion rampant, argent " (heraldic terms for the figure of a lion on its hind legs, worked in silver). The family war-cry was "A Home! a Home!"

63. **Hepburn's mingled banners.** "The Hepburns, a powerful family in East Lothian, were usually in close alliance with the Homes."

69. **Meet,** suitable, fit.

71. **ta'en,** taken, *i.e.* chosen, fixed : cf. 'take a holiday '.

73. **pray'd them dear,** begged them 'dearly ', *i.e.* as though she had set her heart on their consent.

76. **cheer,** hospitality.

77. **bade to feast,** invited to the feast.

79. **Seneschal,** steward. See note on canto iii. 341.

82, 83. 'Howard accepted the invitation; no bolder soldier was ever dubbed a knight.' **Than,** properly a conjunction, here takes after it a pronoun in the objective case like a preposition.

83. **dubb'd,** made a knight by tapping on the shoulder with the flat of the sword.

87. pavilion, tent. (So called from a supposed resemblance to he outspread wings of a butterfly: Lat. *papilio*.)

88. noble Dame, the Duchess of Monmouth: see Introduction o canto i. line 37.

90. Deeming, thinking, considering.

91. set, made.

93. 'Were inspired with no other wish than to shed blood.' Cf. *Acts*, ix. 1, where Saul (afterwards Paul) is said to have been 'breathing out threatenings and slaughter".

97. sate them, reflexive; *sate* would be sufficient of itself.

100. spear is object after **grasp'd:** notice the inverted order.

101. mailed gauntlet, glove covered with a fine steel net-work.

101. clasp'd. The gauntlet is said to 'clasp' the hand which it :overs.

102. interchanged, lit. given in exchange: a curious way of ;aying that hands were 'shaken'.

102. dear, friendly.

103. visors, the movable front parts of the helmets, protecting he face.

105. 'Shared in food and drink in a friendly way.'

106. drove the jolly bowl about. This may mean either (1) passed the wine-cup merrily round, *jolly* in this case being a 'transferred epithet', applied to the bowl because of its effect on the drinkers; or (2) played the game of bowls, a favourite game in England and Scotland. As the next lines contain references to other games it is not improbable that (2) is what Scott meant.

107. chased the day, made the days pass quickly, made the time fly.

109. rout, disorderly throng.

110. 'Eagerly played at football.' So 'pursuit' is used in the sense of an occupation to which a man is devoted. Scott says: "The foot-ball was anciently a very favourite sport all through Scotland, but especially upon the Borders". The same is true at the present day.

115. Had, would have, as in line 117.

119. whinger, a short hanger used as a knife at meals and as a sword in fights.

121. 'Would have been plunged into men's bodies instead of being returned harmlessly to their sheaths.'

122–24. Scott notes that "notwithstanding the constant wa upon the Borders...the inhabitants on either side do not appear have regarded each other with that violent and personal animosi which might have been expected". In times of truce they frequent met in friendly intercourse. Instances of such friendly meeting between rival armies are not uncommon in history, as for instanc during Marlborough's campaigns.

125. But yet. These words imply that, though such terrib things as have just been described might have happened at ar moment at the blast of a bugle, *yet* no such event happened to brin the merriment to a tragic end.

128. wassel, revelry, merriment. Usually spelt *wassail*, fro O. E. *waes hael*, 'be of health', a common drinking salutation.

130. latticed windows, windows made of strips which crosse one another like net-work.

132. Divided square, divided into squares by the lattice-work

133. flakes. Seen from below, the beams of light issuing fron the square panes of glass seemed to overlay one another like flakes

134. Nor less, *i.e.* not less at night than during the day.

135. beakers, goblets, wine-cups. The word appears in differer forms in various languages.

136. frequent, frequently: adj. for adverb.

139. Give should be *gave*, so as to correspond with the past tens *ran*, in line 137. The occasional use of the present tense for th past gives vividness to a narrative, but here it is probably used onl because in the next two lines a present tense, *proclaim*, is wanted, t rime with *name*.

139. watchword. Scott quotes an extract from an old authe who complains of the noisy whooping, whistling, and calling of watcl words with which the Borderers disturbed the night, contrary to th usage of war.

142. fainter still, constantly becoming fainter.

144. you might hear; a kind of impersonal use of *you*, commo enough in modern colloquial speech.

147. The challenge of his watch. It was the duty of th sentinel when he heard footsteps to demand of the comer the watcl word. The 'watch', that is, the company who came to reliev guard, would of course know and give this word.

148. dark profound. There is no doubt that *profound* is here noun, meaning the wide deep space between Branksome hill, wher the imaginary hearer is, and the "nether lawn", from which th sounds ring out.   The word, like the Latin word *profundum* (deep), whence it comes, is thus not seldom used by the poets.   Milton has "the void profound of unessential night" (*Paradise Lost*, ii. 438) and "I travel this profound" (*id.* ii. 980).   Dryden, Wordsworth, Shelley, and Mrs. Browning afford instances, and Pope (*Iliad*, xxiv. 106) has this very phrase:

> "Down plunged the maid (the parted waves resound);
> She plunged, and instant shot *the dark profound*",

where, however, "dark profound" means the sea.

150. nether lawn, the grassy space surrounding the castle. (*Nether*, lower, comparative adj. due to an O. E. adv. *nither*, downward.)

152. pales, palings, stakes, to form the fence.

153. lists, space marked out for the fight, enclosed by barriers.

154. Against, so as to provide for; a sense derived from its proper meaning 'in opposition to.'   Cf. *Genesis*, xliii. 25, "And they made ready the present against Joseph came at noon".

155-165. Notice the picture: Margaret, filled with a strange, ominous anxiety (like Antonio at the beginning of the *Merchant of Venice*), leaving the scene of merriment in which she could not join, and so pre-occupied as not to observe the sighs with which her departure is marked by the noble warriors who are hopelessly in love with her.

161. many a bold ally, subject to *strove to win*, like *many a noble warrior*.

163. All, used intensively, as in "All in a hot and copper sky" (Coleridge, *Ancient Mariner*, 111).

163. bower, private room.   See note on canto i. introd. 28.

165. By times, betimes, *i.e.* by the proper time, early.   *Be* is an old form of *by*.

166. repose.   See note on line 139 above.

173. the livelong yesterday, all the previous day.

178. Blessed Mary! an exclamation which rose naturally to the lips in the 16th century, when nearly everybody was a Roman Catholic.   Such exclamations, of surprise or fear or awe, are not unfrequent in poetry.   Coleridge has "Jesu Maria!", Keats "Good saints!", Wordsworth even "Dear God!"

179. Secure, having the *feeling* of security, without anxiety. (Lat. *se*, for *sine*, without; *cura*, care.)   This use of the word was common in the 16th-18th centuries.

179. Ousenam, or *Oxnam,* between Branksome and Jedburgh.

185. Queen Mary, Mary of Guise, widow of James V., and at this time Regent.

187. buy his life a day, save his life for one day.

188. hazard, risk.

189. bethink you of, remember.

189. spell, a magical form of words.

191. This, *i.e.* the spell.

192. glamour, the magic power by which objects are made to appear different from the reality. See note on canto iii. 103. *Glamour* is used here as an adjective.

193. Hermitage, a castle in Roxburghshire, near the s.w. extremity of the Border. It being the property of the Douglas family, a 'knight from Hermitage' would be welcome at Branksome.

196. For all the vassalage, in spite of all the vassals who were keeping guard. *For all* is a common phrase, *all,* however, not usually qualifying the following noun, but meaning 'all that...could do'. Cf. Milton, *Nativity Hymn,* 69—

> "The stars
> ...will not take their flight,
> For all the morning light".

Vassalage, properly an abstract noun meaning 'the state of being a vassal or dependant', is here used as a collective noun; *-age* is strictly a Norman-French collective affix.

197. quaint, strange, odd. (The word, derived from Lat. *cognitus,* well-known, through O. F. *cointe,* first meant 'known' (cf. acquaint); then 'neat', and so 'pretty', 'nice'. These last meanings are probably due to a fancied derivation from Lat. *comptus,* adorned. The modern meaning is 'odd and old-fashioned'.)

198. azure, blue. (From an Arabic word, the name of a blue-coloured precious stone.)

203. mused, wondered, meditated.

205. To bring, in bringing.

205. round, about.

206. Spenser wrote a poem which he called *Hymn to Heavenlie Love.*

207. sprite, contracted form of *spirit.* Cf. 'spritely'.

215, 216. 'The page's low mind could not understand the purity of their love.'

217-222. Lockhart compares Byron's *Giaour*—

> "Yes, love, indeed, is light from heaven,
> A spark of that immortal fire
> With angels shared, by Alla given,
> To lift from earth our low desire".

219. fantasy, fancy.

224. silver link, silken tie. *Silver* is a symbol of brightness and purity, *silk* of softness and fineness.

224. Cranstoun's visit to Margaret was natural, in view of the fact that he was about to engage in a deadly fight. Scott does not tell us, but it is implied in lines 280-1 and 443-5, that Cranstoun told Margaret at this nocturnal interview of his determination to personate Deloraine.

230. port, "a martial piece of music, adapted to the bagpipe". (A Gaelic word.)

234. Ettrick wood, Ettrick Forest, in Selkirkshire.

237. bandied, exchanged. 'To bandy' is properly 'to beat to and fro', and was a common expression in the game of tennis.

242. The second 'twixt is unnecessary.

243. 'gan is strictly correct without the apostrophe, as the past tense of O. E. *ginnan*, not a shortened form of *began*.

243. to reckon kin and rent, to consider and state the degree of relationship in which they stood to the Ladye's family, and the rent they paid—urging that the nearest in blood and the one who paid highest rent should fight for Deloraine.

244. frowning brow on brow. Cf. *Richard II*. i. 1. 15, "face to face And frowning brow to brow".

249. craved the combat due, begged that the combat might be allowed to take place as arranged.

250. her charm successful, her charm (to have been) successful. See canto iii. stanza xxiii. The Ladye, finding Deloraine wounded after his encounter with Cranstoun, stanched his blood with a charm, and promised

> "That he should be whole man and sound
> Within the course of a night and day".

252. for, in order to reach. See note on canto iv. 28.

257. feats, famous deeds. (O. F. *faict,* Lat. *factum,* from *facere,* to do.)

258. garb, dress. (From an old word meaning 'something got ready'.)

258. Flemish ruff, frilled collar, called 'Flemish' either because actually made in Flanders or because, having been originally made there, ruffs of this kind were generally known as Flemish. In the Middle Ages the Flemings were famous cloth weavers, and Edward III. introduced Flemish weavers into England.

259. doublet, close-fitting garment, so called perhaps because it was wadded and so made doubly thick.

259. buff, properly a kind of leather made from the skin of the ox. It was very thick.

260. slash'd, having openings cut in it, through which the satin lining showed.

262. Poland fur. The Russians and Poles wear thick furs during their long and bitter winter.

263. hose, leg-coverings, reaching from the thighs to the feet.

264. Bilboa blade. Bilbao, a town near the N.E. coast of Spain, was famous for its iron and steel. The fame of its manufactures is shown by the word *bilbo,* used by Shakespeare and other Elizabethan authors for a sword: cf. Scott's *Woodstock,* ch. iii. "My tough old knight and you were at drawn bilbo". Weapons often take their names from the places where they are manufactured: cf. 'Damascus blade', 'Enfield rifle', and 'bayonet' from Bayonne. So "Jedwood-axe" in canto i. 39.

264. Marchmen, dwellers on the 'marches' or borderlands.

265. studded, set with ornamental studs or knobs. These were often of gold or precious stones. Cf. *Taming of the Shrew,* Induction, **2.** 42, where the Lord promises Christopher Sly the tinker that his horses' harness "shall be studded all with gold and pearl".

269. palfrey, a riding-horse. See note to canto i. introd. 13.

270. foot-cloth, a long, often handsomely decorated, covering for a horse.

271. wimple, a covering for the head, sides of the face, and neck, once worn by women out-of-doors, now worn by nuns.

272. chaplet, wreath.

274. Angus. See note on line 52 above.

277. Had strove, would have striven.

280. cause of terror. See note above at line 224.

283. graced, added grace to, honoured.

284. Prize of the field. According to the agreement made (see canto iv. stanza xxxii.), if Deloraine should prove victor the boy was to be restored to his mother; if Musgrave should conquer, the boy was to remain as a hostage with the English.

285. to view, *view* is either a noun or a verb. If a noun, *view* will be used in the same sense as in the phrases 'on view', 'exposed to view'; if a verb, the meaning is that the boy was led out to see the fight on which his fate depended. The former is the more probable explanation.

290. leading-staffs, short sticks or batons carried as marks of their authority. The 'warder' thrown down by King Richard to stop the combat between Bolingbroke and Mowbray (*Richard II.* i. 3. 122) was a similar staff.

291. marshals, officers appointed to manage the combat. (Lit. 'horse-servants', O. F. *mareschal*, from O. Germ. *marah*, horse (cf. mare); *scalh*, a servant. *Marshal* is now a military title.)

291. mortal field, the field in which a deadly fight was about to take place. (Lat. *mors*, death.)

293. 'A similar position with regard to any advantage to be derived from sun and wind.' The fight would not be fair if one combatant was dazzled by the sunlight or troubled by the wind.

295. King of England, **Queen** of Scotland.

296. lasts should be *lasted.*

301. alternate Heralds. *Alternate*, an adjective qualifying *Heralds*, is for 'alternately', an adverb qualifying *spoke*. They spoke *alternately*, that is, in turn, one after the other.

302-318. With these speeches of the Heralds compare similar speeches in *Richard II.* act i. scene 3. Jeffrey says: "The whole scene of the duel, or judicious combat, is conducted according to the strictest ordinances of chivalry, and delineated with all the minuteness of an ancient romancer. The modern reader will probably find it rather tedious; all but the concluding stanzas, which are in a loftier measure."

303. freely born, free-born. *Freely* is quite incorrect, the meaning, 'born a free man', not being expressed by an adverb qualifying *born*. But Scott had no scruple in suiting his metre in this way.

305. despiteous, malicious, cruel. The word, not now in common use, is found in Spenser and Shakespeare and other older poets. In Chaucer it appears in the earlier form *despitous*; he says of his 'poor Parson' (*Prologue*, 516), "He was to sinful man nought despitous", where the word has the meaning 'pitiless'.

305. scathe, harm. (O.E. *sceatha.*)

308. This, this charge, accusation.

311. strain, descent, kindred. (O.E. *stréon,* product.) The word has several forms; in Chaucer it is *streen,* in Spenser, *strene.*

313. coat, *i.e.* coat of arms. A disgrace falling on a family was spoken of as staining their coats of arms. Hence the title of Brown-ing's play, *A Blot on the 'Scutcheon.*

315. That is, prove by giving Musgrave mortal wounds. It was assumed that the conqueror was in the right.

322. poised, balanced on the arm.

323. measured, cautious and slow.

324. did close, came to close quarters, fought hand to hand.

327. to, in response to, under the blows of the axes.

334. claymore, a large broadsword. (Gaelic *claidheamh mor*; the first syllable connected with Lat. *gladius,* sword; the last with Lat. *magnus,* great.)

334. bayonet. Bayonets are said to have been first made at Bayonne, in S.W. France.—For the contest of claymore with bayonet see note on canto iv. 21.

335. through red blood. By a poetical extravagance the war-horse may be said here to dash through *its own* red blood. But perhaps the phrase means 'through heaps of the slain and wounded', as though their blood formed a running stream.

336. reeling strife, men swaying this way and that as they fought. *Strife,* an abstract noun, is put for the men striving.

337. for must be understood differently with *death* and with *life. For death* means 'because of', 'for fear of death'; *for life* means 'on behalf of', 'in order to save his life'.

338–367. These lines contain real instances of the historic present, the use of the present tense making the description more vivid and real.

343. visor, movable front part of the helmet to protect the face.

344. gorget, throat-armour. (F. *gorge,* throat; cf. *corslet* from *corse.*)

346. bootless, useless. (O.E. *bót,* profit.)

46. Friar. The friars (O.F. *frere,* from Lat. *frater,* brother) were originally a preaching brotherhood.

348. shriven. To 'shrive' a man is to hear his confession and give him absolution or pardon. (Hence *Shrove*-Tuesday, the day on which people were shriven before the Lenten fast.) Great importance is attached to this in the Roman Catholic church.

351. naked. This implies that the Friar was one of the poorer brotherhoods. The original friars bound themselves by a vow of poverty, but they soon became rich. Chaucer's "Frere" had no "thredbare cope" like a "poure scoler", but "was lik a maister or a pope".

351. with red, the blood of the knights.

353. the shouts on high, the loud shouts which filled the air. The rough warriors thought nothing of the dying man.

358. the crucifix. For the reason why it was held before him cf. *Marmion*, vi. stanza xxxii.—

> "O look, my son, upon yon sign
> Of the Redeemer's grace divine;
> O, think on faith and bliss".

The death of Marmion has several points of likeness with the death of Musgrave here.

359. darkening eye, eye to which all things are becoming dark in death.

364. Pours, as though the "ghostly comfort" were a healing balm.

364. ghostly, spiritual. (O. E. *gastlic*, of a spirit.)

371. beaver, the mouthpiece of the helmet, which could be moved to allow the wearer to drink. (F. *bavière*, a child's bib. The spelling here is perhaps due to confusion with 'beaver-hat'.)

373. gratulating, congratulating, complimenting on his success.

378. panic, here an adjective, 'in extreme and causeless fear'. From *Pan*, the Greek rural god, who was supposed to cause such fear.)

382. haggard, with pale and worn face. Skeat says that the word, originally *hagged* (*i.e.* like a witch, hag), was mis-spelt through confusion with *haggard*, meaning 'wild', and said of a hawk (O. F. *hagard*, wild).

383. as, as if he were, as being.

384. armed, an epithet transferred from the men who were armed.

387. Vaulted, leapt. (O. F. *volter*, to leap, through Ital. from Lat. *volvere*, to turn round.)

392. this fair prize. We can imagine that Cranstoun had double meaning, referring to the young boy, and also, with a mear ing look at the Ladye, to Margaret.

397. The Ladye had been doubly anxious—anxious that th fight should end in favour of the supposed Deloraine, in order tha she might regain her son; and troubled because, though she ha said that Deloraine should be "whole man and sound", yet sh feared his strength might fail. Her magic powers are of little us to her all through.

400. Me lists not tell, it does not please me to tell, I do nc wish to tell. See note on *list*, canto ii. line 141.

404. feud, quarrel.

404. forgo, give up. The prefix *for* has an intensive force, wit the sense of 'away', as in 'forget', 'forswear', &c.

405. bless the nuptial hour; in prose, consent to their mar riage. (*Nuptial*, from Lat. *nubere*, to marry.)

407. river...hill. Cf. canto i. stanza xv., where the River Spiri and the Mountain Spirit converse.

408. prophecy. Cf. canto i. 177—

"—no kind influence deign they shower
On Teviot's tide and Branksome's tower
Till pride be quell'd and love be free".

410. Not you, including Cranstoun and those who had pleade< his cause.

411. influence, an astrological term, denoting the inflowin; power which the heavenly bodies were supposed to have on th lives of men.

413. quell'd, destroyed, vanquished.

415. might, could.

420. betrothing day. The betrothal was in olden times, an< still is on the Continent, a far more important and binding ceremon than it is now.

The story is now practically finished, but the sixth canto afford an opportunity for the description of the marriage feast and th pilgrimage to Melrose, and for the introduction of the Minstrel' songs, including the beautiful *Rosabelle*.

423. All, even, just; used for emphasis.

428. high, in its figurative sense.

429. gramarye, magic. See note on canto iii. line 140.

430. dight, clad. The proper sense is 'prepared'.

436. in view of day, in daylight. Magic, being unlawful and elieved to be connected with evil spirits, was fitly practised at night.

437. well she thought, she thoroughly determined.

440. Michael's grave, the grave of the wizard Michael Scott at Ielrose Abbey, from which the Book of Magic had been taken by)eloraine at the Ladye's bidding.

441. Needs not, there is no need. *Needs* is used impersonally.

448. some chance, and not the Ladye's magic charms.

450. taught, informed.

456. held him for, 'took' him for, considered him to be.

456. wraith, "the spectral apparition of a living person". The /ord is generally used as meaning the ghost-like form of a person ıst dead or about to die, appearing to some one connected with him.

459. what hap had proved, what the fortune of the combat ad been.

461. debate, strife, contest. (Lat. *de*, down; *batuere*, to beat; hrough O. F. *debatre*.)

462. void of, free from. (Lat. *vidus*, empty.)

462. rancorous, intensely spiteful. (Lat. *rancor*, a bad smell.)

466. meet, fitting (from the Borderer's point of view).

466. for, on account of.

474. epitaph, strictly an inscription on a tomb. (Gk. *epi*, upon; *iphos*, tomb.) Here it is used almost in the sense of 'eulogy', a peech of praise.

477. if, granting that.

478. a sister's son to me, one who was *to me* in the relation-hip of *a sister's son*.

480. Naworth Castle, Howard's castle near Carlisle.

481. mark, worth 13*s.* 4*d.* In expressions of number, weight, &c., he sign of the plural is often omitted as here. Cf. 'ten stone'; also *The Tempest,* i. 2. 53, "Twelve year since, Miranda, twelve year ince".

482. long of, because of; usually 'along of'.

487. rest thee God! may God give thee rest.

490. word, watchword, motto.

490. Snaffle, spur, and spear. Scott says that he took this :om Drayton's *Polyolbion*, song 13—

"The lands that over Ouse to Berwick forth do bear,
　　Have for their blazon had the snaffle, spur, and spear ".

(*Snaffle*, a horse's bridle: Dutch *snavel*, a muzzle.)　This mott
implies the readiness in which the Borderers always kept themselve
and their horses for the sudden outbreaks.

491. to follow gear, to go in pursuit of those who had carrie
off booty. *Gear*, from O. E. *gearwe*, things got ready, was applie
to all kinds of things: armour, tools, dress, &c.

492. as we look'd behind.　Deloraine recalls the time whe
he was one of a marauding party who were being chased by Mus
grave.　The skilful way in which the pursuit was managed extorte
admiration even from the pursued.

493. chase, that which was the object of the chase.

493. wind, track along their winding course.

494. the dark blood-hound.　Scott notes that blood-hound
were employed even up to his own day to track marauders on th
Borders.　They were similarly used in America to track runawa
slaves.

495. rouse the fray, stir up the pursuers to the fight.

499. bowning, going.　In iii. 392 "bowne them" means 'mak
themselves ready to go '.　See note there.

502. levell'd lances, lances ranged horizontally, and either rest
ing on the shoulders of the bearers, or held with hands lowered.

502. four and four, referring to the bearers, not the lances
Sets of four men took it in turns to carry the body.

504. upon the gale.　There has been no mention of a storm,
so that *gale*, properly meaning 'a furious storm ', here means '
gentle breeze ', as in Milton's *Paradise Regained*, ii. 364, "winds o
gentlest gale Arabian odours fanned ", and in Keble's hymn—

　　　"Softer than gale at morning prime,
　　　　Hovered His holy Dove ".

505. the Minstrel's plaintive wail.　It does not seem prob
able that there was only *one* minstrel.　Hence *the Minstrel* must b
taken as a general or collective term.　*Wail*, the wailing, mournfu
sound produced by the musical instruments.

506. in sable stole.　The 'stole' was properly a long tunic
reaching to the ground. Spenser and Milton, however, use the word
as meaning 'hood '; cf. *Il Penseroso*, 35—

　　　" And *sable stole* of cypress lawn,
　　　　Over thy decent *shoulders* drawn ".

This is perhaps what is meant here, though the ecclesiastical stole is strictly "a long narrow scarf, with fringed ends", worn about the neck and hanging down in front over each shoulder.   sable, black, from the black-furred animal of that name.

507. requiem, a solemn hymn in which God is asked to give rest to the souls of the dead.   It is so called from the first word of the Latin: *Requiem aeternam dona eis, Domine* ('Rest eternal give to them, O Lord').   (Lat. *requies*, rest.)

509. trailing pikes, pikes reversed and trailed along the ground, as a sign of mourning.

511. Leven, a small river in Cumberland.

512. Holme Coltrame or **Cultram**, in N. Cumberland, on the Solway Firth.   It had a famous Cistercian abbey (probably the "lofty nave" mentioned here), within whose precincts, and not at Melrose, Michael Scott the wizard was, according to one tradition, buried.

512. nave, church.   Strictly, only the body of the church, without the aisles; as Skeat says, "by the common similitude which likened Christ's church to a ship".   (Lat. *navis*, ship.)

515. Continue the music in imitation of the dead march or funeral music played at the funeral of Musgrave.   This stanza admirably expresses the effect of the Minstrel's music on the fair listeners.   As he played, they seemed to be able to see the mournful procession crossing mountain and valley, then entering the church, and then the burial amid the solemn strains of the full choir.

516. a-near, a poetical word, found also in Coleridge's *Ancient Mariner*, 310—

> "And soon I heard a roaring wind :
>   It did not come anear".

The *a-* is a corruption of the preposition *on*, as in 'amain'.

517. eludes, avoids as though mockingly.   (Lat. *e*, out; *ludere*, to play.)

520. Seems, *i.e.* it seems.

521. loads the gale, fills the air.   See note on line 504.

523. stave, song, stanza.   This sense of the word has nothing to do with *stave* as meaning the series of parallel lines on which music is written.

524. they, the Duchess and her ladies.

527. Wander, used here transitively.   So we can say 'roam the land', 'walk the street', 'sail the sea'.

527, 528. poor and thankless soil ... generous Southern Land. Though here the soil is mentioned, the disposition of the inhabitants is meant. As a matter of fact, the soil of England is richer than that of Scotland, and the Scotch are said to be correspondingly less open-handed than the English. Yet Scottish hospitality is proverbial.

530. howsoe'er, although.

534. scornful jeer, rather a strong expression to be applied to the ladies' remarks. The Duchess, too, was a Scotswoman. However, the complaint serves as an introduction to the splendid patriotic outburst at the opening of the next canto.

535. Misprised, slighted, set at a low price. (The word is also spelt 'misprized', the *s* being due to its derivation from Latin through O. F. *mespriser*.)

536. High, of lofty indignation.

CANTO SIXTH.

I.

BREATHES there the man, with soul so dead,
Who never to himself hath said,
  This is my own, my native land!
Whose heart hath ne'er within him burn'd,
As home his footsteps he hath turn'd,   5
  From wandering on a foreign strand!
If such there breathe, go, mark him well;
For him no Minstrel raptures swell;
High though his titles, proud his name,
Boundless his wealth as wish can claim;   10
Despite those titles, power, and pelf,
The wretch, concentred all in self,
Living, shall forfeit fair renown,
And, doubly dying, shall go down
To the vile dust, from whence he sprung,   15
Unwept, unhonour'd, and unsung.

II.

O Caledonia! stern and wild,
Meet nurse for a poetic child!
Land of brown heath and shaggy wood,
Land of the mountain and the flood,   20
Land of my sires! what mortal hand
Can e'er untie the filial band,
That knits me to thy rugged strand!
Still, as I view each well-known scene,
Think what is now, and what hath been,   25
Seems as, to me, of all bereft,
Sole friends thy woods and streams were left;
And thus I love them better still,
Even in extremity of ill.
By Yarrow's streams still let me stray,   30
Though none should guide my feeble way;
Still feel the breeze down Ettrick break,
Although it chill my wither'd cheek;
Still lay my head by Teviot Stone,
Though there, forgotten and alone,   35
The Bard may draw his parting groan.

III.

Not scorn'd like me! to Branksome Hall
The Minstrels came, at festive call;
Trooping they came, from near and far,
The jovial priests of mirth and war;   40
Alike for feast and fight prepared,
Battle and banquet both they shared.
Of late, before each martial clan,
They blew their death-note in the van,
But now, for every merry mate,   45
Rose the portcullis' iron grate;
They sound the pipe, they strike the string,
They dance, they revel, and they sing,
Till the rude turrets shake and ring.

IV.

Me lists not at this tide declare   50
   The splendour of the spousal rite,
How muster'd in the chapel fair
   Both maid and matron, squire and knight;
Me lists not tell of owches rare,
Of mantles green, and braided hair,   55
And kirtles furr'd with miniver;
What plumage waved the altar round,
How spurs and ringing chainlets sound;
And hard it were for bard to speak
The changeful hue of Margaret's cheek;   60
That lovely hue which comes and flies,
As awe and shame alternate rise!

V.

Some bards have sung, the Ladye high
Chapel or altar came not nigh;
Nor durst the rites of spousal grace,   65
So much she fear'd each holy place.
False slanders these:—I trust right well
She wrought not by forbidden spell;
For mighty words and signs have power
O'er sprites in planetary hour: 70
Yet scarce I praise their venturous part,
Who tamper with such dangerous art.
   But this for faithful truth I say,
     The Ladye by the altar stood,

Of sable velvet her array, 75
  And on her head a crimson hood,
With pearls embroider'd and entwined,
Guarded with gold, with ermine lined;
A merlin sat upon her wrist
Held by a leash of silken twist. 80

VI.

The spousal rites were ended soon:
'Twas now the merry hour of noon,
And in the lofty archéd hall
Was spread the gorgeous festival.
Steward and squire, with heedful haste, 85
Marshall'd the rank of every guest;
Pages, with ready blade, were there,
The mighty meal to carve and share:
O'er capon, heron-shew, and crane,
And princely peacock's gilded train, 90
And o'er the boar-head, garnish'd brave,
And cygnet from St. Mary's wave;
O'er ptarmigan and venison,
The priest had spoke his benison.
Then rose the riot and the din, 95
Above, beneath, without, within!
For, from the lofty balcony,
Rung trumpet, shalm, and psaltery:
Their clanging bowls old warriors quaff'd,
Loudly they spoke, and loudly laugh'd; 100
Whisper'd young knights, in tone more mild,
To ladies fair, and ladies smiled.
The hooded hawks, high perch'd on beam,
The clamour join'd with whistling scream,
And flapp'd their wings, and shook their bells, 105
In concert with the stag-hounds' yells.
Round go the flasks of ruddy wine,
From Bourdeaux, Orleans, or the Rhine;
Their tasks the busy sewers ply,
And all is mirth and revelry. 110

VII.

The Goblin Page, omitting still
No opportunity of ill,
Strove now, while blood ran hot and high,
To rouse debate and jealousy;

Till Conrad, Lord of Wolfenstein,   115
By nature fierce, and warm with wine,
And now in humour highly cross'd,
About some steeds his band had lost,
High words to words succeeding still,
Smote, with his gauntlet, stout Hunthill;   120
A hot and hardy Rutherford,
Whom men called Dickon Draw-the-sword.
He took it on the page's saye,
Hunthill had driven these steeds away.
Then Howard, Home, and Douglas rose,   125
The kindling discord to compose:
Stern Rutherford right little said,
But bit his glove, and shook his head.—
A fortnight thence, in Inglewood,
Stout Conrad, cold, and drench'd in blood,   130
His bosom gored with many a wound,
Was by a woodman's lyme-dog found;
Unknown the manner of his death,
Gone was his brand, both sword and sheath;
But ever from that time, 't was said,   135
That Dickon wore a Cologne blade.

VIII.

The dwarf, who fear'd his master's eye
Might his foul treachery espy,
Now sought the castle buttery,
Where many a yeoman, bold and free,   140
Revell'd as merrily and well
As those that sat in lordly selle.
Watt Tinlinn, there, did frankly raise
The pledge to Arthur Fire-the-Braes;
And he, as by his breeding bound,   145
To Howard's merry-men sent it round.
To quit them, on the English side,
Red Roland Forster loudly cried,
"A deep carouse to yon fair bride!"—
At every pledge, from vat and pail,   150
Foam'd forth in floods the nut-brown ale;
While shout the riders every one;
Such day of mirth ne'er cheer'd their clan,
Since old Buccleuch the name did gain,
When in the cleuch the buck was ta'en.   155

IX.

The wily page, with vengeful thought,
   Remember'd him of Tinlinn's yew,
And swore, it should be dearly bought
   That ever he the arrow drew.
First, he the yeoman did molest,   160
With bitter gibe and taunting jest;
Told, how he fled at Solway strife,
And how Hob Armstrong cheer'd his wife;
Then, shunning still his powerful arm,
At unawares he wrought him harm;   165
From trencher stole his choicest cheer,
Dash'd from his lips his can of beer;
Then, to his knee sly creeping on,
With bodkin pierced him to the bone:
The venom'd wound, and festering joint,   170
Long after rued that bodkin's point.
The startled yeoman swore and spurn'd,
And board and flagons overturn'd.
Riot and clamour wild began;
Back to the hall the Urchin ran;   175
Took in a darkling nook his post,
And grinn'd, and mutter'd, " Lost! lost! lost!"

X.

By this, the Dame, lest farther fray
Should mar the concord of the day,
Had bid the Minstrels tune their lay.   180
And first stept forth old Albert Græme,
The Minstrel of that ancient name:
Was none who struck the harp so well,
Within the Land Debateable;
Well friended, too, his hardy kin,   185
Whoever lost, were sure to win;
They sought the beeves that made their broth,
In Scotland and in England both.
In homely guise, as nature bade,
His simple song the Borderer said.   190

XI.

ALBERT GRÆME.

It was an English ladye bright,
   (The sun shines fair on Carlisle wall,)

F 2

And she would marry a Scottish knight,
    For Love will still be lord of all.

Blithely they saw the rising sun,   195
    When he shone fair on Carlisle wall;
But they were sad ere day was done,
    Though Love was still the lord of all.

Her sire gave brooch and jewel fine,
    Where the sun shines fair on Carlisle wall;   200
Her brother gave but a flask of wine,
    For ire that Love was lord of all.

For she had lands, both meadow and lea,
    Where the sun shines fair on Carlisle wall,
And he swore her death, ere he would see   205
    A Scottish knight the lord of all!

XII.

That wine she had not tasted well,
    (The sun shines fair on Carlisle wall,)
When dead, in her true love's arms, she fell,
    For Love was still the lord of all!   210

He pierced her brother to the heart,
    Where the sun shines fair on Carlisle wall:—
So perish all would true love part,
    That Love may still be lord of all!

And then he took the cross divine,   215
    (Where the sun shines fair on Carlisle wall,)
And died for her sake in Palestine,
    So Love was still the lord of all.

Now all ye lovers, that faithful prove,
    (The sun shines fair on Carlisle wall,)   220
Pray for their souls who died for love,
    For love shall still be lord of all!

XIII.

As ended Albert's simple lay,
    Arose a bard of loftier port;
For sonnet, rhyme, and roundelay,   225
    Renown'd in haughty Henry's court:

There rung thy harp, unrivall'd long,
Fitztraver of the silver song!
  The gentle Surrey loved his lyre—
    Who has not heard of Surrey's fame?   230
  His was the hero's soul of fire,
    And his the bard's immortal name,
And his was love, exalted high
By all the glow of chivalry.

XIV.

They sought, together, climes afar,   235
  And oft, within some olive grove,
When even came with twinkling star,
  They sung of Surrey's absent love.
His step the Italian peasant stay'd,
  And deem'd, that spirits from on high,   240
Round where some hermit saint was laid,
  Were breathing heavenly melody;
So sweet did harp and voice combine,
To praise the name of Geraldine.

XV.

Fitztraver! O what tongue may say   245
  The pangs thy faithful bosom knew,
When Surrey of the deathless lay,
  Ungrateful Tudor's sentence slew?
Regardless of the tyrant's frown,
His harp call'd wrath and vengeance down.   250
He left, for Naworth's iron towers,
Windsor's green glades, and courtly bowers,
And faithful to his patron's name,
With Howard still Fitztraver came;
Lord William's foremost favourite he,   255
And chief of all his minstrelsy.

XVI.

FITZTRAVER.

'Twas All-souls' eve, and Surrey's heart beat high;
  He heard the midnight bell with anxious start,

Which told the mystic hour, approaching nigh,
  When wise Cornelius promised, by his art,   26(
  To show to him the ladye of his heart,
Albeit betwixt them roar'd the ocean grim;
  Yet so the sage had hight to play his part,
That he should see her form in life and limb,
And mark, if still she loved, and still she thought o
     him.   26

XVII.

Dark was the vaulted room of gramarye,
  To which the wizard led the gallant Knight,
Save that before a mirror, huge and high,
  A hallow'd taper shed a glimmering light
  On mystic implements of magic might;   27(
On cross, and character, and talisman,
  And almagest, and altar, nothing bright:
For fitful was the lustre, pale and wan,
As watchlight by the bed of some departing man.

XVIII.

But soon, within that mirror huge and high,   27
  Was seen a self-emitted light to gleam;
And forms upon its breast the Earl 'gan spy,
  Cloudy and indistinct, as feverish dream;
  Till, slow arranging, and defined, they seem
To form a lordly and a lofty room,   28
  Part lighted by a lamp with silver beam,
Placed by a couch of Agra's silken loom,
And part by moonshine pale, and part was hid in gloom

XIX.

Fair all the pageant—but how passing fair
  The slender form, which lay on couch of Ind! 28
O'er her white bosom stray'd her hazel hair,
  Pale her dear cheek, as if for love she pined;
  All in her night-robe loose she lay reclined,
And, pensive, read from tablet eburnine,   28
  Some strain that seem'd her inmost soul to find:-
That favour'd strain was Surrey's raptured line,
That fair and lovely form, the Lady Geraldine.

XX.

Slow roll'd the clouds upon the lovely form,
  And swept the goodly vision all away—
So royal envy roll'd the murky storm   295
  O'er my belovéd Master's glorious day.
  Thou jealous, ruthless tyrant! Heaven repay
On thee, and on thy children's latest line,
  The wild caprice of thy despotic sway,
The gory bridal bed, the plunder'd shrine,   300
The murder'd Surrey's blood, the tears of Geraldine!

XXI.

Both Scots, and Southern chiers, prolong
Applauses of Fitztraver's song;
These hated Henry's name as death,
And those still held the ancient faith.—   305
Then, from his seat, with lofty air,
Rose Harold, bard of brave St. Clair;
St. Clair, who, feasting high at Home,
Had with that lord to battle come.
Harold was born where restless seas   310
Howl round the storm-swept Orcades;
Where erst St. Clairs held princely sway
O'er isle and islet, strait and bay;—
Still nods their palace to its fall,
Thy pride and sorrow, fair Kirkwall!—   315
Thence oft he mark'd fierce Pentland rave,
As if grim Odin rode her wave;
And watch'd, the whilst, with visage pale,
And throbbing heart, the struggling sail;
For all of wonderful and wild   320
Had rapture for the lonely child.

XXII.

And much of wild and wonderful
In these rude isles might fancy cull;
For thither came, in times afar,
Stern Lochlin's sons of roving war,   325
The Norsemen, train'd to spoil and blood,
Skill'd to prepare the raven's food;
Kings of the main their leaders brave,
Their barks the dragons of the wave.

And there, in many a stormy vale,   330
The Scald had told his wondrous tale;
And many a Runic column high
Had witness'd grim idolatry.
And thus had Harold, in his youth,
Learn'd many a Saga's rhyme uncouth,—   335
Of that Sea-Snake, tremendous curl'd,
Whose monstrous circle girds the world;
Of those dread Maids, whose hideous yell
Maddens the battle's bloody swell;
Of Chiefs, who, guided through the gloom   340
By the pale death-lights of the tomb,
Ransack'd the graves of warriors old,
Their falchions wrench'd from corpses' hold,
Waked the deaf tomb with war's alarms,
And bade the dead arise to arms!   345

With war and wonder all on flame,
To Roslin's bowers young Harold came,
Where, by sweet glen and greenwood tree,
He learn'd a milder minstrelsy;
Yet something of the Northern spell   350
Mix'd with the softer numbers well.

XXIII.

HAROLD.

O listen, listen, ladies gay!
  No haughty feat of arms I tell;
Soft is the note, and sad the lay,
  That mourns the lovely Rosabelle.   355

—"Moor, moor the barge, ye gallant crew!
  And, gentle ladye, deign to stay!
Rest thee in Castle Ravensheuch,
  Nor tempt the stormy firth to-day.

"The blackening wave is edged with white: 360
  To inch and rock the sea-mews fly;
The fishers have heard the Water-Sprite,
  Whose screams forbode that wreck is nigh.

"Last night the gifted Seer did view
  A wet shroud swathed round ladye gay;   365

Then stay thee, Fair, in Ravensheuch:
    Why cross the gloomy firth to-day?"—

"'T is not because Lord Lindesay's heir
    To-night at Roslin leads the ball,
But that my ladye-mother there   370
    Sits lonely in her castle-hall.

"'T is not because the ring they ride,
    And Lindesay at the ring rides well,
But that my sire the wine will chide,
    If 't is not fill'd by Rosabelle."—   375

O'er Roslin all that dreary night,
    A wondrous blaze was seen to gleam;
'T was broader than the watch-fire's light,
    And redder than the bright moon-beam.

It glared on Roslin's castled rock,   380
    It ruddied all the copse-wood glen;
'T was seen from Dryden's groves of oak,
    And seen from cavern'd Hawthornden.

Seem'd all on fire that chapel proud,
    Where Roslin's chiefs uncoffin'd lie,   385
Each Baron, for a sable shroud,
    Sheathed in his iron panoply.

Seem'd all on fire within, around,
    Deep sacristy and altar's pale;
Shone every pillar foliage-bound,   390
    And glimmer'd all the dead men's mail.

Blazed battlement and pinnet high,
    Blazed every rose-carved buttress fair—
So still they blaze, when fate is nigh
    The lordly line of high St. Clair.   395

There are twenty of Roslin's barons bold
    Lie buried within that proud chapelle;
Each one the holy vault doth hold—
    But the sea holds lovely Rosabelle!

And each St. Clair was buried there,   400
    With candle, with book, and with knell;
But the sea-caves rung, and the wild winds sung,
    The dirge of lovely Rosabelle.

XXIV.

So sweet was Harold's piteous lay,
  Scarce mark'd the guests the darken'd hall,   405
Though, long before the sinking day,
  A wondrous shade involved them all:
It was not eddying mist or fog,
Drain'd by the sun from fen or bog;
  Of no eclipse had sages told;   410
And yet, as it came on apace,
Each one could scarce his neighbour's face,
  Could scarce his own stretch'd hand behold.
A secret horror check'd the feast,
And chill'd the soul of every guest;   415
E'en the high Dame stood half aghast,
She knew some evil on the blast;
The elvish page fell to the ground,
And, shuddering, mutter'd, " Found! found! found!"

XXV.

Then sudden, through the darken'd air,   420
  A flash of lightning came;
So broad, so bright, so red the glare,
  The castle seem'd on flame.
Glanced every rafter of the hall,
Glanced every shield upon the wall;   425
Each trophied beam, each sculptured stone,
Were instant seen, and instant gone;
Full through the guests' bedazzled band
Resistless flash'd the levin-brand,
And fill'd the hall with smouldering smoke,   430
As on the elvish page it broke.
  It broke, with thunder long and loud,
  Dismay'd the brave, appall'd the proud,—
    From sea to sea the larum rung;
  On Berwick wall, and at Carlisle withal,   435
    To arms the startled warders sprung.
When ended was the dreadful roar,
The elvish dwarf was seen no more!

XXVI.

Some heard a voice in Branksome Hall,
Some saw a sight, not seen by all;   440
That dreadful voice was heard by some,
Cry, with loud summons, " GYLBIN, COME!"

And on the spot where burst the brand,
  Just where the page had flung him down,
Some saw an arm, and some a hand,   445
  And some the waving of a gown.
The guests in silence pray'd and shook,
And terror dimm'd each lofty look.
But none of all the astonish'd train
Was so dismay'd as Deloraine;   450
His blood did freeze, his brain did burn,
'T was fear'd his mind would ne'er return;
For he was speechless, ghastly, wan,
Like him of whom the story ran,
Who spoke the spectre-hound in Man.   455
At length, by fits, he darkly told,
With broken hint, and shuddering cold—
  That he had seen, right certainly,
A shape with amice wrapp'd around,
With a wrought Spanish baldric bound,   460
  Like pilgrim from beyond the sea;
And knew—but how it matter'd not—
It was the wizard, Michael Scott.

XXVII.

The anxious crowd, with horror pale,
All trembling heard the wondrous tale;   465
  No sound was made, no word was spoke,
  Till noble Angus silence broke;
    And he a solemn sacred plight
    Did to St. Bride of Douglas make,
  That he a pilgrimage would take   470
  To Melrose Abbey, for the sake
    Of Michael's restless sprite.
Then each, to ease his troubled breast,
To some bless'd saint his prayers address'd:
Some to St. Modan made their vows,   475
Some to St. Mary of the Lowes,
Some to the Holy Rood of Lisle,
Some to our Ladye of the Isle;
Each did his patron witness make,
That he such pilgrimage would take,   480
And monks should sing, and bells should toll,
All for the weal of Michael's soul.
While vows were ta'en, and prayers were pray'd,
'T is said the noble dame, dismay'd,
Renounced, for aye, dark magic's aid.   485

XXVIII.

Nought of the bridal will I tell,
Which after in short space befell;
Nor how brave sons and daughters fair
Bless'd Teviot's Flower, and Cranstoun's heir:
After such dreadful scene, 't were vain   490
To wake the note of mirth again.
　　More meet it were to mark the day
　　　Of penitence and prayer divine,
　　When pilgrim-chiefs, in sad array,
　　　Sought Melrose' holy shrine.   495

XXIX.

With naked foot, and sackcloth vest,
And arms enfolded on his breast,
　　Did every pilgrim go;
The standers-by might hear uneath,
Footstep, or voice, or high-drawn breath,   500
　　Through all the lengthen'd row:
No lordly look, nor martial stride,
Gone was their glory, sunk their pride,
　　Forgotten their renown;
Silent and slow, like ghosts they glide   505
To the high altar's hallow'd side,
　　And there they knelt them down:
Above the suppliant chieftains wave
The banners of departed brave;
Beneath the letter'd stones were laid   510
The ashes of their fathers dead;
From many a garnish'd niche around,
Stern saints and tortured martyrs frown'd.

XXX.

And slow up the dim aisle afar,
With sable cowl and scapular,   515
And snow-white stoles, in order due,
The holy Fathers, two and two,
　　In long procession came;
Taper and host, and book they bare,
And holy banner, flourish'd fair   520
　　With the Redeemer's name.
Above the prostrate pilgrim band
The mitred Abbot stretch'd his hand,
　　And bless'd them as they kneel'd;

With holy cross he sign'd them all,   525
And pray'd they might be sage in hall,
  And fortunate in field.
Then mass was sung, and prayers were said,
And solemn requiem for the dead;
And bells toll'd out their mighty peal,   530
For the departed spirit's weal;
And ever in the office close
The hymn of intercession rose;
And far the echoing aisles prolong
The awful burthen of the song,—   535
  DIES IRÆ, DIES ILLA,
  SOLVET SÆCLUM IN FAVILLA;
While the pealing organ rung;
  Were it meet with sacred strain
  To close my lay, so light and vain,   540
Thus the holy Fathers sung.

XXXI.

HYMN FOR THE DEAD.

That day of wrath, that dreadful day,
When heaven and earth shall pass away,
What power shall be the sinner's stay?
How shall he meet that dreadful day?   545

When, shrivelling like a parchéd scroll,
The flaming heavens together roll;
When louder yet, and yet more dread,
Swells the high trump that wakes the dead!

Oh! on that day, that wrathful day,   550
When man to judgment wakes from clay,
Be THOU the trembling sinner's stay,
Though heaven and earth shall pass away!

HUSH'D is the harp—the Minstrel gone.
And did he wander forth alone?   555
Alone, in indigence and age,
To linger out his pilgrimage?
No; close beneath proud Newark's tower,
Arose the Minstrel's lowly bower;
A simple hut; but there was seen   560
The little garden hedged with green,
The cheerful hearth, and lattice clean.

There shelter'd wanderers, by the blaze,
Oft heard the tale of other days;
For much he loved to ope his door,   565
And give the aid he begg'd before.
So pass'd the winter's day; but still,
When summer smiled on sweet Bowhill,
And July's eve, with balmy breath,
Waved the blue-bells on Newark heath;   570
When throstles sung in Harehead-shaw,
And corn was green on Carterhaugh,
And flourish'd, broad, Blackandro's oak,
The aged Harper's soul awoke!
Then would he sing achievements high,   575
And circumstance of chivalry,
Till the rapt traveller would stay,
Forgetful of the closing day;
And noble youths, the strain to hear,
Forsook the hunting of the deer;   580
And Yarrow, as he roll'd along,
Bore burden to the Minstrel's song.

NOTES.

CANTO SIXTH.

The main interest of the poem ceased with the betrothal of Margaret and Lord Cranstoun. But the Goblin page, who had played a more or less important part in the story, was left unaccounted for, and Scott determined to get rid of him in another canto, which he made of suitable length by the description of the wedding festivities in which the songs of the minstrels are introduced, and of the final ending of the feud by the pilgrimage to Melrose.

The first two stanzas, containing Scott's famous patriotic lines, were skilfully led up to at the close of the fifth canto. They are an indignant response to the question of the listening ladies, why the Minstrel wandered through Scotland, "a poor and thankless soil", when he might have been gaining rich rewards and honour in "the more generous Southern land".

1. Breathes there the man, *i.e.* does there live any such man?

1. with soul so dead, so incapable of the higher feelings.

2. who is used with reference to the antecedent *man*, as though the words "with soul so dead" had not occurred. It here = 'as that he', the 'as' corresponding to 'so' being implied.

4. within him burn'd. Cf. *St. Luke*, xxiv. 32, "Did not our heart burn within us?"

6. strand, shore, is used for 'country', a part for the whole.

8. no minstrel raptures swell. *Raptures* is here probably used in the sense of the rapturous or joyful strains of music which express his feelings. So Comus says of the Lady's song (Milton, *Comus*, 247)—

> "with these raptures moves the vocal air
> To testify his hidden residence".

11. Despite, notwithstanding.

11. pelf, wealth. The word is only applied contemptuously. (O. F. *pelfre*, booty.)

12. concentred all in self, selfish in all his thoughts, aims, and desires, which are all fixed on himself, as (*e.g.*) all the spokes of a wheel meet in one *centre*.

14. doubly dying, *i.e.* dying in his body, and all remembrance of him dying too. So in canto v. line 20, "Whose memory feels a *second death*".

15. vile, common, worthless; expressing the worthlessness of men's bodies and their material possessions compared with their souls. Cf. "Dust thou art, to dust thou shalt return".

17. O Caledonia! This begins what is technically called an apostrophe, an address to an inanimate thing that is personified.

18. nurse. In Shakespeare's *Richard II.* Bolingbroke calls England his "nurse". The poet Spenser called London his "most kindly nurse". In this way they expressed their affection for the country and the town in which their early life was passed, and their early impressions were received. Scotland, a land of varied scenery, is a land where the young poet's imagination may be fed and stimulated. Observe what influence Scottish scenery had on Scott himself, on Burns, and on Wordsworth when he visited the country.

19-21. These lines contain an example of the figure of speech called *climax* (Gk. *klimax*, a ladder), so called because it consists of a series of exclamations gradually rising in strength. Scott rises from "land of brown heath" to "land of the mountain" and then "land of my sires".

22. the filial band, the bond of affection which unites him to his country as a son to his mother. (Lat. *filius*, a son.)

26. Seems as, it seems as if.

26, 27. Arrange these lines in prose order.

29. extremity of ill, the deepest misfortune.

31. guide my feeble way, *i.e.* guide me as I feebly go on my way.

32. down Ettrick break, blow in gusts down the valley of the Ettrick.

33. "The preceding four lines now form the inscription on the monument of Sir Walter Scott in the market-place of Selkirk."

37. Not scorn'd like me! See the note on canto i. 7, where it is pointed out that in earlier times the Minstrel had been held in high favour.

40. **priests of mirth and war,** *i.e.* the celebration in song of the festivities of peace and the glories of war was almost a religious duty to them.

43. **Of late,** recently, that is when the two hostile armies were face to face before Branksome.

44. **death-note,** such music as should stir up the soldiers to mortal fight.

44. **in the van,** in the front of the armies (*van*, or 'vanguard', from Fr. *avant-garde, avant* meaning 'before').

46. **portcullis,** an iron grating, which could be let down in front of the gateway of the castle.

49. **rude,** rough; meaning that the turrets were more used to rough scenes of violence than to merry scenes.

50. **Me lists not,** I do not wish to: see note to canto ii. line 141.

51. **spousal rite,** wedding ceremonies.

54. **owches,** golden ornaments in which precious stones are set. Cf. *Exodus*, xxviii. 11, "Thou shalt make them to be set in ouches of gold". The true form of the word is 'nouch', from O.F. *nouche*, a buckle. 'A nouch' became 'an ouch', just as 'a nadder' became 'an adder'.

56. **miniver,** a white fur spotted with black. (O.F. *menu vair*; Lat. *minutus*, small; and *varius*, varied.)

57. **plumage,** collectively for the plumes of the assembled knights. The meaning is, 'what knights there were, whose plumes waved around the altar'.

58. **chainlets,** small chains, probably those holding up the knights' swords or the ladies' trains. The word was coined by Scott.

59. **hard it were,** it would be a difficult task.

59. **speak,** describe.

68. Scott notes that popular belief made a distinction between magicians, who were supposed to *command* evil spirits, and wizards, who were supposed to be *under the control of*, or in equal partnership with, evil spirits. The Ladye's magic was of the former kind, and was feeble enough.

70. **sprites,** spirits.

70. in planetary hour. In the Middle Ages it was believed that the stars had some influence on the lives and destinies of men. People of all classes used to consult astrologers to ascertain what star they were born under, and no one would undertake any important course of action unless he was assured that his stars were favourable. *In planetary hour* therefore means the time at which the particular planets concerned were favourable to the exercise of the "mighty words and signs".

71. scarce I praise, I can hardly give praise to.

78. Guarded, edged.

78. ermine, the fur of a small animal.

79. merlin. Scott notes: "A merlin, or sparrow hawk, was actually carried by ladies of rank, as a falcon was, in time of peace, the constant attendant of a knight or baron". He also quotes a complaint by an old author of "the common and indecent custom of bringing hawks and hounds into churches".

80. leash, a loose string or strap. (Lat. *laxus*, slack.) The word is usually applied to the strap by which a hunting-dog was held.

84. gorgeous, splendid. "The sense of 'gorgeous' was originally proud, from the swelling of the throat in pride. The derivation is from F. *gorge*, throat." (Skeat.)

86. 'Conducted the guests to their places, according to their rank.'

87. with ready blade. The *pages* were ready: *ready* is a 'transferred epithet'.

89. capon, a fattened cock-chicken.

89. heron-shew, a young heron. Also spelt 'heronshaw', 'hernshaw', 'handsaw' (cf. the phrase 'to know a hawk from a handsaw'). From O. F. *herounçeau*, a form of *herouncel*, diminutive of *hairon*.

90. peacock. Scott notes: "The peacock was considered, during the times of chivalry, not merely as an exquisite delicacy, but as a dish of peculiar solemnity. After being roasted, it was again decorated with its plumage, and a sponge, dipped in lighted spirits of wine, was placed in its bill."

91. boar-head. Scott notes: "The boar's head was also a usual dish of feudal splendour. In Scotland it was sometimes surrounded with little banners, displaying the colours and achievements of the baron at whose board it was served."

91. garnish'd, ornamented. See previous note.

91. brave, adj. for adverb; finely. This is the original sense of 'brave', cf. Scottish 'braw'.

92. cygnet, young swan.

92. St. Mary's wave, St. Mary's Loch, at the head of the river Yarrow. There were often flights of wild swans upon it. *Wave* is put, by the figure of speech called synecdoche, for the lake on which the waves were.

94. spoke his benison, said grace, asked a blessing. *Spoke*, short for spoken. *Benison*, blessing; a doublet of 'benediction', the latter being derived direct from Lat. *benedictio*, the former being the O. F. *benison*.

98. shalm, a musical instrument something like an oboe or clarinet, in which the note is produced by the breath of the player striking against a thin reed. (O. F. *chalemie*, Lat. *calamus*, a reed. The word is also written 'shawm', as in the Prayer Book version of Psalm xcviii. 6, "with trumpets also and shawms".) It was sometimes wrongly supposed to be an instrument of the cornet kind.

98. psaltery, a stringed instrument, like a harp. (Through F. and Lat. from Gk. *psalterion*.)

99. clanging, that is, either when they placed them roughly upon the table, or when they struck them one against another as they drank toasts.

103. hooded. When the hawks were not actually employed in hunting, they had little caps or hoods upon their heads. These were withdrawn when they were let fly.

103. on beam, *i.e.* on the beams which crossed the "lofty arched hall" supporting the roof.

105. bells, small bells fastened to the birds' wings.

107. Note that Scott here changes his construction from the past to the present tense.

108. Bourdeaux, s.w. of France. Orleans, in central France. the Rhine, the river flowing through Germany and Holland into the North Sea. The wines of Bourdeaux and the Rhine are still celebrated.

109. sewers, servants whose duty it was to bring in the dishes and wait at table. Formerly they had to taste the food, in order to assure their master that it was not poisoned. (From an old word *sewen*, to set meat, from O. E. *seaw*, juice.)

115. Conrad, the officer of the German mercenaries.   See canto iv. stanza xviii.

117. in humour highly cross'd, much vexed in temper.

119. ' Angry words said by one provoking angry words from another.'

122. " Dickon Draw-the-sword was son to the ancient warrior called in tradition the Cock of Hunthill, remarkable for leading into battle nine sons, gallant warriors, all sons of the ancient champion." (Scott.) Nicknames or surnames expressing some quality or occupa· tion of the persons to whom they were applied were once common. The Norman champion at the battle of Hastings was Taillefer, *i.e.* cut-iron.   In *Ivanhoe* one of the knights is Front de Bœuf, *i.e.* ox-forehead.

123. He, Conrad.

123. saye, word.   *Saye* is here a noun, the final *e* giving it an old appearance like the O. E. *sage*, whence it comes.

125. Howard, Home, and Douglas, natural enemies, English and Scotch, but joining on this festive day to keep the peace.

126. compose, set at rest.   (Lat. *componere*, to lay down.)

128. bit his glove, a pledge of mortal revenge.

132. lyme-dog, hound held in by a leam or lym, *i.e.* a leash. (O. F. *lien*, Lat. *ligamen*, a band.)

136. It is here hinted that Dickon slew Conrad and appropriated his sword.   **Cologne** (accented here on first syllable), applied as an adjective to blade, does not imply that swords made at Cologne (in Germany) were famous like those of Toledo or Bilbao in Spain. It implies no more than that the sword in Dickon's possession was of foreign make, and in fact the one that Conrad formerly wore.

139. buttery, where the provisions were kept.

142. selle, seat.   (Through F. from Lat. *sella*.)

143, 144. raise The pledge to, raise his goblet and drink to the health of, or pledge.

144. Arthur Fire-the-Braes, an Elliot who lived in Liddesdale. He got this name because he was noted for setting fire to the 'braes' or hills.   Being an Elliot, he was connected with the Carrs, who were the mortal enemies of the Scotts and therefore of Watt Tinlinn. But on this occasion the feud was forgotten.

145. as by his breeding bound, as required by good manners. It was the custom for one whose health had been drunk to pledge some one else, the goblet perhaps being passed from hand to hand.

146. Howard's merry-men, the English soldiers commanded by Lord Howard.

146. it, the goblet.

147. To quit them, to discharge their obligation in turn. Them = 'themselves' and refers to the English.

149. carouse, a full glass. (From Germ. *gar aus*, quite out. The usual meaning is a noisy drinking festival.)

150. vat, large wooden tank or tub.

152. riders, moss-troopers, raiders.

154, 155. Scott notes: "Two brethren, natives of Galloway, having been banished from that country for a riot, came to Rankleburn in Ettrick Forest", where they were welcomed by the keeper "on account of their skill in winding the horn and in the other mysteries of the chase. Kenneth MacAlpin, then King of Scotland, came soon after to hunt in the royal forest, and pursued a buck from Ettrick-heugh to the glen now called Buckcleugh....Here the stag stood at bay; and the king and his attendants, who followed on horseback, were thrown out by the steepness of the hill and the morass. John, one of the brethren from Galloway, had followed the chase on foot, and now coming in, seized the buck by the horns, and being a man of great strength and activity, threw him on his back, and ran with his burden about a mile up the steep hill, to a place called Cracra-Cross, where Kenneth had halted, and laid the buck at the sovereign's feet."

155. cleuch, "a strait hollow between precipitous banks, or a hollow descent on the side of a hill". (Jamieson.)

157. Remember'd him of = remembered. *Him* is used reflexively. Cf. the phrase, often heard in Scotland, 'mind of' = remember.

157. Tinlinn's yew, the bow of yew from which Tinlinn had shot the arrow that pierced the page's shoulder: see canto iv. 274–281.

158, 159. it should be...arrow drew, that Tinlinn should pay dearly for having drawn the arrow. *It* is used in anticipation of the true subject, which is the noun clause "That...drew".

161. gibe, mocking joke.

161. Solway strife, the affair of Solway Moss, where in 1542 a large Scotch army was seized with panic and disgracefully fled before a few hundred English horsemen. The shame of this flight is said to have hastened the death of James V., father of Mary Queen of Scots.

166. trencher, wooden plate on which food was cut. (O. F. *trencher*, to cut, carve.)

165. cheer, *i.e.* food.

168. sly, *i.e.* slily.

169. bodkin, small dagger. (W. *bidogyn*, diminutive of *bidog*, dagger.)

171. rued, was the worse for.

172. spurn'd, kicked, stamped. (This is the literal meaning of the word. In Mod. E. it is used solely in its metaphorical sense, 'reject'.)

176. darkling, dark, gloomy (an adjective). The word is usually an adverb, meaning 'in the dark'. Cf. *King Lear*, i. 4. 237, "So, out went the candle and we were left darkling". It occurs as an adjective in Keats' *Eve of St. Agnes*, 355, "Down the wide stairs a darkling way they found".

178. By this, *i.e.* by this time.

180. tune their lay, *i.e.* tune their harps and begin their songs.

181. Græme, the Scots pronunciation of 'Graham'.

182. of that ancient name. Scott in his note gives particulars of the family. They were notorious freebooters, descended from John Græme, second son of Malice Earl of Monteith, who lived in the reign of Henry IV.

183. Was none, there was none.

184. the Land Debateable, a part of the Border lands lying partly in England and partly in Scotland, and claimed by both kingdoms. It was finally divided between the two by commissioners appointed by both nations.

185. Well friended, being well served by friends; well befriended.

186. The Græmes, living in the Land Debateable, and therefore belonging to neither nation, sometimes sided with the English, sometimes with the Scotch. They were outlaws, but made friends on both sides of the Border by giving intelligence of raids to English or Scotch as it suited them. Hence they would always contrive to profit by the victory of either side.

187. beeves, oxen. (O.F. *bœuf*, Lat. *bos*, an ox.) "A saying is recorded of a mother to her son, *Ride, Rowley, hough 's i' the pot*; that is, the last piece of beef was in the pot, and therefore it was high time for him to go and fetch more." (Scott.)

189. In homely guise, in simple style.

189. as nature bade. Being one of a rough freebooting family, Albert Græme's song would not exhibit much refinement.

190. said. This is not an appropriate word, but Scott wanted a word to rime with 'bade'.

191–222. This song is a simple narrative, varied only by the refrain of the second and fourth line of each stanza. It is as plain as one of the old ballads, from one of which Scott adopted the refrain—

> "She lean'd her back against a thorn,
> The sun shines fair on Carlisle wa';
> And there she has her young babe born,
> And the lyon shall be lord of a'".

193. would, meant to; was resolved to.

195. Blithely, gaily; gladly.

202. For ire, because of his anger at the choice of his sister. (Lat. *ira*, anger.)

203. meadow and lea. These words in poetry and in common speech often mean the same. *Meadow* is strictly land on which the grass is mown (O. E. *mædu*, from *mǽwan*, to mow). *Lea* is properly barren or fallow land, but is here applied to land used for pasture (O. E. *leáh*).

207. not tasted well, in prose, 'not well tasted', *i.e.* scarcely tasted. There was poison in it.

213. all would, all who would. The nominative relative is omitted.

215. took the cross divine. To 'take the cross' was a common phrase meaning to go on a crusade. The Crusaders wore the figure of a cross woven upon their garments, in token that they were engaged in a holy war on behalf of the tomb of Christ.

221. their souls, the souls of them.

224. of loftier port, of more distinguished appearance. Cf. 'portly', as in Tennyson's *Miller's Daughter*—

> "I see the wealthy miller yet,
> His double chin, his portly size".

225. sonnet, a short poem of fourteen lines, each of five feet, riming, and the rimes arranged in a particular way. It was originally an Italian form of poem, introduced into England by Surrey and Sir Thomas Wyatt in the reign of Henry VIII. Splendid sonnets have been written by Shakespeare, Milton, Wordsworth, and Keats.

The following is a fine sonnet by Wordsworth, composed early one September morning on Westminster Bridge.

> " Earth has not any thing to show more fair:
> Dull would he be of soul who could pass by
> A sight so touching in its majesty:
> The City now doth, like a garment, wear
> The beauty of the morning; silent, bare,
> Ships, towers, domes, theatres, and temples lie
> Open unto the fields, and to the sky;
> All bright and glittering in the smokeless air.
> Never did sun more beautifully steep,
> In his first splendour, valley, rock, or hill;
> Ne'er saw I, never felt, a calm so deep!
> The river glideth at his own sweet will:
> Dear God! the very houses seem asleep;
> And all that mighty heart is lying still."

225. rhyme (the correct spelling of which is ' rime') is probably used here in the sense of verse in general, whether rimed or not (blank verse): cf. *Lycidas*, 10—

> "he knew
> Himself to sing and build the lofty rhyme".

The word is so used by Chaucer in the sense of a tale in verse. (The spelling ' rhyme' is due to confusion with ' rhythm', from Gk. *rhythmos*. ' Rime' is O. E. *rim*.)

225. roundelay, properly a dancing-song, in which the same line comes round again. (The word is from O. F. *rondelet*, diminutive of *rondel*. The *-let* is corrupted into *-lay*, as though it means ' song'.)

226. haughty Henry, Henry VIII.

228. silver song. ' Silver' is applied to soft sweet sounds, probably because bells of silver are imagined to give forth tones of peculiar clearness and sweetness. Spenser in his *Shepheards Calender* has "of fayre Elisa be your silver song", which was imitated from a Greek phrase in Hesiod. Also Milton in his *Nativity Ode* speaks of the "silver chime" of the music of the spheres.

229. The gentle Surrey. "The gallant and unfortunate Henry Howard, Earl of Surrey, was unquestionably the most accomplished cavalier of his time; and his sonnets display beauties which would do honour to a more polished age. He was beheaded on Tower Hill in 1546, a victim to the mean jealousy of Henry VIII., who could not bear so brilliant a character near his throne." (Scott.) He was an admirable poet, who with Sir Thomas Wyatt shares the honour of introducing into England various Italian forms of poetry, such as the sonnet, which English poets carried to great perfection.

231. soul of fire, *i.e.* burning with high and noble thoughts and desires.

235. Though Surrey imitated the Italian poets, he was never in Italy. The story contained in stanzas xvi.–xx. below is a fabrication, first published in the year 1594 by Nashe.

235. climes afar, far countries. Surrey was often in France on state business.

236. olive grove. Italy is famous for its olives.

238. Surrey's absent love. This lady, the Geraldine mentioned in line 244, is supposed to have been Lady Elizabeth Fitzgerald, daughter of the Earl of Kildare, whom Surrey is said to have seen and become attached to before his imprisonment at Windsor in 1537. At that date the lady was a girl of nine years. Surrey was married, and deeply attached to his wife. It was very common among the poets in the 14–15th centuries to inscribe their poems to some lady, of whom they were not necessarily the lover. Thus the great Italian poet Petrarch wrote some beautiful poetry to 'Laura', a lady who was married, and the mother of a large family. Surrey may very well have followed this fashion.

239–242. That is, the simple Italian peasant, hearing the sweet music of Surrey and his companion, stopped to listen, and fancied that angelic spirits were singing around the grave of some holy man.

246. knew, felt.

247. of the deathless lay, whose poems would never die. Cf. "bard's immortal name" (line 232). *Of* is here used descriptively.

248. Surrey was executed on a charge of treasonable designs. In 1546 Henry VIII. was dying, and it was disputed who should be protector of the young prince, Edward. Surrey, in order to assert the superiority of his family over the Seymours, caused the arms of Edward the Confessor, which he was entitled to wear, to be quartered upon his own. This was the only evidence that could be brought against him.

251. Naworth's iron towers, the strongly fortified castle of the Howards, near Carlisle. The use of the epithet 'iron' implies that the towers were strong, as they need be in the disturbed Border district.

252. Much of Surrey's poetry was written while he was a prisoner at Windsor.

253. The minstrel was faithful to the successors of his patron.

256. minstrelsy, collectively, the body of minstrels; just as 'chivalry' means the body of knights.

257–301. Fitztraver's song is much more elaborate than Albert Græme's. It gives a carefully drawn picture of a single scene, and it is written in a stanza differing from that of the simple ballad. This stanza is known as the Spenserian stanza, because it was first used in English by Edmund Spenser (1552–1598). It consists of nine lines, the first eight having five feet, the last having six feet and being known as an Alexandrine, probably from the name of an old French poet, who used the line of six feet. The nine lines contain three sets of rimes, the rimes occurring thus:—ABABBCBCC. The stanza has been used by several poets since Spenser, the most successful being Thomson in *The Castle of Indolence,* Byron in *Childe Harold,* Keats in *The Eve of St. Agnes,* and Shelley in *Adonais.*

"The song of the supposed bard is founded on an incident said to have happened to the Earl in his travels. Cornelius Agrippa, the celebrated alchemist, showed him in a looking-glass the lovely Geraldine, to whose service he had devoted his pen and his sword. The vision represented her as indisposed, and reclining upon a couch, reading her lover's verses by the light of a waxen taper." (Scott.)

257. All-souls' eve, the day before the Festival of All Souls, November 2nd. But Scott probably meant the eve of All Saints' day, November 1, known as Hallowe'en. Spirits were supposed to walk abroad on that night, and it was the best time for consulting magicians and witches.

259. the mystic hour. Spirits were supposed to be let loose from their confinement, and to have influence upon men, from midnight to cock-crow.

260. Cornelius, Cornelius Henry Agrippa (1486–1535), who was by turns secretary to the Emperor Maximilian I., a soldier in Italy, and a magician and alchemist.

262. albeit, although.

63. **sage,** wise man.

263. **hight**, promised. (O. E. *hèht*, past tense of *hátan*, to command, promise. *Hight* also means 'was or is called', this being from *hatte*, the past tense of O. E. *hátan*, to be called.)

264. **in life and limb**, that is, exactly as she was, a living lady.

266. **gramarye**, magic. See note to canto iii. line 140.

269. **hallow'd taper**, a taper which had been consecrated (probably by magical, not by religious rites).

270. **implements**, tools. (Low Lat. *implementum*, an accomplishing; from Lat. *implere*, to fill in.)

271. **character**, magical sign, especially the symbol used by astrologers to represent a planet.

271. **talisman**, a magical image.

272. **almagest**, a great collection of problems in astronomy and geometry, made by Claudius Ptolemy (140 A.D.). The Greek name was *Hē megalē syntaxis*, which means 'the great collection'. The Arabs, believing it to be the greatest work on the subject, prefixed their article *al*, the, to the Greek superlative adj. *megistē*, thus forming the word almagest.

272. **nothing**, no whit, not at all.

274. **watchlight**, a dim slow-burning light used by persons sitting up at night.

276. **self-emitted**, not apparently proceeding from any luminous object, but arising of itself. It was a magic mirror.

277. **upon its breast**, a curious phrase for the face of the mirror.

277. **gan**, see note on canto i. line 253.

278. **as feverish dream**, like the images men see in their dreams.

231. **silver beam**, pure bright light.

232. **Agra's silken loom.** The loom is a weaving instrument; hence *silken*, which properly means made of silk, is a transferred epithet: the loom which weaves silken stuff. Agra is in India, and the Indian silks were and are famous.

284. **Fair all the pageant**, the whole scene was beautiful.

284. **passing**, surpassingly, excellently.

285. **Ind**, India.

289. pensive, thoughtful.

289. eburnine, made of ivory. (Lat. *ebur*, ivory.)

290. strain, poetry.

290. that seem'd...find, that seemed to touch her very deeply.

291. raptured line, poem written under strong emotion.

295. royal envy. See note on line 248 above.

295, 296. roll'd...day. Henry is represented as having for ever put an end to the glorious sunshine of Surrey's life by causing the dark storm-clouds of death to roll across his sky.

297. ruthless, without pity. (O. E. *hreow*, pity.)

299. caprice, changeable conduct. (Said to be derived from Lat. *caper*, a goat, changeable conduct being likened to the frisking of a goat. Cf. 'to cut a *caper*'.)

299. despotic sway, rule of an absolute master.

300. The gory bridal bed. Henry VIII. married Jane Seymour the very day after Anne Bullen's execution. Hence his bed is described as being stained with blood.

300. the plunder'd shrine. This refers to the dissolution of the monasteries. Henry VIII. and his servant Cromwell dismissed the monks, and took all their property.

304. These, *i.e.* the Southern chiefs, among whom was Howard, a relative of the Earl of Surrey.

305. those, *i.e.* the Scots. The Reformation was accomplished in Scotland later than in England and was then much more thorough.

305. ancient faith, *i.e.* Roman Catholicism.

308. feasting high at Home, being a guest at Home Castle, where splendid banquets were held in his honour.

311. Orcades, the Latin name of the Orkney Islands.

312. "The St. Clairs are of Norman extraction, being descended from William de St. Clair, second son of Walderne Compte de St. Clair, and Margaret, daughter to Richard Duke of Normandy. He married Elizabeth, daughter of Malice Spar, Earl of Orkney and Stratherne, in whose right their son Henry was in 1379 created Earl of Orkney by Haco King of Norway. In exchange for this earldom the castle and domains of Ravenscraig or Ravensheuch were conferred on William St. Clair, Earl of Caithness." (Scott.)

312. erst, at one time. (O. E. *ǽrest*, superlative of *ǽr*, soon.)

315. "The Castle of Kirkwall was built by the St. Clairs while Earls of Orkney." Kirkwall is the capital of the Orkney Islands. The castle is called its 'pride' because it stands as a reminder of the former glories of the earldom. It is called its 'sorrow' because of its ruined condition, which is a sad reminder of the past.

316. fierce Pentland, the Pentland Frith, between the Orkneys and the mainland.

317. Odin, or Woden, the chief god of the Norsemen. The Orkneys at one time belonged to Norway.

318. the whilst, at the same time.

319. the struggling sail, the struggles of the ships in the frith against the winds which sweep through the channel. Notice how the description of these sea-scenes leads up to the Minstrel's song.

320, 321. 'Everything that was wild and wonderful had a charm for the lonely boy's imagination.' These lines apply well to Scott himself.

323. cull, gather, select. (O.F. *cuillir*, Lat. *colligere*.)

325. This line is in apposition to "The Norsemen" in line 326, and is explained by these words : 'the men of Scandinavia, devoted to roving and fighting upon the sea'. **Lochlin,** the Gaelic name of Scandinavia.

326, 327. 'Trained to war and plunder, and skilful in fight, thus providing food (in the bodies of the slain) for the birds of prey.' Ravens hover over battle-fields and eat the dead bodies. Perhaps Scott had in mind too the fact that the Danish standard bore the figure of a raven.

328, 329. "The chiefs of the *Vakingr*, or Scandinavian pirates, assumed the title of *Sækonungr*, or Sea-kings. Ships, in the inflated language of the Scalds, are often termed the serpents of the ocean." (Scott.)

330. there, in the Orkneys.

331. Scald, the name of the Scandinavian minstrel.

332. Runic column, stone upon which were cut or marked inscriptions in the runes, or letters of the Norse alphabet. These characters, sixteen in all, were arranged in certain combinations, which then formed charms.

333. grim idolatry. The columns are supposed to mark spots where heathen rites were performed. The word *grim* probably implies that human sacrifices formed part of these rites, as they did in the Druid worship.

335. Saga, the name given to the tales of Scandinavian heroes. The word is connected with 'say', and with 'saw' ("wise *saws* and modern instances"); *g* in O. E. becoming *y*; so O. E. *dæg* is Mod. E. *day*. (Icelandic *saga*, a tale.)

335. uncouth, rude, unpolished. (Properly 'unknown'; O. E. *un*, not; *cuth*, past participle of *cunnan*, to know.)

336, 337. "The *jormungandr*, or Snake of the Ocean, whose folds surround the earth, is one of the wildest fictions of the Edda [a collection of the Scandinavian mythical tales]. It was very nearly caught by the god Thor, who went to fish for it with a hook baited with a bull's head." (Scott.)

336. tremendous curl'd, curled up in a tremendous circle.

338. those dread Maids, "the *Valcyriur*, or Selectors of the Slain, despatched by Odin from Valhalla [the Scandinavian heaven] to choose those who were to die and to distribute the contest. They are well known to the English reader as Gray's Fatal Sisters." (Scott.) They correspond to the classical Furies or *Parcae*.

340–345. "The Northern warriors were usually entombed with their arms and their other treasures....Their ghosts were not wont tamely to suffer their tombs to be plundered; and hence the mortal heroes had an additional temptation to attempt such adventures; for they held nothing more worthy of their valour than to encounter supernatural beings." (Scott.)

341. death-lights, lights, like that of Michael Scott (see canto ii. stanzas xvii. and xviii.), which were continually burning in the tombs.

346. 'Excited by these tales of war and wonder.'

347. Roslin, by the Frith of Forth. It means 'promontory of the linn', or waterfall (Gaelic *ros*, a headland; *linn*, a pool).

350, 351. In spite of his having learnt a more refined kind of song through his residence in the South, yet the influences of his early life in the wild North are traceable in his song.

351. numbers, verses, because in poetry the lines consist of a definite number of syllables.

352–403. As the second song was superior to the first, so this third song is superior to the other two. In metre it is just as simple as the first; as a picture it is as clearly drawn as the second; but in style it is far more vigorous and powerful. Lord Jeffrey said of it: "The third song is intended to represent that wild style of composition which prevailed among the bards of the Northern Continent, somewhat softened and adorned by the minstrel's residence in the south. We prefer it, upon the whole, to either of the two former, and shall give it entire to our readers, who will probably be struck with the poetical effect of the dramatic form into which it is thrown, and of the indirect description by which everything is most expressively told, without one word of distinct narrative." Mr. Hales says: "The pictures tell their own story, and tell it so vividly and thrillingly that nothing more is needed."

The ballad, though headed 'Harold', is usually known as 'Rosabelle'.

355. Rosabelle, a family name in the house of St. Clair.

356–375. These five stanzas contain a conversation between Rosabelle and another person on the sea-shore.

358. Rest thee. In prose one would say 'rest'. *Thee* is used reflexively, as in 'hie thee', 'haste thee', &c.

358. Castle Ravensheuch, "a large and strong castle, now ruinous, situated on a steep crag washed by the Firth of Forth. ... It was long a principal residence of the Barons of Roslin".

359. tempt, try, *i.e.* try to cross.

361. inch, island.

362. Water-Sprite. "The *water-sprite* is heard often in old poems, and the poems that imitate or refer to these." It is sometimes called the water-wraith, and the water-kelpie. It was supposed to be a spirit which gave warning by shrieks and groans of the destruction of ships and the people on board.

364. Seer, literally, one who *sees.* It is the name by which prophets are often called in the Bible. In a special sense, it means one gifted with second sight, the power of seeing future events.

365. shroud, a sheet in which a dead body is wrapt.

365. swathed, wrapt round.

366. stay thee, reflexive.

366. Fair, adjective used as noun.

368–375. Although Rosabelle denies that "Lord Lindesay's heir" is concerned in her wish to return, her denial only assures us that such is at anyrate partly the fact. She modestly wishes to conceal her motive.

372. the ring. 'At the ring' is the correct phrase as in line 373. "A ring was suspended, not tightly fastened, but so that it could be easily detached, from a horizontal beam resting on two upright posts. The players rode at full speed through the archway thus made, and as they went under, passed their lance points, or aimed at passing them, through the ring and so bore it off." (Hales.)

374. sire, father.

374. the wine will chide, will grumble at the wine.

375. 'tis, it is: that is, the goblet.

376–395. These five stanzas correspond with the previous five. They give the second picture—Roslin chapel all ablaze. The first picture shows the stormy firth and the group gathered upon its shore; that is the *natural* foreboding of ill. The second picture,—the mysteriously lighted chapel—gives us the *supernatural* foreboding of ill.

381. ruddied, give a ruddy glow to.

382. Dryden's groves of oak, the oak woods of Dryden house, south of Roslin.

383. Hawthornden, a mansion and park on the left bank of the Esk about 12 miles south of Edinburgh. It is famous as the residence of the poet Drummond, who is known chiefly by his notes of conversations with Ben Jonson. Beneath the mansion are some large caverns, hewn out of the solid rock, and connected with each other by long passages.

384. chapel. The chapel was founded in 1446 by William St. Clair, Earl of Orkney, and Lord of Roslin. Beneath it the barons of Roslin were until the end of the 17th century buried in complete armour. It was a superstitious belief that on the night before the death of any of the Lords of Roslin the chapel appeared in flames.

387. panoply, full armour. (Gk. *pan*, all; *hopla*, arms.)

389. Deep sacristy, the chamber where the sacred robes and vessels were kept. *Deep* may perhaps mean 'lofty', or probably 'remote', or 'far-extending'.

389. altar's pale, the enclosure in which the altar was.

390. foliage-bound, having carvings of leaves and flowers wound about them. See the description of Melrose Abbey in canto ii.

392. pinnet, a pointed ornament on the roof of a building, pinnacle. (A diminutive of Lat. *pinna*, feather.)

394. still, always; or perhaps 'yet'.

396-403. The last two stanzas draw the connection between the two parts of the poem. The disaster foretold by the blazing chapel was the drowning of Rosabelle.

396-7. In those two lines one subject, "twenty ... barons bold", serves for two verbs, "are" and "lie buried", or the relative (*who*) may be regarded as omitted before the latter verb.

397. chapelle. The French form of the word 'chapel' is used because it is accented on the second syllable, and so provides the required rime with 'Rosabelle'.

401. That is, with all the due ceremonies, such as the carrying of lighted candles in the funeral procession, the reading of the funeral service from the service-book, the solemn tolling of the bell. The contrast is drawn between the peaceful orderly burial of the warlike barons, and the wild tumults which rage over the watery grave of the gentle lady.

405. In prose: 'that the guests scarcely noticed how dark the hall had become'.

407. involved, literally, rolled up in. (Lat. *in*; *volvere*, to roll.)

408. eddying, whirling, moving about.

411. apace, rapidly.

417. 'She knew that the blast was bearing some misfortune with it.'

419. The only thing that the page has said hitherto has been "Lost! lost! lost!" He probably means now that he has been found by the magician, Michael Scott, or that he has at last found a place where he will abide for ever.

424. Glanced, flashed.

426. trophied beam, the wooden beams supporting the roof on which were fixed trophies, that is, spoils of war or of the chase, such as armour or flags or the tusks of boars.

427. instant seen, seen for an instant.

427. instant gone, gone instantly, in an instant.

428. the guests' bedazzled band, the company of guests who were dazzled by the bright light. The prefix *be-* strengthens the main verb.

429. levin-brand, flash of lightning. See note on canto iv. 319.

434. larum, the call to arms which was raised by everybody who heard the sudden strange sound. (Shortened from *alarum*, another form of *alarm*. Ital. *all' arme*, to arms.)

435. withal, as well, in addition to Berwick and the other places.

442. Gylbin. The goblin's name was Gylbin or Gilpin Horner. See note on canto ii. 353.

444. flung him, flung himself: reflexive.

450. Deloraine, it will be remembered, was the knight who had ridden to Melrose for the magic book, and had seen the corpse of Michael Scott.

454, 455. Scott quotes a story about a soldier in the Isle of Man, who, in a fit of drunken daring, went out at night to face an apparition called the Manthe Doog, which appeared in the shape of a large black spaniel, and was thought to be an evil spirit. The soldier went out, but soon returned sober to the guard-room, could not speak a word, and died in agony three days after.

459–461. These lines are repeated from canto ii. 214–216, where see the notes.

462. but how it matter'd not. That is, Deloraine told the company that it was Michael Scott, but when pressed to say how he knew, he replied that it did not matter. His journey to Melrose was a secret between himself and the Ladye.

468. plight, promised. The word is another form of 'pledge'.

469. St. Bride of Douglas, "favourite saint of the house of Douglas, and of the Earl of Angus in particular".

471, 472. He thought that by going on a solemn pilgrimage to Melrose they might enable the wizard to rest quietly in his grave.

477. Holy Rood, the image of the Cross. Rood is the same word as rod.

479. make has two objects, *patron* and *witness*: 'each knight made his own special saint a witness of his vow'.

482. weal, welfare.

487. 'Which took place soon afterwards.'

490, 491. The Minstrel says that after describing the dreadful cene (which, however, docs not have a very horrifying effect on the eader) it is impossible to sing of joyful subjects.

491. meet, fitting.

491. were, would be.

491. to mark, to pay special attention to.

496. sackcloth. The custom of wearing clothes of very coarse loth as a sign of mourning is very old. It is mentioned often in he Bible.

499. might hear uneath, could scarcely hear. (O. E. *eath*, easy.)

500. high-drawn breath. This curious expression probably neans that the pilgrims were sighing deeply but inaudibly.

506. high altar. The high or principal altar stands at the east nd of a church. In large Roman Catholic churches it is usual to lave more than one altar, the smaller ones being dedicated to ndividual saints.

509. departed brave, *i.e.* brave warriors who have died. *Brave* is .n adjective used as a noun, but as a rule the definite article would ie placed before it, as in "None but the brave deserves the fair".

510. letter'd stones, the tombstones on which were engraved r painted inscriptions.

512. garnish'd niche, decorated recess in the wall.

513. The statues of the saints and martyrs are said to frown from heir recesses along the wall. It is a kind of poetical fancy that the old stone figures are in sympathy with the solemn purpose of the ilgrims.

515. cowl, a large hood forming part of the monk's gown.

515. scapular, a part of the monk's dress, consisting of two ands of woollen stuff crossing the shoulders, one hanging behind, ne before. (Lat. *scapula*, shoulder-blade.)

516. stoles: see note to canto v. 506.

516. in order due, placed in order of rank.

519. host, the consecrated bread, which is believed by Catholics ɔ become the actual body of Christ, and is offered up as a sacrifice ι the mass. (Lat. *hostia*, victim, sacrifice.)

520. flourish'd fair, having fairly woven or embroidered on it.

523. mitred, having upon his head the mitre, a kind of pointed cap.

526. sage in hall, wise in the counsel chamber.

527. in field, on the battle-field.

528. mass, the name given to the celebration of the communion in the Roman Catholic church. See note on canto ii. 65.

529. requiem. See note on canto v. 507.

532. in the office close, at the conclusion of the various parts of the service.

535. burthen, the conclusion of a stanza, which is repeated after other stanzas. This is the strict meaning; but here the word may be loosely used for the song itself.

535. the song. The Latin hymn of which the first words are here given, and which is known as the *Dies Irae*. It was composed in 1230 by Thomas of Celano, and consists of 17 three-lined stanzas.

536, 537. Literally: 'The day of wrath, that day, shall the world melt in ashes'.

539–541. The Minstrel apologizes for closing his tale of love and fight and magic with the sacred words.

542–553. Many translations have been made of the *Dies Irae*, and in the nature of the case none of them if rimed can be strictly literal. Scott's is a good paraphrase.

543. For the anticipation of the Last Day, cf. *2 Peter*, iii. 10, "the day of the Lord will come as a thief in the night; in the which the heavens shall pass away with a great noise, and the elements [*i.e.* the sky] shall melt with fervent heat; the earth also, and the works that are therein, shall be burnt up".

549. the high trump. Cf. *1 Corinthians*, xv. 25, "The trumpet shall sound, and the dead shall be raised incorruptible".

554–582. The Minstrel's song is now over. These lines form what we might call the epilogue or after-piece, giving an account of how the Minstrel fared—just as the Introduction told how he came to sing his song before the Duchess and her ladies.

554. the Minstrel gone, *i.e.* gone from the ladies' "room of state" in Newark Castle, where he had sung his lay. See the introductory lines.

555-557. These questions are asked for the purpose of drawing a stronger contrast between what is suggested in them and the treatment which the Minstrel actually received.

556. indigence, want. (Lat. *indigens*, needy.)

557. 'To spend his last years in weariness and pain.' Life is often compared to a toilsome pilgrimage.

558. Lockhart quotes from Wordsworth's *Yarrow Visited*—

"the vale unfolds
Rich groves of lofty stature,
With Yarrow winding through the pomp
Of cultivated nature:
And, rising from those lofty groves
Behold a ruin hoary,
The shattered front of Newark's towers,
Renown'd in Border story.

Fair scenes for childhood's opening bloom,
For sportive youth to stray in;
For manhood to enjoy his strength,
And age to wear away in."

560-566. Notice the charming simplicity of these lines, particularly line 561.

568. 'Summer' is personified, and said to 'smile' on Bowhill. The beautiful change which summer causes in the appearance of the earth is aptly compared to a smile.

568. Bowhill, "a seat of the Duke of Buccleuch. It stands immediately below Newark Hill, and above the junction of the Yarrow and the Ettrick". (Lockhart.) In Scott's time it was the residence of the beautiful Lady Dalkeith, who suggested the subject of his *Lay*.

569. July, to be accented, as usual in Scotland, on the first syllable.

569. with balmy breath. Here is another instance of personification. The calm breezes of the summer evening, laden with the sweet scent of flowers, are compared to breath.

571. throstles, thrushes.

571. shaw, a wood.

572. haugh, hill.

575. sing, *i.e.* sing of. The word is thus frequently used b poets.

575. achievements, deeds; warlike feats.

576. circumstance, the accompaniments and details of.

577. rapt, carried away; charmed.

582. Bore burden to, seemed to add music to.   See note o ' burthen', line 535 above.

Of the closing lines of the *Lay* Lockhart says: " In these charr ing lines he has embodied what was, at the time when he penne them, the chief day-dream of Ashestiel.   From the moment that hi uncle's death placed a considerable sum of ready money at hi command, he pleased himself, as we have seen, with the idea c buying a mountain farm, and becoming not only the ' sheriff' (as h had in former days delighted to call himself), but ' the *laird* of th cairn and the scaur '."